OECD Studies on Tourism

Tourism Policy Review of Mexico

OECD
BETTER POLICIES FOR BETTER LIVES

Please cite this publication as:
OECD (2017), *Tourism Policy Review of Mexico*, OECD Studies on Tourism, OECD Publishing, Paris.
http://dx.doi.org/10.1787/9789264266575-en

ISBN 978-92-64-26656-8 (print)
ISBN 978-92-64-26657-5 (PDF)

Series: OECD Studies on Tourism
ISSN 2223-9790 (print)
ISSN 2223-9804 (online)

Photo credits: Cover © vectomart/Shutterstock.com

Corrigenda to OECD publications may be found on line at: *www.oecd.org/about/publishing/corrigenda.htm*.

Preface

Tourism plays a crucial role for Mexico's economy, and has performed strongly in recent years. Tourism accounts directly for 8.5% of GDP and generates higher than average value for the economy. It also provides employment for millions of Mexicans. While official data indicate that the sector directly supports 2.3 million jobs (5.8%), the real figure is significantly higher when informal jobs are taken into account. Growth in tourism has surpassed growth in many other advanced and emerging tourism economies in recent years, and has contributed to a healthy travel balance, helping to compensate for weaker oil revenues.

However, tourism's potential to promote inclusive and sustainable growth, as well as local and regional development in Mexico, remains largely unrealised and the sector is faced with many competitiveness and sustainability issues. Key policy challenges include the need to adapt the model of tourism development to make it more inclusive; strengthen the governance of tourism; increase support to small and micro businesses; and connect new markets and destinations.

In this context, the *OECD Tourism Policy Review of Mexico* recommends that Mexico: strengthen the governance of tourism by promoting a more strategic and integrated approach to tourism policy; boost air connectivity from high potential source markets to support market diversification, and develop a more integrated transport system to move visitors around the country; adapt the model of tourism development to respond to market trends and better spread the benefits of tourism by promoting inclusive tourism growth, product diversification and destination development; and target financing to innovative tourism projects offering the strongest potential, including to small and micro enterprises.

Through this review, the Mexican authorities have engaged in a proactive and welcome effort to develop and further strengthen the contribution of tourism to the Mexican economy and society. The review prepared by the OECD Centre for Entrepreneurship, SMEs, Local Development and Tourism as part of the Tourism Committee's Programme of Work, is the result of a rich and co-operative policy dialogue with the Mexican authorities. It is our hope that it will provide inspiration to policy makers in other countries facing similar challenges, and help advance the policy debate on sustainable and inclusive tourism development in OECD member and partner countries.

Angel Gurría

Secretary-General of the OECD

Foreword

This publication presents the OECD country review of tourism issues and policies in Mexico. It forms part of the programme of work of the OECD Tourism Committee and has been prepared by the Secretariat of the OECD Centre for Entrepreneurship, SMEs, Local Development and Tourism. The report is part of a series of reviews on tourism issues and policies undertaken by the OECD in countries that express an interest in co-operating on an external assessment of their policy challenges. Tourism policy reviews aim to: enhance tourism performance, competitiveness and innovation; increase knowledge about tourism policy design and evaluation; diffuse evidence-based lessons and good practices; and strengthen policy coherence and linkages. The present review has been prepared at the request of the Government of Mexico.

This review provides an assessment of tourism-related policies, programmes and plans to support a competitive and sustainable tourism development in Mexico. The structure, profile and performance of tourism are examined, along with the policy making environment and governance arrangements for tourism. This report also includes chapters of special relevance to Mexico: transport connectivity; inclusive tourism growth and infrastructure development; and investment and SME financing. The OECD Tourism Committee peer-reviewed and approved the report at its meeting on 6 October 2016.

The review has been possible thanks to the support and co-operation of the Mexican authorities, including the numerous officials, experts and representatives from Federal and state government and the private sector who provided valuable written and oral inputs, and in other ways participated in the review process. The OECD is particularly grateful to Minister Enrique de la Madrid Cordero, Under Secretary María Teresa Solís Tejo, Javier Guillermo Molina and officials at the Ministry of Tourism (SECTUR), and Ambassador Dionisio Pérez-Jácome Friscione and Aldo Aldama from the Permanent Delegation of Mexico to the OECD, and officials at the Ministry of Foreign Affairs (SRE), for their continuous support throughout the review process.

Jane Stacey co-ordinated the review and led the drafting of the report, under the direction of Alain Dupeyras, Head of the OECD Tourism Unit. Drafting contributions were provided by Alain Lumbroso, International Transport Forum (Chapter 3) and external experts Aidan Pender (Chapter 4) and Virginia Robano (Chapter 5). Peter Haxton participated in the mission and provided feedback on early drafts. Laetitia Reille managed the statistical component. María Castaño provided research and logistical assistance. Julie Pilato provided administrative support and prepared the manuscript for publication.

The review has also benefitted from contributions, feedback and guidance from the peer-review countries, represented by: Veronica Kunze, Ministry of Economy, Development and Tourism, Chile; Sérgio Guerreiro, Turismo de Portugal; and Isabel Hill, US Department of Commerce. The representatives of Portugal and the United States participated in the review mission.

Lamia Kamal-Chaoui
Director, Centre for Entrepreneurship, SMEs, Local Development and Tourism

Table of Contents

Tables

Figures

Boxes

Acronyms and abbreviations

APEC	Foro de Cooperación Económica Asia-Pacífico Asia-Pacific Economic Co-operation
Bancomext	Banco Nacional de Comercio Exterior Mexican Foreign Trade Bank
Banobras	Banco Nacional de Obras y Servicios Públicos National Bank of Public Works and Services
Banxico	Banco de México Bank of Mexico
CDI	Comisión Nacional para el Desarrollo de los Pueblos Indígenas Commission for the Development of Indigenous People
CKD	Certificados de Capital de Desarrollo Capital Development Certificate
CNET	Consejo Nacional Empresarial Turístico National Tourism Business Council
CPTM	Consejo de Promoción turística de México Mexican Tourism Board
COFEMER	Comisión Federal de Mejora Regulatoria Federal Commission for Regulatory Improvement
CONANP	Comisión Nacional de Areas Nacionales Protegidas National Commission of Natural Protected Areas
DATATUR	Sistema Nacional de la Información Estadística del Sector Turismo de México National Tourism Statistical Information System
FDI	Inversión extranjera directa Foreign Direct Investment
FIBRA	Fideicomiso de Infraestructura y Bienes Raíces Infrastructure and Real Estate Trust
FND	Financiera Nacional de Desarrollo Agropecuario, Rural, Forestal y Pesquero National Financial Institute for Agricultural, Rural, Forestry and Fisheries Development
FONATUR	Fondo Nacional de Fomento al Turismo National Fund for Tourism Development
GDP	Producto Interior Bruto Gross Domestic Product

INADEM	Instituto Nacional del Emprendedor National Institute for Entrepreneurship
INEGI	Instituto Nacional de Estadística y Geografía National Institute of Statistics and Geography
MXN	Peso Mexicano Mexican Peso
NAFIN	Nacional Financiera National Financial Institute
NAFTA	Tratado de Libre Comercio de América del Norte North American Free Trade Agreement
PND	Plan Nacional de Desarrollo National Development Plan
PNI	Programa Nacional de Infraestructura National Infrastructure Plan
PPP	Participación público-privada Public Private Partnership
ProMéxico	Agencia para la Promoción de Inversión y Comercio Trade and Investment Promotion Agency
PROSECTUR	Programa Sectorial de Turismo Sectoral Programme for Tourism
PROMAGICO	Programa de Pueblos Mágicos Magic Towns Programme
PRODERMAGICO	Programa de Desarrollo Regional Turístico Sustentable y Pueblos Mágicos Regional Sustainable Tourism Development and Magic Towns Programme
SCT	Secretaría de Comunicaciones y Transportes Ministry of Communications and Transport
SE	Secretaría de Economía Ministry of Economy
SEDATU	Secretaría de desarrollo agrario, territorial y urbano Ministry of Agrarian, Territorial and Urban Development
SECTUR	Secretaría de Turismo Ministry of Tourism
SEDESOL	Secretaría de desarrollo social Ministry of Social Development
SEGOB	Secretaría de Gobernación Ministry of the Interior
SEMARNAT	Secretaría de Medio Ambiente y Recursos Naturales Ministry of Environment and Natural Resources
SHCP	Secretaría de Hacienda y Credito Público Ministry of Finance and Public Credit

SMEs	Pequeña y Mediana Empresa Small and medium-sized enterprises
TNC	Transport Network Company
TSA	Cuenta Satélite del Turismo Tourism Satellite Account
UNESCO	Organización de las Naciones Unidas para la Educación, la Ciencia y la Cultura United Nations Educational, Cultural and Scientific Organization
UNWTO	Organización Mundial del Turismo United Nations World Tourism Organization

Executive summary

Tourism is an important economic sector in Mexico, and the country plays a prominent role in tourism globally. The sector directly accounts for 8.5% of GDP, 5.8% of full-time paid employment (in the formal sector), and 77.2% of service exports. It contributes positively to Mexico's Balance of Payments, and generates higher than average value to the economy. A record 32.1 million international tourists contributed MXN 246.1 billion (USD 15.5 billion) to the economy in 2015, with growth in people and monetary flows to the country outstripping growth in many advanced and emerging tourism economies in recent years. This follows a prolonged period of more modest growth. Domestic tourism is also significant, contributing 88 of every 100 Mexican pesos consumed by tourists in the country and supporting employment and development in regions which do not attract international visitors.

The sector quickly adjusted and recovered to pre-crisis GDP growth levels following the impact of the international financial crisis and H1N1 influenza outbreak in 2009. International tourist arrivals have also performed strongly. However, tourism growth has lagged overall growth in the wider economy over the last decade. Mexico's travel and tourism sector has faced several difficulties, including challenging economic conditions in key source markets, natural disasters, health scares and security concerns. Tourism's potential to promote local and regional development remains largely unrealised, and the sector faces competitiveness and sustainability challenges.

This review focuses on priority areas to help strengthen Mexico's tourism sector and take advantage of opportunities with strong potential for economic growth, investment and development, including: the policy making environment and governance; transport, mobility and connectivity; inclusive growth, regional and destination development, and product diversification; and investment and SME financing.

Tourism is high on the policy agenda in Mexico, and is identified as one of six priority economic sectors in the National Development Plan 2013-18. The country has a remarkable range of well-articulated tourism plans and programmes which aim to spur investment and economic growth, promote balanced regional development and stimulate more productive, inclusive and sustainable growth. Ensuring these plans and programmes are effectively co-ordinated and implemented will be vital to realising Mexico's tourism development potential, and delivering on these objectives. This requires a stronger and more efficient governance framework, and an integrated and well co-ordinated approach across many government departments, at different levels of government, and with closer involvement of the private sector. Mexico would particularly benefit from a more strategic policy approach to tourism development, and a stronger focus on implementation. The recent public sector spending cuts makes this situation more challenging, but also more necessary.

Transport is a key enabler of tourism, and the Mexican transport system has a vital role to play in moving domestic and international tourists from their place of residence to, and around, their final destination. While the transport system appears to work well for visitors to coastal resort destinations, it gets more complex outside of these tourism zones. Closer inspection reveals areas requiring attention and policy co-ordination, including taking steps to strengthen air connectivity (particularly with emerging markets in Asia), make ground transportation more user-friendly for visitors, and improve inter-modal connectivity. Mexico's challenge is to develop a transport system that is both global and local in reach, and is safe, secure and simple to navigate, easy to understand and accessible. Addressing this challenge of better connecting tourists with destinations, and on to various attractions, is necessary if Mexico is to diversify its tourism offer and source markets, strengthen tourism in regional areas, and better spread the benefits.

Mexico has a well-established model of tourism development, which has benefited from significant public investment to successfully leverage the country's natural climate and coastline endowment. Attention over the last four decades has mainly focused on the development of highly concentrated coastal resorts, which in turn is reflected in tourism demand, marketing and promotion. This model is now maturing, and is vulnerable to challenge, including from changing consumer demand patterns, and environmental considerations. It is unlikely that this model, in its current form, can support tourism policy objectives to promote more inclusive and sustainable growth. Mexico will need to evolve the model to compete in the changing tourism marketplace and support more inclusive, sustainable growth. It will mean greater involvement by government agencies with a more diverse and fragmented group of small and micro-enterprises, and policies to support smaller scale projects and small tourism businesses. This will require a deliberate and market-led policy focus on destination development and product diversification, supported by private sector investment.

Access to finance is one of the key underlying conditions required if tourism in Mexico is to deliver on its economic potential. Mexico has in place a comprehensive public framework to provide finance for tourism-related projects under the existing model of tourism development, but public sector financing supports will need to be adjusted if they are to encourage greater supply-side innovation and support a more diversified model. Opportunities exist to better target financing to viable tourism projects of all scales, and to mobilise private sector funds to finance product and destination diversification. Small and micro-enterprises face particular financing constraints on the supply (small scale of funding relative to transaction costs) and demand side (lack of financial knowledge, culture and collateral, high informality). Financial and non-financial public supports have an important role to play in this context, to capture the wider economic and social benefits and support the finance needs of firms in regional areas.

Key policy recommendations

- **Promote a more integrated approach and stronger governance for tourism policy.** Develop a more strategic approach to tourism in Mexico. Improve the effectiveness of the Tourism Cabinet as a strategic tool for integrated policy development. Strengthen the linkages between policy, product and promotion, and promote a more participative, market-led approach to tourism policy. Strengthen the evidence base to support policy development.
- **Boost connectivity to support market diversification and move visitors around the country.** Better align transport and tourism policy from point of origin to destination, and make the transport system integrated and seamless for visitors and residents alike. Continue efforts to liberalise air service agreements to

better support tourism and increase connectivity for all Mexican airports. Improve road transport by making it safer, more secure and more efficient for tourists.

- **Promote inclusive tourism growth, product diversification and destination development.** Evolve the model of tourism development. Target policies and interventions to support businesses in a more fragmented, smaller-scale tourism sector. Support a consumer-centric, market-drive approach to product and destination development.
- **Target investment and SME financing to support supply-side innovation.** Direct financing to tourism projects offering the strongest potential and ensure more strategic and efficient use of public monies. Support better uptake and use of financing opportunities by small and micro-enterprises. Capitalise on the capacity for the National Fund for Tourism Development to be a pivotal actor in financing and engineering a new model of tourism development.

Assessment and recommendations

Tourism is an important economic sector in Mexico, and the country plays a prominent role in tourism globally. The sector directly contributed 8.5% of GDP to Mexico's economy in 2014, double the OECD average (4.1%), and one of the highest direct shares of GDP among OECD countries. Tourism's impact on employment is significant, directly supporting 2.3 million full-time equivalent jobs, or 5.8% of full-time paid employment, not counting those employed in the significant informal tourism economy. Tourism's share of trade in services is also substantial, as international travel receipts accounted for 77.2% of service exports in 2015, significantly ahead of the OECD average (21.3% in 2014).

Tourism has risen in importance relative to some other sectors of the economy in recent years, notably oil. The sector quickly adjusted and recovered to pre-crisis GDP growth levels, following the impact of the international financial crisis and H1N1 influenza outbreak in 2009. International tourist arrivals have also performed strongly. However, tourism growth has lagged overall growth in the wider economy, and Mexico's travel and tourism sector has faced several difficulties, including challenging economic conditions in key source markets, natural disasters, health scares and security concerns. Recent public sector spending cuts are also impacting the resources available to develop and implement tourism policies in the short and longer term.

Tourism's potential to promote local and regional development remains largely unrealised, and the sector faces competitiveness and sustainability challenges. Attention to date has mainly focused on the development of highly concentrated coastal resorts, which in turn is reflected in tourism demand, marketing and promotion. Mexico will need to evolve this model to compete in the changing global tourism marketplace, and to spread the economic and social development benefits more widely. National tourism policy aims to encourage investment and economic growth, promote balanced regional development and stimulate more productive, inclusive and sustainable growth.

Against this background, this review provides an assessment of tourism-related policies, programmes and plans to support sustainable tourism development in Mexico. Policy recommendations focus on priority areas to help strengthen Mexico's tourism sector and take advantage of opportunities with strong potential for economic growth, investment and development, with a particular focus on the following areas: policy making environment and governance arrangements; transport, mobility and connectivity to bring visitors to and around the country; inclusive tourism growth, regional and destination development, and product diversification; and investment and SME financing.

Profile and performance of tourism in Mexico's economy

Mexico has recorded moderate economic activity in recent years, with GDP growth projected to be 2.6% in 2016 (OECD, 2016a). This follows three decades marked by slow growth, low productivity, pervasive labour market informality and high income inequalities in Mexico (OECD, 2015a). Despite lower oil prices and softer external demand, the OECD (2016a) expects GDP growth to strengthen to 3% in 2017, as transitory downward pressures on US demand fade away and the current government's broad and deep reform agenda begins to boost investment.

Mexico is experiencing a boom in international tourism at the moment - 2015 was a record year with 32.1 million international tourists contributing MXN 246.1 billion (USD 15.5 billion) to the economy. Since 2014, growth in people and monetary flows to Mexico has outstripped growth in many advanced and emerging tourism economies. The sharp depreciation of the Mexican peso has improved the price competitiveness of tourism exports in Mexico's main source markets, particularly in the important US market. This follows a prolonged period of modest growth in inbound tourism, relative to other countries.

Travel-related exports have made a positive contribution to Mexico's balance of payments position over the last two decades, and generate higher than average value for the economy (91% of tourism exports consist of domestically generated added value, higher than the OECD average of 80%). Tourists who travel beyond the border zone ("non-border tourists") are a higher value and more promotable market as they spend more, stay longer, and make a relatively more important, and expanding, contribution to the Mexican economy, compared to the large number of short-stay cross-border visitors. In 2015, non-border tourists accounted for 21% of international visitors, but contributed 84.4% of visitor receipts.

By virtue of its geographic location, Mexico benefits from the proximity of the United States, which is the second largest outbound market in the world, and Mexico's most important source market by a long way. While the number of tourist arrivals from the United States continues to rise and Mexico has grown its share of US outbound travel, the US share of arrivals to Mexico has fallen over the last decade (down from 87.3% in 2005 to 79.6% in 2014). Arrivals from other source markets have risen over the same period, notably Colombia which has grown by 41% each year since 2012. This points to some source market diversification and a reduced dependence on the US market. This has been helped by measures to ease visa restrictions and facilitate travel, along with improved connectivity and promotional efforts.

Domestic tourism is the mainstay of Mexico's tourism sector, contributing 88 of every 100 Mexican pesos consumed by tourists in the country. Domestic tourists are more evenly spread across the territory and make an economic contribution in regions which do not attract international visitors. International demand is heavily concentrated in sun-sea-sand destinations, including Cancún, the Riviera Maya and Los Cabos. Quintana Roo in the south-southeast region alone accounts for almost half of all international arrivals (47.5%) and almost two thirds of international overnights (62%). By comparison, 4% of domestic arrivals and 5.7% of domestic overnights are recorded in this state.

Towards a more integrated approach and stronger governance for tourism policy

Tourism is high on the policy agenda in Mexico. The National Development Plan 2013-18 identifies tourism as one of six priority sectors and sets out a strategic agenda to modernise and reposition Mexico's tourism industry globally and better harness the economic potential of the sector. The Sectoral Programme for Tourism 2013-18 details the strategies and actions to achieve this. Tourism is also a core pillar of the National Infrastructure Plan 2014-18, which recognises the need to take tourism into account in infrastructure planning and includes a dedicated tourism investment portfolio for the first time, while the Regional Development Programmes 2014-18 contain plans to harness the sector's capacity to stimulate regional economies and support local communities.

The tourism dimensions of these strategies and plans are ambitious and wide-ranging, and provide the general policy framework for tourism development in Mexico. Ensuring these plans and actions are effectively co-ordinated and implemented will be vital to realising Mexico's tourism development potential and delivering on these ambitions. This requires a stronger and more efficient governance framework and an integrated and well-co-ordinated approach across many government departments, at different levels of government, and with closer involvement of the private sector.

Mexico would particularly benefit from a more strategic approach to tourism development, and a stronger focus on implementation. The country has a remarkable range of well-articulated tourism plans, programmes and initiatives, but the strategic framework to identify policy priorities and implement actions to address these is weak. Limited information is available assessing the extent to which initiatives are prioritised and implemented, the outcomes measured and evaluated, and lessons drawn to improve future policy. More effective implementation is essential to make the most of tourism policies and programmes and deliver on Mexico's tourism policy objectives.

The current resource constraints facing policy makers in Mexico makes this situation more challenging, but also more necessary. Budgetary realities are impacting on Mexico's ability to deliver on the national tourism plans, strategies and programmes, linked with the public-sector spending and resource cuts introduced following the sharp reduction in oil-related government revenues. Staff turnover and loss of expertise is impacting the development of effective joined-up tourism policy. The political cycle also makes it difficult to develop and implement a longer-term vision for the tourism sector beyond the term of each administration.

Safety and security are important concerns for tourists around the world. Mexico has developed a suite of measures to help provide a safe and secure environment for tourists. Continued attention to these challenges is needed to respond to the evolving situation in the country, and to realise the economic and regional development potential of tourism.

As part of the wider reform agenda, Mexico has taken steps to strengthen the legal and institutional framework for tourism, and improve the regulatory environment in which the sector operates. This has included an internal restructuring of the Ministry of Tourism (SECTUR) to better respond to the changing demands of the tourism sector, and the introduction of new rules of procedure, both of which were accomplished in 2014. A further restructuring process is currently underway and is expected to be completed by the end of 2016. These reforms should focus on modernising and streamlining the institutional arrangements for tourism and more closely aligning the demand- and supply-side perspectives to ensure tourism policy is close to the market.

Mexico's multi-level government structure has implications for the governance of tourism, and the implementation of tourism policy. Strengthening co-ordination with each level of government, and the private sector, and adopting a more participative and collaborative approach would provide for more effective policy making. Such horizontal and vertical co-ordination is legally underpinned by the General Tourism Law 2009, but is challenging to achieve in practice.

Established in 2013, the Federal Tourism Cabinet is intended to be a strategic policy instrument focused on tourism policy priorities and provides a framework to support a more integrated approach to tourism policy making across government at federal level. The large number of working groups and limited progress made on some activities suggests that the Cabinet would benefit from refocusing its energies and resources on a smaller number of core priority areas. Stronger application of the criteria established to prioritise the policy issues addressed by the Cabinet, closer monitoring of progress and advance planning for transitioning projects out of the Cabinet would also help improve its effectiveness. Awareness of the impacts arising from the activities of the Cabinet is also key to ensuring continuity through political cycles.

Under Mexico's federal government structure, certain tourism policy, planning and development activities are under the responsibility of the state and municipal authorities, which play a central role in implementing national tourism policy. The Sectoral Programme for Tourism 2013-18 provides the policy framework for state and municipal level tourism plans and programmes. Co-ordination between different levels of government mainly occurs within the context of specific programmes and initiatives, notably the Programme for Sustainable Regional Tourism Development and Magic Towns (PRODERMAGICO). However, this co-ordination is not institutionalised and appears to take place largely at the technical rather than the strategic level, indicating there is significant room for improvement. Strengthening vertical co-ordination will be essential to better align policy priorities across the three levels of government, and support more effective policy implementation.

Private sector participation has been instrumental in the development and implementation of certain initiatives. However, while individual instances of successful co-ordination can be identified, engagement with industry and civil organisations does not currently take place on a regular or systematic basis, and such engagement with industry in the development and delivery of policy objectives is limited. This is largely consistent with the wider framework conditions and the strong role played by the Federal Government in planning, developing and financing tourism in Mexico over the last four decades. One of the challenges in seeking industry level policy input in Mexico is the range of industry bodies that represent different types of businesses and branches in the sector, making it difficult for tourism to speak with one voice.

Recommendations

- **Develop a more strategic approach to tourism in Mexico.** Adopt a more coherent framework for identifying policy priorities and implementing actions in the short, medium and long term. Put in place mechanisms to better align strategic policy priorities across the various plans and programmes, and the three levels of government. Enhance the focus on implementation and ensure sufficient resources are allocated to priority actions. Clearly articulate a long-term vision for tourism policy to 2030 and beyond, to provide an over-arching framework for tourism plans, programmes and initiatives.

- **Improve the effectiveness of the Tourism Cabinet as a strategic tool for integrated policy development.** Strengthen the focus on core policy priorities and reduce the number of work groups and activities within the Cabinet to align with these priorities. Enhance engagement with sub-national levels of government and the private sector. Consider creating a Working Group on Implementation to guide, evaluate and monitor progress on key aspects of policy implementation. Build on existing engagement with competent authorities to further strengthen co-ordination and address safety and security issues impacting tourism.

- **Strengthen the linkages between policy, product and promotion, and promote a more participative, market-led approach to tourism policy.** Take advantage of the current re-organisation of the Ministry of Tourism to simplify and modernise the institutional framework for tourism. Clearly set out the roles, responsibilities and linkages between the different functions within the Ministry, and strengthen the relationship with, and between, the National Fund for Tourism Development (FONATUR) and the Mexico Tourism Board (CPTM). Adopt private sector engagement strategies to encourage more active and institutionalised involvement in policy making and improve the impact of policy. Consider establishing a National Tourism Industry Council to act as the main industry interlocutor on policy matters.
- **Strengthen the evidence base to support policy development.** Enhance the integration, availability and use of robust tourism statistics to inform policy development, guide implementation and support monitoring and evaluation. Strengthen the relationship between statistical providers and users, including the National Institute for Statistics and Geography (INEGI), Bank of Mexico and the Ministry of Tourism.

Boosting connectivity to support market diversification and move visitors around the country

Mexico is ranked ninth in the world in terms of international tourist arrivals, which could not have been achieved without a strong, dynamic transport sector. Close proximity to two important source markets, the United States and Canada, provide a natural comparative advantage for Mexico which has been leveraged to build the dynamic industry that exists today. However, while the transport system appears to work well for visitors to coastal resorts, its gets more complex outside of these tourism zones. A closer look at the tourism transportation situation in Mexico reveals areas of concern requiring attention and policy co-ordination.

Connectivity for Mexico has to be examined through an end-to-end lens bringing tourists from their point of origin to a Mexican gateway, and beyond this to the multiple places and attractions they wish to experience. This implies greater global transport connectivity to tourism source markets, domestic transport options that cater to domestic, international and mobility-reduced tourists alike, and a seamless integration and co-ordination between the outward- and inward-facing transport networks and services to allow tourists to customise their trips and discover Mexico's attractions that lie beyond its popular beaches. Domestically, it implies the need for greater point-to-point services, bypassing the country's leading hubs and making better use of low cost carriers.

Mexico enjoys excellent air connectivity between its main markets of origin, the United States and Canada, and its main tourism destinations, with Cancún, Puerto Vallarta and Los Cabos all well served. Where direct flights do not exist, connections via Mexico City or other North American hubs provide one-connection routings for most passengers. Air connectivity from Europe, Latin American and in particular Asia is weaker, and the limited direct connectivity reduces the attractiveness of destinations other than Cancún and Mexico City.

While more liberalised air service agreements with the United States and Canada will help improve connectivity with these markets, restrictions still favour the interest of Mexican carriers over that of the tourism industry and the overall economy. Saturation of

Mexico City's Benito Juárez International Airport is also preventing new route development and limiting the full potential of Mexico as a hub connecting Latin America to Asia and the rest of the world, an issue that will remain until the new airport opens in late 2020. Domestic air connectivity appears to be good, with a mix of low cost carriers and a network carrier. However, it is articulated around a few key hubs which makes travel between two secondary markets longer and may require connections. Finally, airports should be connected not only to other airports but also to their city. While Mexican airports have good road connection to their city, albeit sometimes with heavy congestion like in Mexico City, there are few public transport options that would be viable for tourists carrying luggage.

Cruise ship traffic has started to recover after steep declines in the beginning of the decade but passenger numbers in 2015 remained 11% below the 6.7 million peak recorded in 2010. Cozumel is the second busiest cruise port in the world and is continuing to grow. However, cruising activity is increasingly concentrated in a smaller number of ports, with Cozumel, Ensenada and Majahual accounting for around three quarters of cruise passenger traffic. With the limited exception of Ensenada, Mexican ports are mainly ports-of-call. This limits the economic windfall that this activity provides.

Aside from air, road transport is the main option available to move visitors around the country. Also, with 57 official border crossings spread over 3 145km, road travellers have multiple options available for driving between the United States and Mexico. The road network constitutes the backbone of Mexico's transport system, but is better developed in the north and centre of the country than in the south-southeast region, reflecting the economic centre of gravity and main population centres. Mexico enjoys a well-developed and high quality inter-city bus network which offers wide coverage of destinations. However, road quality is more variable, while road safety and security are also issues.

Ground transportation can be challenging and even at times daunting for independent tourists. Accessing information and understanding the bus network is not always easy, while available public transport is not very user friendly, especially for international visitors. Tourists are often strongly encouraged to avoid public transport and rely on more expensive hotel taxis and transportation network companies for their urban mobility. Accessible transportation is also not well organised and not tourist friendly. Improving the accessibility of transport will cater to the growing number of people with impaired mobility linked with aging populations in Mexico's main source markets, as well as benefiting local people.

Against this backdrop stands a national tourism policy that seeks to bring tourists to inland destinations, diversify source markets beyond North America and offer tourists a more varied experience. With many other nearby destinations offering sun and beach vacations, Mexico's comparative advantage is the rich mix of other experiences it is able to offer visitors. In order to fully take advantage of this, Mexico requires the transport infrastructure and services to connect noteworthy communities with key global tourism markets, as well as major Mexican cities which can be significant domestic tourism generators in their own right. Lack of adequate transport infrastructure can lead to these lesser known destinations being entirely bypassed. Even when infrastructure exists, it must be clearly indicated for tourists to find it, hence the importance of wayfinding initiatives like the National Tourism Signage Programme.

The Mexican transport system must cater to the very different needs of these domestic and international tourists. This means a transport system that is both global and local in reach, and is safe, secure and simple to navigate, easy to understand with information available in multilingual formats, makes use of modern technologies, and accessible. Transforming this aspirational goal into a realistic plan requires the transport system to be more responsive to the user's needs and make an effective use of modern communication technology to remove obstacles to seamlessness within the system.

Mexico's challenges in transport policy are to go beyond the basics and become a global leader. This will help Mexico to diversify its tourism offer and source markets, as well as strengthen tourism in regional areas and spread the benefits. Tourism stands to benefit from the significant allocations for transport under the National Infrastructure Programme 2013-18, while addressing the infrastructure gaps can also provide socio-economic opportunities for local communities in under-served regions.

Recommendations

- **Better align transport and tourism policy from point of origin to destination, and make the transport system integrated and seamless for visitors and residents alike.** Develop integrated transport offerings to connect tourists with regions and attractions, including bundling the purchase of transport and tourism services, developing tourism routes and designing travel itineraries. Align local transport to the needs of tourists and properly plan public transport access to the country's main gateways, especially the new Mexico City Airport. Leverage transport to better distribute the economic benefits of tourism across the country.
- **Continue efforts to liberalise air service agreements to better support tourism and increase connectivity for all Mexican airports.** Build on the recent air service agreements with the United States and Canada. Focus on enhancing connectivity with key and emerging source markets offering the greatest potential. Make better use of low cost carriers to encourage more point-to-point domestic services. Encourage air carriers to co-ordinate schedules and improve transfer times to open up connectivity with Asia and other source markets, where current demand is insufficient to support a direct air service.
- **Improve road transport by making it safer, more secure and more efficient for tourists.** Enhance road connectivity between secondary destinations across the country and the main tourism centres and gateways, especially in the south-southeast region. Provide better information on ground transport (inter-city buses, taxi, public transport) to tourists who are planning to travel to Mexico, and real-time information during their trip. Significantly improve accessibility for people with disabilities and mobility impairments.

Promoting inclusive tourism growth, product diversification and destination development

Mexico has a well-established model of tourism development based on a strong sun-sea-sand offer, largely built around the creation of centrally planned integrated coastal resorts. This model has benefited from significant public investment over the last four decades and is designed to leverage the country's natural climate and coastline endowment. It has been very successful in attracting international demand to destinations like Cancún and Los Cabos; however, attempts to replicate this success in other destinations have met with more mixed results. Concerns have also been raised about the highly concentrated impacts of this type of development, and limited return on public investment in terms of economic and social development.

This model is now maturing, its economic impacts are very localised and its capacity to contribute to regional development and spread the benefits of tourism more widely is limited. The scale of these developments also has significant consequences for the natural and cultural environment. The existing product is strongly tailored to the traditional North American market and a lack of supply-side innovation is limiting Mexico's potential to compete in other markets. In the long term, this model is vulnerable to challenge, including from changing consumer demand patterns, environmental considerations and competitiveness issues.

A focus of tourism policy and planning in Mexico is to secure the future development of the tourism industry on a basis that is more competitive, inclusive and sustainable. It is unlikely that the existing dominant model of the resort-based sun-sea-sand product can support these three outcomes. This will require a deliberate and market-led policy focus on destination development and product diversification, supported by private sector investment. Mexico would benefit from a move to a more geographically distributed model of tourism development and the implementation of regional dispersal measures focused on developing new tourism products, routes and clusters across the country. This type of tourism development relies heavily on co-operation between different levels of government and different actors, as well as the provision of supporting infrastructure and facilities.

Such a diversification strategy should be complementary to the existing sun-sea-sand product, and should not be considered to replace it. This product will continue to be core to Mexico's tourism offer. Mexico has an opportunity to build on this to develop a more diversified, higher value tourism offer. In the future, tourism development will require two things – a refresh of the existing product, and a focus on Mexico's considerable asset base to facilitate product diversification, greater regional spread of tourism and greater inclusivity in terms of tourism employment. Maintaining competitiveness in both mature and emerging tourism products will therefore be a key challenge and priority over the medium term.

Mexico has strong alternatives for tourism development. It enjoys a considerable asset base in terms of its natural, built and cultural heritage which goes beyond its coastal environment. The potential to package new and innovative tourism experiences based on this rich and unique resource base is significant. Looking beyond conventional tourism hubs, this asset base represents an opportunity to consider tourism destination development in new locations which will better support the regional spread of the economic gains associated with tourism. This in turn will better support local jobs and incomes and open up new employment and entrepreneurship opportunities, including for women and indigenous populations, as well as providing micro-enterprises with better prospects of accessing local supply chains. A further positive feature associated with this model of tourism product diversification is that around the world, tourists are moving in this direction too.

Diversifying the tourism product and securing greater regional spread of the economic gain associated with tourism will require different policies and supports. It will mean greater involvement by government agencies with a more diverse and fragmented group of small and micro tourism enterprises. This will require government agencies to develop a new and more nimble skill-set focused on the business development needs of small businesses. Most importantly it will require new management and leadership skills that will help overcome the inherent fragmentation in the tourism sector, and also skills that will support small businesses to integrate and cluster, so as to build some local economic scale. The fragmentation of the tourism industry tends to limit the efficacy of centrally planned policy interventions –locally based tourism entities can remain beyond the influence of central government planning.

Infrastructure development will be key to achieving a tourism industry profile based on a more diversified portfolio of tourism products, with investment in tourism-supporting infrastructure equally as important as tourism-centric investment. Ensuring tourism is taken into account in wider infrastructure planning, notably transport and internet connectivity, is required to address the infrastructure deficits currently limiting tourism's development potential, particularly in regional areas. Realising the tourism infrastructure projects in the National Infrastructure Plan 2014-18 and other programmes will also be important. Mechanisms are also needed to develop visitor services, product development and marketing, and enhance information provision.

Opportunities exist to build on existing initiatives to diversify the tourism product based on a wider and more varied asset base and promote higher value tourism markets, including developing tourism clusters associated with cultural, natural and built assets (e.g. Magic Towns, gastronomic and medical and ecotourism initiatives), as well as expand existing sub-sectors with growth potential such as gastronomy and meetings, incentives, conference and events (MICE). It is important these developments are informed by demand-side trend intelligence and by a market-led understanding of product needs, gaps and opportunities. This requires a consumer-centric, market driven approach to tourism planning, development and marketing.

Pursuing a destination development model on the basis of product diversification will thus require investment in marketing and market research. Whereas the sun-sea-sand product typically targets a homogeneous mass-market base, the market for consumers seeking a different experience of Mexico is more niche and fragmented. This will require more extensive market analysis and detailed intelligence on consumer behaviour and decision-making, including the motivating factors that prompt consumers to research and book a trip to Mexico. More information is also required on the background and characteristics of these visitors, their travel and consumption patterns, and their expectations and satisfaction with different aspects of their experience. Consumer insight and increased market segmentation and analysis should be the starting point for all tourism development programmes.

Investment in skills and capacity building is also required. A more diversified industry will be characterised by the participation of a greater number of small businesses which may lack the resources, experience and know-how of larger firms. A specific programme of supports will be necessary to promote entrepreneurship, and to assist the owners of small and micro-enterprises. It will also be necessary to develop capacity building initiatives to support policy makers at federal and state level. An emerging tourism development paradigm based on a growing level of product diversification will require new skills in the areas of strategic planning, policy implementation, horizontal and vertical co-ordination, and integration of action plans. At local government level, it will also require a strengthened model of collaboration between local government, business groups and civil society.

Recommendations

- **Evolve the model of tourism development. Identify different destination development models, based on a geographically distributed offer and supported by tourism clusters.** Develop a more diversified, higher value market-led portfolio of tourism products and make the most of Mexico's diverse tourism assets including gastronomy, eco, adventure and MICE tourism. Evolve and rejuvenate the existing model to offer more value to consumers and open up greater opportunities to explore, encounter local experiences and take part in new activities. Promote regional tourism initiatives in existing and new destinations to stimulate local economic and social development. Capitalise on the experience with Magic Towns and other existing initiatives (e.g. medical clusters, ecotourism) as part of this new approach. Review and adjust the role of the Ministry of Tourism, FONATUR and the Mexico Tourism Board to support the new model of tourism development.

- **Target policies and interventions to support businesses in a more fragmented, smaller-scale tourism sector.** Develop the capacity and ability of public authorities at each level of government to support a new model of tourism development, based on greater regional spread, local clusters and more routine interaction with SMEs. Promote entrepreneurship and support SMEs to grow their business and integrate into tourism value chains. Incentivise SMEs to cluster to support destination development and enhance market profile, and build capacity to deliver (and capture) scale effects, efficiencies and organisational capacity to compete in tourism supply chains. Strengthen collaboration between public and private actors, with the public sector providing a leadership role and acting as an enabler of private sector-led tourism development.

- **Support a consumer-centric, market-driven approach to product and destination development.** Ensure policy, planning, development and marketing is based on strong demand-side analysis and insight. Strengthen the capacity of government agencies to commission, analyse and utilise market-facing consumer research. Develop a mechanism to co-ordinate consumer research, monitor consumer trends in relation to lifestyle, tourism and travel, and convert research into actionable insights. Consider introducing an annual visitor survey to better understand the profile, needs and behaviours of visitors, and assess levels of satisfaction with visitor services.

- **Better align infrastructure and tourism policies.** Ensure tourism-supporting infrastructure planning is informed by a new tourism orientation to a more diverse product, which is regionally dispersed and clustered. Improve broadband access for rural tourism SMEs. Influence and inform infrastructure planning and development undertaken at federal and state level of government.

Targeting investment and SME financing to support supply-side innovation

Mexico has in place a comprehensive public framework to finance large and small tourism projects, which have different finance needs requiring different approaches. Even where the finance opportunities are not tailored for tourism firms, they are accessible, although informality remains a barrier for many tourism businesses seeking to access external financing, particularly micro-enterprises. However, these public financing supports cater mainly to the current model of tourism development and will need to be adjusted if they are to encourage greater supply-side innovation and support a more diversified model.

Opportunities exist to better target financing to viable tourism projects of all scales and reach small and micro-firms to support product and destination diversification. This requires more rigorous assessment and evaluation to ensure funding is targeted at market-led tourism projects offering the greatest potential. It entails improved co-ordination between the different actors and levels of government, and follow-up supports to enhance the capacity of public and private actors to deliver on this potential and ensure optimal use of public funds. Financing a new model of tourism development also involves the public sector moving from a direct investment role to a more supporting role as a private sector investment facilitator.

Mexico has a well-developed tourism investment model which operates through FONATUR and supports the dominant sun-sea-sand offer. Developed over 40 years ago, this supply-side model finances large-scale, centrally-planned tourism projects, particularly in the resort hotel sector, using these investments to leverage private sector participation. However, the model has struggled in recent years to replicate its early success in attracting investors to new tourism developments. FONATUR finances have deteriorated, linked with the global financial crisis, underlying weaknesses in the business model and other demand-side conditions. Following a financial and organisational restructure in 2012, FONATUR is modifying its business model to promote a broader set of destinations, and finance smaller-scale investment projects, including SMEs. This re-orientation should be supported and strengthened, in order to harness FONATUR experience and know-how to support a new model of tourism development.

The public component of financing tourism development in Mexico is more significant compared to other OECD countries. There are well-known structural reasons that explain such intervention, at least on a temporary basis (e.g. high levels of financial exclusion and underdeveloped credit and capital markets). Tourism development has benefited from significant government investment, and public development banks play a strong role in providing credit, sometimes at subsidised rates which risk crowding out the private sector. The recent reduction and reconfiguration of public budget allocations is constraining the capacity of several ministries and agencies, including the Ministry of Tourism and the National Institute for Entrepreneurship (INADEM), to provide funding to viable private sector-led tourism projects, and also complicates long-term planning. Insufficient funding to meet demand may also reflect a lack of prioritisation or strategic approach to ensure financing is directed to projects with the strongest potential.

Financial reforms are strengthening the role of public banks in counter-cyclically financing SMEs, and creating products capable of increasing participation in the finance market, including women. These reforms are benefiting tourism firms, with an increase in both the level of credit and number of firms financed through the Mexican Foreign Trade Bank (Bancomext). The reforms will also support the diversification of the tourism offer, including in rural areas and communities. The creation and uptake of new capital market investment finance vehicles, including infrastructure and real estate trust vehicles (FIBRAs) and capital development certificates (CKDs), have strongly contributed to attracting private sector-led investment in the tourism real estate market (e.g. the creation of hotels in agro-industrial corridors). However, these instruments are better suited to the development of hotels which are part of an international chain and cater to the business market, rather than all-inclusive resorts and independent hotels which account for the majority of the sector in Mexico and are more likely to cater to the leisure market.

Mexico can build on its experience using public-private partnerships (PPPs) to leverage network infrastructure investments (roads, connectivity, water and sewage treatment) to strengthen future tourism-related PPPs, which can provide the necessary funding, expertise and demand-side view for potential projects. However, horizontal and vertical co-ordination remain a challenge, as these activities are decided and financed at the sub-national level, often with support from the federal government, while the capacity to implement these activities at local level is an issue.

Mexico is promoted as a destination for foreign direct investment (FDI) in large-scale commercial tourism-related projects, but has seen declines in FDI inflows in the sector, which are subject to the macroeconomic conditions in the both the host and source country. This limits in part the scope for Mexico to influence FDI inflows for tourism. Attracting FDI also has the potential to indirectly benefit tourism SMEs, but to secure these benefits Mexico has to ensure that FDI investments connect with local firms, promote knowledge transfer and create local linkages that will enable SMEs integrate into global value chains.

For tourism SMEs and entrepreneurs, Mexico has a wide range of dedicated and general finance instruments available. Financing constraints on the supply (small scale of funding relative to transaction costs) and demand side (lack of financial knowledge, culture and collateral, high informality) mean that tourism SMEs are unlikely to be financed through the commercial banking system. Public supports play an important role in this context, to capture the wider economic and social benefits and support the finance needs of firms in certain geographic areas. Mexico offers standard loans and credit guarantee programmes with public support through the private credit market, as well as programmes providing access to venture capital and credit to fund start-ups or expand SMEs and innovative micro-enterprises. However, access to finance is only part of the story as issues remain around the uptake and effective use of these instruments. Non-financial supports are also important for tourism SMEs. To address this, the finance products available make provision for technical assistance and mentoring.

Since 2012, the INADEM promotes entrepreneurship development and provides comprehensive support for SMEs in all sectors. Tourism SMEs are covered by these supports, but INADEM does not have a specific tourism mandate or budget, unlike Bancomext. There is potential to strengthen INADEM role to match viable tourism-related projects with finance opportunities, provide capacity building and mentoring, and help small firms integrate into value chains and enterprise networks, to benefit from economies of scale. Strengthening and expanding the role of the Tourism Enterprise Attention Centres and Rapid Business Start-up System (CAET-SARE) can reduce informality and is a starting point to build on financing tourism SMEs.

Recommendations

- **Direct financing to tourism projects offering the strongest potential and ensure more strategic and efficient use of public monies.** Undertake more robust assessment and evaluation of public investment in tourism. Examine the cost and potential welfare gains of using subsidies to finance tourism-development projects, particularly in the context of overall constrained resources. Establish ex-ante fiscal caps on public sector finance provision. Improve co-ordination between levels of government and implementing agencies. Capitalise on Mexico's experience using public-private partnerships to finance basic infrastructure to support tourism development. Consider the provision of finance for tourism projects within a wider destination context, to support the creation of routes, clusters and strategic destination developments.
- **Support better uptake and use of financing opportunities by small and micro-enterprises.** Strengthen the role of INADEM in providing financial and

non-financial supports to small and micro tourism enterprises. Improve the financial capacity of small and micro-enterprises through technical assistance and mentoring. Encourage tourism enterprises to formalise and move out of the informal economy, including through administrative simplification and expanding the role of the Tourism Enterprise Attention Centres and Rapid Business Start-up System. Explore the potential of alternative financing sources (channelling remittances through crowdfunding, micro-finance) that bring a private sector perspective to the selection and funding of projects.

- **Capitalise on the capacity for FONATUR to be a pivotal actor in financing and engineering a new model of tourism development.** Support FONATUR in driving the implementation of a new model of tourism development from design to evaluation, under the leadership of the Ministry of Tourism. Build synergies between FONATUR, INADEM and other financing actors to foment and support product and destination diversification. Strengthen Mexico's leadership on tourism development in Latin America by exporting FONATUR know-how in tourism engineering and providing advisory services to countries in the region.

Chapter 1
Profile and performance of tourism in Mexico

Tourism is an important economic sector in Mexico and plays a key role in stimulating growth, generating export revenues and supporting jobs. The country is experiencing a boom in international tourism at the moment – 2015 was a record year for international arrivals and receipts, with growth outstripping many advanced and emerging tourism economies. Domestic tourism is also important. This chapter examines the performance and competitiveness of tourism in Mexico over the last decade, within the broader economic context. The major challenges and opportunities facing the Mexican tourism sector are discussed, and the importance of robust statistical information on tourism to better drive business and policy decision-making is highlighted.

Tourism in the economy

Tourism is an important economic sector in Mexico, and plays a key role in stimulating growth, generating export revenues and supporting jobs. However, the potential for tourism to promote local and regional development remains largely unrealised, and the sector faces competitiveness and sustainability challenges. Attention to date has mainly focused on the development of highly concentrated integrated coastal resorts. Mexico is currently looking to evolve this model to compete in the changing tourism marketplace, and to spread the benefits more widely across the territory and support more inclusive, sustainable growth.

This chapter considers the role of tourism in the economy and examines the performance and competitiveness of tourism in Mexico over the period 2005-15. It situates tourism in the broader economic context, and discusses some of the major challenges and opportunities currently facing Mexican tourism and its development potential. The analysis is primarily based on official statistics from the National Tourism Statistical Information System, DATATUR, and the National Institute of Statistics and Geography, INEGI.

Macroeconomic environment

Tourism is influenced by changing economic conditions in both the national and global economy, and in major generating source markets. When economies grow, levels of disposable income also increase, resulting in higher spending on tourism and travel. Economic growth also means more resources are available in both the public and private sector to invest in infrastructure and encourage the development of the travel and tourism sector. Wider macro-economic conditions also influence the business environment in which tourism enterprises operate.

Eight years after the financial crisis, recovery remains weak with growth rates well below pre-crisis norms. Global GDP growth is projected by the OECD (2016a) to be 3% in 2016, unchanged from 2015, with only a modest improvement foreseen in 2017. Many emerging market economies have lost momentum and deep recessions persist in Brazil and Russia, while the upturn in advanced economies remains modest. Such a prolonged period of slow growth has damaged the longer-run supply-side potential of economies, via the scarring effect of extended unemployment, foregone investment and adverse impact of weak trade growth on productivity.

Mexico has recorded moderate economic activity in recent years and the OECD (2016a) has projected GDP to grow by 2.6% in 2016, following the 2.5% growth recorded in 2015. This is due to weakening global growth, policy uncertainty in some other emerging market economies, concerns about divergent monetary policies in advanced economies and downward pressures on commodity prices (OECD, 2016a). It follows three decades marked by slow growth, low productivity, pervasive labour market informality and high income inequality in Mexico, with one in five Mexicans living in poverty, compared to one in ten in OECD economies (OECD, 2015a).

Despite lower oil prices and softer external demand, the OECD (2016a) expects GDP growth in Mexico to strengthen to 3% in 2017, as transitory downward pressures on US demand fade away and the government's broad reform agenda begins to boost investment. The sharp depreciation of the peso has improved export competitiveness, including for tourism, and resilient domestic demand continues to support economic activity. Inflation has remained below the central bank's target, and monetary policy remains focused on achieving inflation stability and avoiding upward price pressures from currency weakness. Public sector spending cuts are being implemented following the sharp reduction in oil-related government revenues, as the significant decline in oil prices has impacted the state of the public finances. This has implications for Mexico's infrastructure investment programme, and is negatively impacting the resources available to develop and implement tourism policies in the short and longer term.

Economic contribution of tourism

Tourism directly contributed MXN 1.4 billion or 8.5% of GDP to Mexico's economy in 2014 (down from 9.3% in 2005 in current prices), based on Tourism Satellite Account (TSA) data. By comparison, the construction and mining sectors each accounted for 7.3% of GDP, while financial services and agriculture contributed 4.5% and 3.1% respectively. Tourism's indirect and induced GDP effects are also important, but it is extremely difficult to obtain evidence of such effects from the application of a consistent approach to measurement.

Tourism's direct share of GDP in Mexico is double the OECD average of 4.1%, and is one of the highest among OECD countries. Mexico's tourism GDP is made up of: transport services 16.8%, crafts and other goods 15.5%, restaurants, bars and nightclubs 10.1%, accommodation 8.8% and time share and second homes 4.6%, with other miscellaneous activities making up the remainder.

Figure 1.1. Direct contribution of tourism to the Mexican economy, 2014

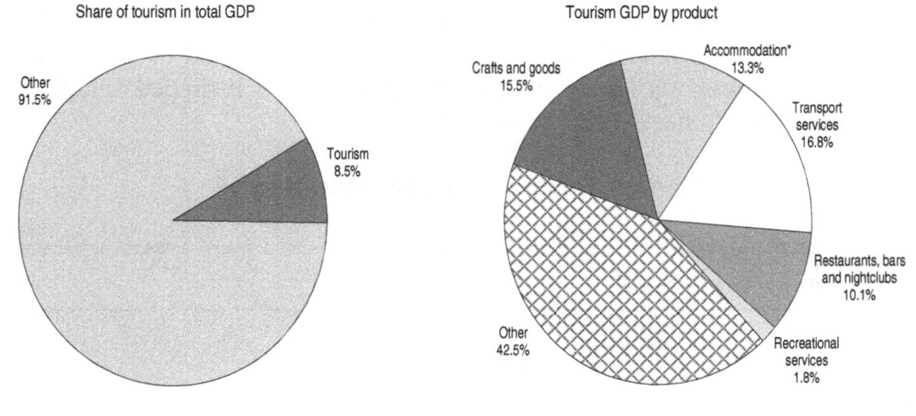

* Includes timeshare and second home.

Source: INEGI, extract May 2016.

The value of tourism in the economy has grown slightly behind overall GVA growth in real terms over the period of the review (21.7% compared with 23.3% between 2005 and 2014, at constant prices). This averages at 2.2% growth each year in real terms, compared with 2.4% growth in the economy as a whole. The sector contracted by 4.5% in 2009, linked with the global financial crisis and the H1N1 flu pandemic, but quickly adjusted and has recovered to pre-crisis growth levels.

Tourism's share of GDP has declined slightly over this period. However, tourism's importance relative to some other sectors of the economy has risen in recent years, notably oil. The sector has also grown ahead of the construction sector, but behind financial services over the period of the review.

Figure 1.2. GDP contribution of tourism relative to other sectors, 2005-14

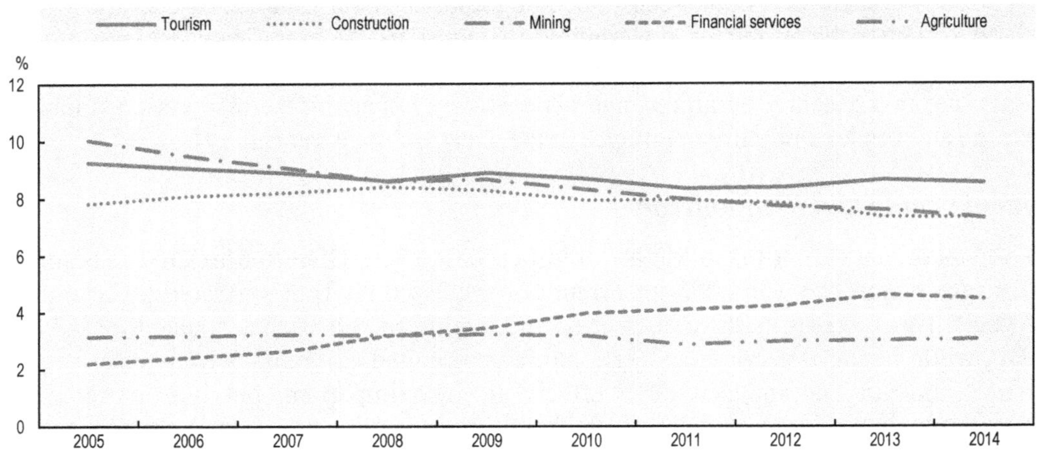

Source: INEGI, extract May 2016.

Tourism exports, travel balance and contribution to domestic value added

Tourism's share of trade in services is significant. The sector is an important export-driver and source of foreign exchange earnings in Mexico. International travel receipts accounted for 77.2% of service exports and 4.3% of total exports in 2015, in current prices. The significance of tourism's share of service exports in Mexico is apparent when compared the OECD average of 21.3%, and a global average of 25.6% (UNWTO, 2016a). Tourism's share of total exports has fallen over the period of the review, while the share of service exports has expanded overall (although it dipped sharply in 2013 linked with growth in "other export" revenues).

Figure 1.3. Travel-related exports, 2005-15

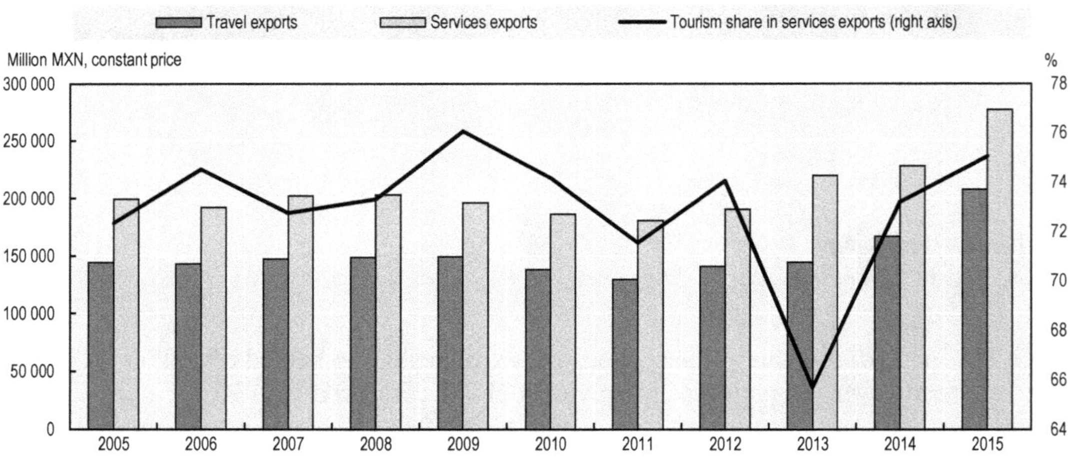

Base year 2008.

Source: INEGI and OECD calculations.

Travel-related exports contribute positively to Mexico's balance of payments position. Over the last two decades, Mexico has consistently recorded a travel balance surplus, as growth in receipts from international visitors (exports) has outpaced expenditure of Mexican residents travelling to other countries (imports).

This situation was accentuated since 2013, as growth in inbound tourism has helped to compensate for weaker oil revenues. Travel-related exports rose from MXN 178.2 billion in 2013 to MXN 215.8 billion in 2014 and MXN 276.7 billion in 2015, an increase of 43.8% in real terms. The travel surplus rose from MXN 61.6 billion in 2013 to MXN 87.9 billion in 2014 and MXN 116.6 billion in 2015, or by 75.1% in real terms over this same period.

Figure 1.4. Tourism contribution to balance of payments, 2005-15

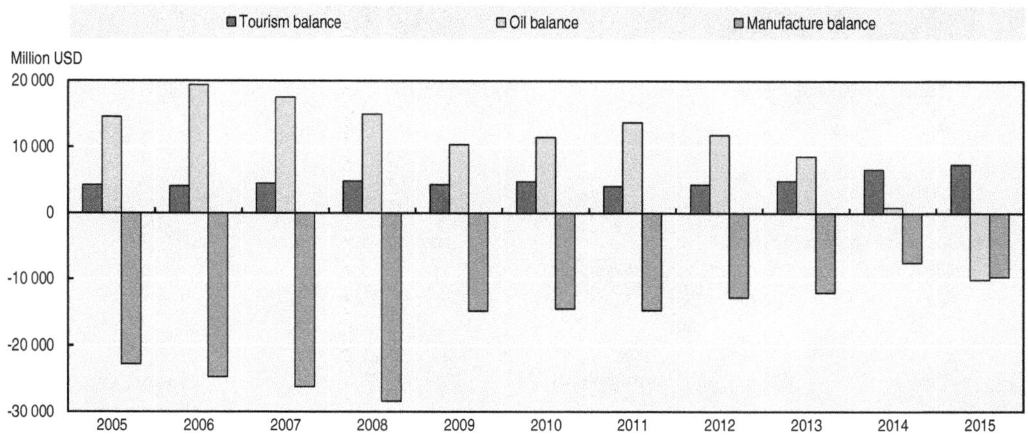

Source: Bank of Mexico, extract May 2016.

Tourism exports are economically important as they contribute to the value added of the economy and have significant upstream impacts. While not all tourism exports result in increases in domestic value added, initial figures from the OECD-WTO Trade in Value Added (TiVA) analysis indicates that tourism receipts generate higher than average value-added for receiving countries, and have significant upstream effects in both the recipient country, and in other countries.

According to TiVA estimates, approximately 91% of Mexican tourism exports consist of domestically generated value added (in Mexico). This is higher than the OECD average of 80%. The remaining 9% resulted in value created in other countries (imports). Tourism expenditures also generate significant upstream effects in Mexico, with every EUR 1 of value added in tourism-related industries estimated to result in 33 cent additional value added in upstream industries in Mexico. This last figure is lower than the OECD average (of 56%), mainly reflecting that, in particular, the Mexican services industries (transport, other services) have a relatively high direct value added content in their sales, i.e. are less likely to outsource inputs from (domestic) suppliers but provide their own.

Consumption by domestic and inbound tourists

TSA data for Mexico indicates that internal tourism consumption amounted to MXN 2.1 billion in 2014, in current prices. The domestic market contributed approximately 88 of every 100 Mexican pesos consumed by tourists in the country. This share of tourism consumption is above the OECD average of 77%, underlining the significant economic role played by domestic tourism in Mexico. This share has remained relatively stable over the period of the review.

Figure 1.5. Internal tourism consumption by type of tourism and product, 2014

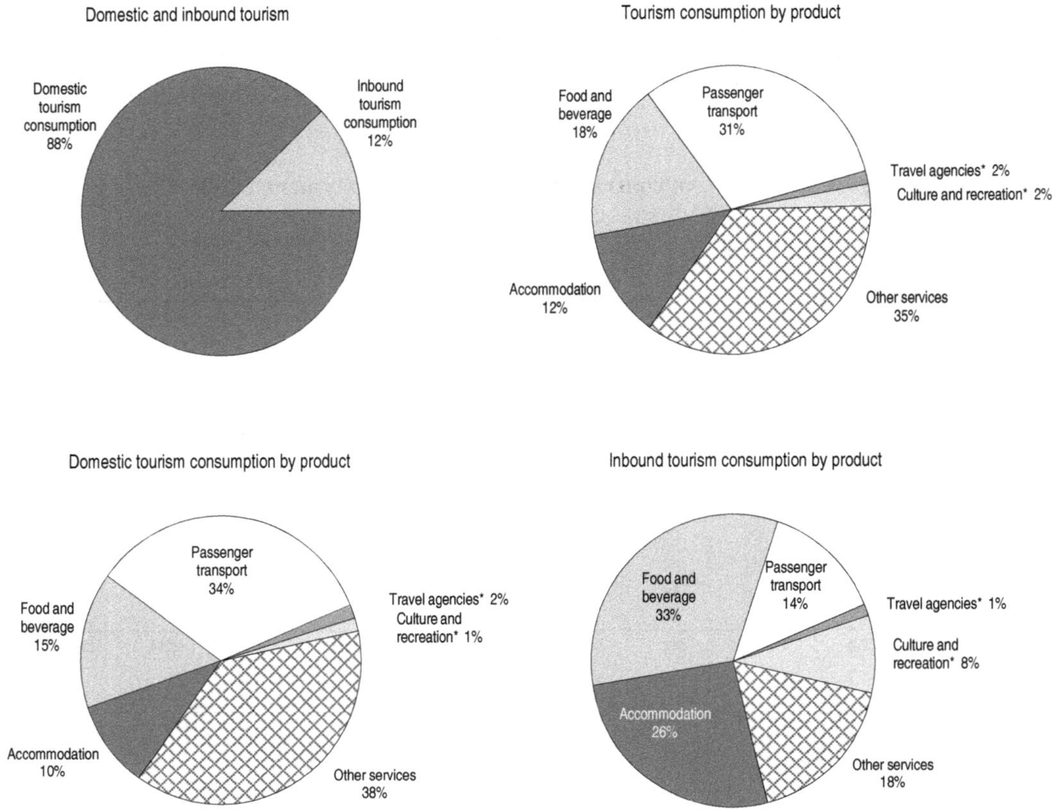

* Travel agencies include other reservation services. Culture and recreation include sports.

Source: INEGI, Tourism Satellite Account, 2014.

For its part, consumption linked with outbound travel by Mexican residents amounted to MXN 168 million in current prices, bringing total tourism consumption in Mexico to MXN 2.3 billion in 2014, up 3.7% from MXN 2.2 billion in 2013.

TSA data demonstrates the different consumption patterns of domestic and international tourists, with significant variations observed. Overall, transport accounts for the single largest share of internal tourism consumption (30.9% in 2014) followed by food and beverage (17.6%) and accommodation services (12.2%). However, transport represents a smaller share of inbound tourism consumption (13.7%), while accommodation (26.3%) and food and beverage services (32.7%) account for a larger share. The opposite is true of consumption by domestic tourist. This is linked with the fact that the domestic market makes more frequent but short trips, and is more likely to stay with friends and families. Also, for inbound tourists, spending on leisure tourism was the most important component of inbound tourism consumption (62.7%), with business travel accounting for 6.7%. For domestic tourists, leisure and business travel accounted for 33.2% and 22.3% respectively.

Impact of tourism on employment

The impact of tourism on employment is significant in Mexico. Measuring the complete range of jobs directly and indirectly linked to tourism is challenging. Tourism is a heterogeneous industry representing a wide variety of types and sizes of businesses. Two measures provide data on tourism employment in Mexico.

TSA provides a comprehensive picture of tourism employment, based on full-time equivalent paid jobs. It uses a tourism ratio to estimate the number of paid jobs directly linked to tourism demand. According to the latest available data, tourism directly supports over 2.3 million jobs or 5.8% of full-time paid employment in Mexico. This compares to 5.9% on average in OECD.

While employment in the sector has increased in absolute terms over the past decade, up 4.6% from 2.2 million in 2005, tourism's share of total employment is slightly down on the 2005 level of 6.1%. The biggest share of tourism employment is provided by restaurants, bars and nightclubs at just over a third (36%), followed by 16.2% in passenger transport, 13.1% in crafts and other goods, and 8% in accommodation, timeshare, second home and recreational services, with 26.6% in other services. According to TSA data, total tourism remuneration was MXN 244.2 billion in 2014, while the average annual wage in tourism is MXN 106 150, below the economy-wide average of MXN 118 149.

Figure 1.6. Number of paid jobs in tourism, 2005-14

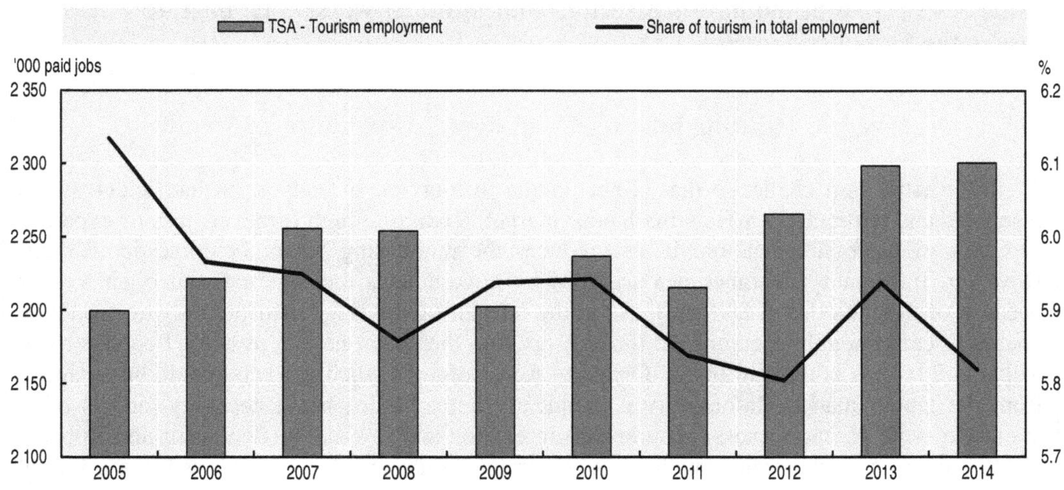

Source: INEGI, TSA.

DATATUR's employment data provides an alternative, but related measure. It measures the number of occupied people working in the sector. It is constructed based on the National Occupation and Employment Survey and weights tourism characteristic and related categories based on the equivalent paid jobs in the TSA. According to this measure, an estimated 3.7 million people are employed in the tourism sector in Mexico in 2015, equivalent to 8.2% of total employment. Tourism employment has grown steadily over the period of the review, rising on average 2.5% each year up from 2.97 million in 2006.

Figure 1.7. Number of people[1] employed in tourism, 2006-15

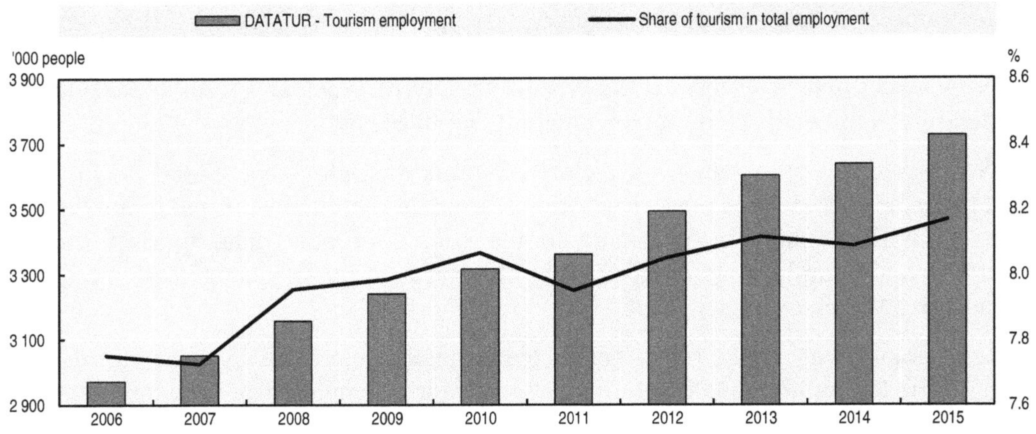

1. Data refers to self-employed workers, subordinates and paid workers in quarter 4.

Source: DATATUR based on Encuesta Nacional de Ocupación y Empleo (ENOE) INEGI.

These measures only present a partial picture of tourism employment in Mexico. They do not capture employment in the informal tourism economy, which is sizeable in Mexico. INEGI estimates that over half (54%) of accommodation and food service businesses operate in the informal sector, with informal workers earning 40% less than those in the formal sector (Box 1.1).

Box 1.1. Tackling informality in the tourism sector in Mexico

Informality is a challenge that is not unique to tourism. It leads to an inefficient use of resources and particularly affects the labour market, leading to high turnover, loss of expertise and lack of professionalisation. It also reduces the purchasing power in domestic markets. However, informality is sometimes accepted by governments and international organisations because of the idea that it favours those at the left tail of the wage distribution who would be unable to earn enough to contribute through taxes to the social benefit system (Bentancor and Robano, 2014). It is thought that if formality were enforced, such workers would be excluded from the labour market. Informality is frequently not a choice but a necessity, and is often associated with precariousness, geographic segregation and low-skills (Bentancor and Robano, 2014). For most workers, informality is a constraint, as had they been employed in the formal sector, these informal workers would have been net recipients of social security, given their low skills and salary. In an effort to bring tourism businesses into the formal economy in Mexico, the Ministry of Tourism has put in place a strategy to register craft and street vendors at beach and other tourism destinations. The implementation of the Tourism Enterprise Attention Centres and Rapid Business Start-up System (CAET-SARE) is also helping to address informality. Moving to the formal sector can benefit employees and help firms in tourism-related activities to access finance from formal lenders.

Tourism profile and performance

Mexico's travel and tourism sector has faced several challenges over the past decade, including the impact of the global economic crisis, natural disasters (Hurricane Odile) and health scares (H1N1, Zika). Tourism is also more vulnerable to external events than many other sectors of the economy. Despite this, the sector has remained resilient and has continued to expand. However, the Sectoral Programme for Tourism 2013-18 notes that Mexico's performance across the main tourism indicators has been moderate compared to other countries over the past three decades.

International tourism

Trade in international tourism services attracts policy attention in many countries due to the potential to support export-driven growth and stimulate the economy. Mexico plays a prominent role in tourism globally, and 2015 was a record year for international tourism to the country, both in terms of arrivals and receipts.

International arrivals

Mexico appears to be experiencing something of a tourism boom at the moment, as strong arrivals performance since 2014 has outstripped growth in many advanced and emerging tourism economies. However, data for the period 2005-13 reveals a much more modest performance relative to other countries.

Over the period 2005-15, international tourist arrivals to Mexico rose by 46.7% overall to reach 32.1 million in 2015, growing at an average rate of 3.9% each year. This is in line with annual growth recorded globally (3.9%) and in the Americas (3.7%) as a whole over the same period, but behind growth of around 5% elsewhere in Latin America.

The overall trend for international tourist arrivals between 2005 and 2013 was one of moderate if uneven growth, marked by a downturn in 2009 followed by a strong return to growth in 2010. During this period, overnight trips to Mexico rose by 10.2% or 1.2% on average each year. This was followed by exceptional growth of 21.5% in 2014. Continued strong performance in 2015 saw a further increase of 9.5%. This recent strong arrivals growth is linked with positive external factors, notably the favourable US dollar exchange rate.

Figure 1.8. Inbound arrivals to Mexico, 2005-15

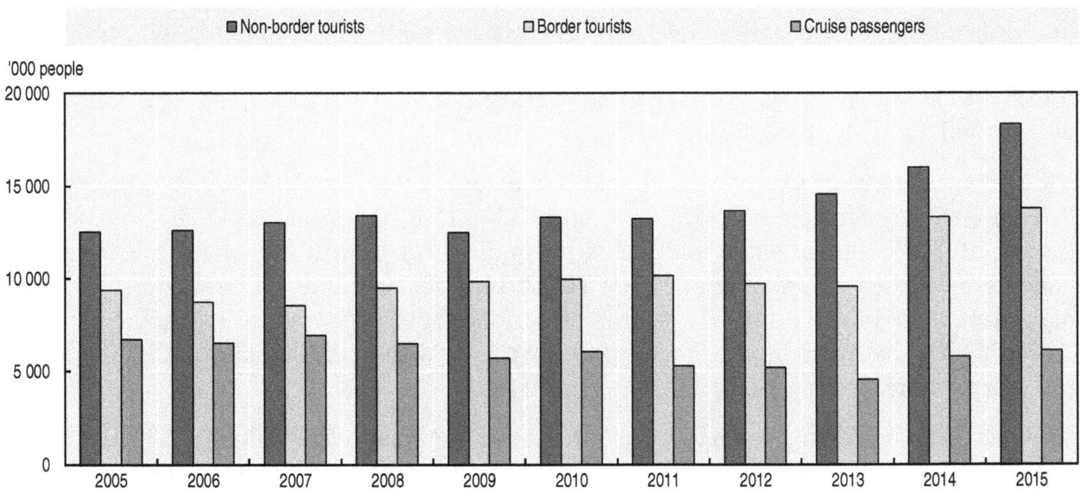

Source: Bank of Mexico.

The share of international tourist arrivals as part of total visitor arrivals has risen over this period, from 21.2% in 2005 to 30.9% in 2013, and 36.9% in 2015, as the number of international visitors (overnight and same-day) fell to a low of 75.7 million in 2011 and remains 15.4% lower than peak levels of 103.1 million in 2005 (87.2 million in 2015).

A significant share of recent arrivals growth in 2014 comes from an extraordinary rise (39.2%) in "border tourists" (overnight visitors to the border zone, who do not travel further than an area 25-30 km land border with the United States to the north, and a shorter border with Belize and Guatemala to the south. Around 13.8 million international tourists (15.8%) crossing these borders in 2015 did not travel beyond the narrowly defined border zone, from a total of 62.8 million border visitors. The flows of visitors to the border zone are relatively volatile, and are influenced by changes in the peso-dollar exchange rate and relative price of goods and services, and border control measures, among other things. Many of cross-border visitors are also visiting friends and relatives.

In contrast, non-border tourism grew by 27.7% from 12.6 million in 2005 to 16 million in 2014, growing at an average annual rate of 2.7% between 2005 and 2014. Non-border tourist arrivals again rose strongly in 2015 to reach 18.4 million, up 46.4% on 2005, equivalent to 3.9% growth per year. Non-border tourist arrivals were more affected by the economic crisis and flu pandemic, falling by 6.9% in 2009 (compared with 2.5% fall in overall tourist arrivals), but recovered well, rising by 6.6% in 2010 (compared with 4.2%), and have recorded consistent growth since. Available data indicates that non-border tourists are a higher value market, as they spend more and stay longer, and are also a more promotable target than border tourists. The majority of non-border tourism to Mexico is for leisure purposes (59.7% in 2014), followed by visiting friends and relatives (25.3%), with 7.8% visiting for business purposes.

Cruise passengers are not counted in the international tourist arrivals data. In 2014, Mexico welcomed 5.8 million cruise passengers, up 27% on 2013, and grew by a further 5.7% to reach 6.1 million in 2015. However, cruise passenger numbers have fallen by 8.8% over the review period (2005-15) and have fluctuated on an annual basis, peaking in 2007, followed by double-digit falls recorded in 2009, 2011 and 2013.

International receipts

Monetary flows are a significant performance indicator when assessing the economic contribution of tourism. Over the period 2005-15, international visitor receipts to Mexico rose by 44% in real terms, growing at an average rate of 3.7% each year. This is in line with growth in international tourist arrivals.

International visitors (overnight and same-day) generated MXN 276.7 billion in foreign currency receipts in 2015, up from MXN 215.8 billion in 2014. This equates to growth of 24.4% in real terms in 2015, strongly ahead of growth in global travel receipts which grew by 3.6% in real terms (UNWTO, 2016a). It also builds on growth of 15.6% in real terms in 2014. This follows on from a period where performance was more mixed, during which international receipts recorded weak growth over the period 2005-09, then fell sharply in real terms in 2010 (7.4%) and 2011 (6.3%).

Overnight visitors accounted for 36.9% of international visitors in 2015, but contributed 88.9% of visitor receipts, or MXN 246.1 billion to the Mexican economy. This is up from 21.2% of visitors and 77.5% of receipts in 2005. Growth in international tourism receipts (3.1% annual growth in real terms) has largely performed in line with the observed growth in tourist arrivals (3.3% annually) over the period 2005-14, but outpaced arrivals growth in 2015.

Non-border tourists in particular accounted for 21% (18.4 million, an increase of 14.7% compared to 2014) of international visitors in 2015, but contributed 84.4% of foreign currency receipts. This is up from 12.2% of visitors and 72% of receipts in 2005. Non-border tourist spending rose (68.7% in real terms over the period 2005-15) ahead of non-border tourist arrivals (46.4%), while spending by border tourists (up 19.6% in real terms) lagged growth in arrivals (47%). Same-day visitor spending fell (29.3% in real terms) slightly behind the fall in arrivals (32.2%). This highlights the relatively higher, and expanding, contribution of tourists to the Mexican economy, and non-border tourists in particular, compared to the large number of short-stay cross border visits.

Figure 1.9. Visitor and tourist arrivals and spending, 2005-15

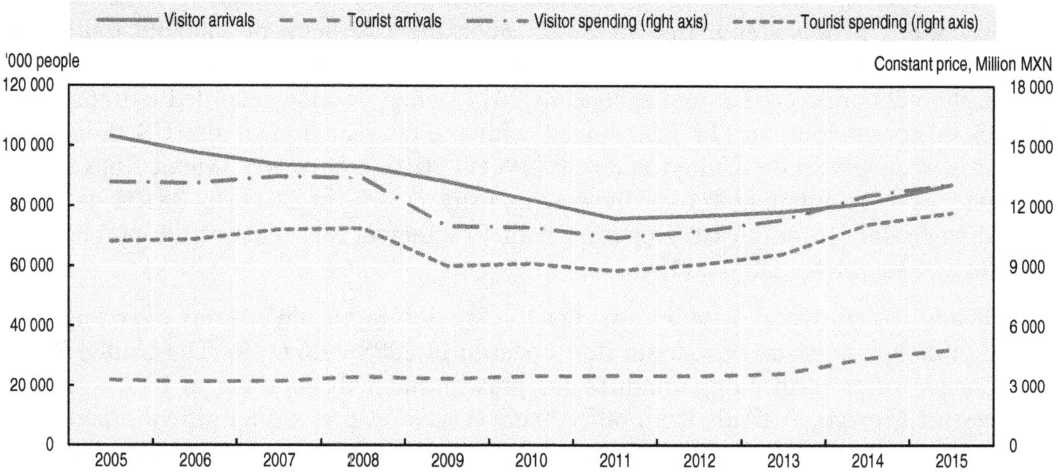

Base year 2008.

Source: Bank of Mexico.

Market share, global rankings and exchange rate fluctuations

In line with the growth in international arrivals and receipts, Mexico has risen in the global rankings. At the same time, Mexico has seen its market share of both arrivals and receipts expand while recording growth in the volume of both people and monetary flows. In terms of people flows, Mexico accounted for 2.7% of global tourism arrivals and was ranked 9th in the world in 2015, up from a 2.6% share and 10th in the world in 2014. In terms of monetary flows, Mexico accounted for 1.4% of global travel receipts and was ranked 16th in the world in 2015, up from a 1.2% share and 22nd in the world in 2014 (UNWTO, 2016b). The comparatively large difference in Mexico's place in both rankings is explained by the fact that many of its international tourist arrivals are still short-stay cross-border visits (UNWTO, 2016a). The usefulness of the market share concept, and global rankings, for analysing the competitiveness of destinations should not however be overestimated.

The recent depreciation of the Mexican peso has influenced inbound tourism flows as it improved the price competitiveness of Mexico in its main source markets. In particular, the peso depreciated by 4.1% against the US dollar in 2014, and by a further 19.2% in 2015, making Mexico relatively cheaper as a destination and helping boost US visitor arrivals and receipts to Mexico.

Main source markets and diversification

By virtue of its geographic location, Mexico benefits from the proximity of the large North American market. The United States is the second largest outbound market in the world and Mexico's most important source market by a long way, followed by Canada. In 2014, 12.7 million or 79.6% of non-border tourists were from the United States, with a further 0.9 million or 5.5% from Canada. Around 64.5% of US visitors and 5.4% of Canadian visitors arrive by air. By this air arrivals measure, around 76.6% of visitors arrive from the United States, with a further 6.5% from Canada.

While the absolute number of non-border tourists from the United States rose by 16.4% between 2005 and 2014, the US share of tourist arrivals to Mexico has actually fallen (down from 87.3% to 79.6%), declining annually by on average 1.7%. Two years are exceptions to this trend: first in 2009, when the US share of inbound tourists to Mexico rose (perhaps linked with trend to stay closer to home, spend less on holidays during the economic crisis); and second in 2014, when Mexico recorded extraordinary growth in border tourism (14.7%), linked with the appreciation of the US dollar and economic recovery in the United States (UNWTO 2016a). However, Mexico has grown its share of US outbound travel, increasing from 33.9% in 2011 to 38.4% in 2014 according to data from the US Department of Commerce, and remains the number one tourism destination for US travellers.

Canada has grown as a source market for Mexico in absolute terms over the same period, although its share of tourism flows peaked in 2008 with 6.1%. The United States and Canada offer further opportunities for growth and will continue to be key source markets for Mexico. Arrivals from other markets have also recorded growth, increasing their share of non-border visitors from 9.8% in 2005 to 14.8% in 2014. This indicates some source market diversification over the past decade, helped by improved connectivity and promotional efforts.

Figure 1.10. Main source markets to Mexico, based on non-border visitor arrivals, 2005-2014

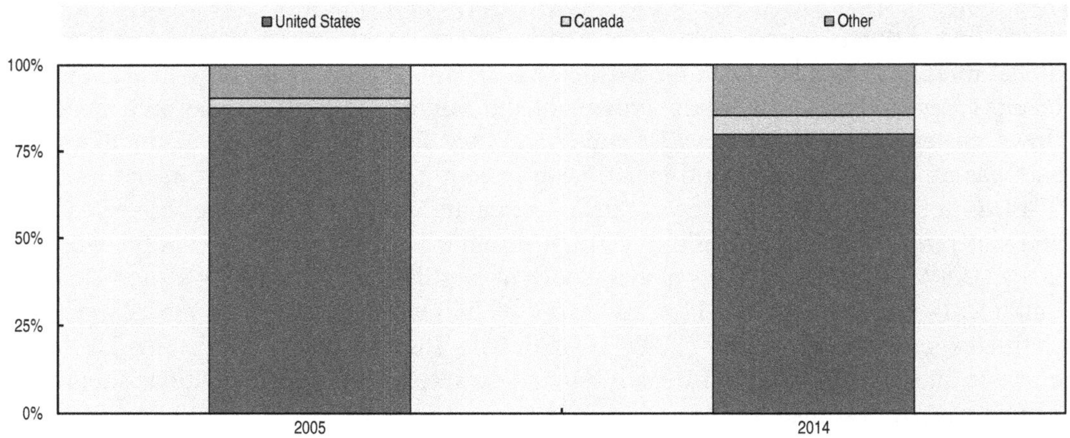

Source: DATATUR, Compendium, extract May 2016.

After the United States and Canada, the United Kingdom, Colombia and Argentina completed the top five main origin markets in 2015, based on air arrivals by country of residence. Arrivals from the United Kingdom have risen by around 12% a year since 2012, at a time when the Mexican peso has depreciated against the pound sterling (by

9.5% in 2014 and 10.7% in 2015). Arrivals from other European countries including Spain, Germany, France, Italy and Sweden have also grown, but at a lower rate. Europe's market share has contracted over the period of the review, from 15% in 2005 to 13% in 2015 (based on air arrivals by nationality). Other OECD countries which are source markets for Mexico include Australia, Chile, Korea and Japan.

Emerging markets offer strong potential, as the pace of tourism growth in many emerging economies is outpacing growth in advanced economies even with the recent economic slowdown and softening of international tourism demand from many emerging markets in 2015. China, for example, led outbound tourism growth in 2015, and is the number one outbound market in terms of both number of trips and expenditure. Air arrivals from China have grown by around 29% a year since 2012, but it remains a very small source market for Mexico (0.4% share).

Latin America has increased its market share from 5% to 13% over the period 2005-15. Growth from Colombia has been particularly strong in recent years, rising by around 41% a year since 2012 to become the fourth largest source market in 2015 (up from 10th in 2012). Arrivals have also risen from the other Pacific Alliance members Chile and Peru. Mexico has taken steps in recent years to remove visa restrictions and facilitate travel from these countries, and from other emerging markets. A number of other Latin American countries including Costa Rica, Guatemala, Panama and Ecuador also recorded growth. However, arrivals from Brazil fell by 4.7% in 2015, while the Venezuela market has also contracted, linked with challenging economic conditions in these countries which are impacting outbound travel flows.

Domestic tourism

Domestic tourism is the mainstay of Mexico's tourism sector and remains the country's most important market. Domestic tourism makes an economic contribution in regions which do not attract international visitors, as well as being less vulnerable to external events.

Awareness of the economic importance of domestic tourism has grown significantly in recent years. However, building an accurate picture of this market is challenging. Data from various sources helps to create a profile of the tourism activities of Mexican residents, including accommodation statistics and household survey data. TSA data also demonstrates the different consumption patterns of domestic tourists, compared to international tourists (e.g. spend less on hotels), as discussed above. The importance of this market varies across different destinations and sub-sectors that make up the tourism sector in Mexico.

The National Household Tourism Spending Survey provides information on the number, purpose and duration of trips by Mexican residents, the type of accommodation and transport used, and level of expenditure. According to the 2013 survey, 59% of Mexican households took a trip in 2013. In 45.4% of cases, at least one member of the household took an overnight trip only, with a further 31.8% taking a same-day trip only. Just over a fifth of households (22.8%) took both an overnight and same-day trip. The main destinations for domestic trips (overnight and same-day) are Mexico City (11.3%), followed by Jalisco (7.9%), Mexico and Veracruz (6.4% each).

Households spent on average MXN 1 013 per day on same-day trips, and MXN 1 222 per day on overnight trips (or MXN 5 610 per overnight trip lasting on average 4 nights). Visiting friends and families (41.1%) is the main motive for taking an overnight trip, with more than half of households (53.9%) staying with friends and families. A further 39.4% stayed in hotels. The other main motives for overnight trips were for a leisure break or holiday (40.3%), with business trips accounting for a further 7.1% of trips. The three peak travel periods for overnight trips were the Summer (18.2% of trips), Winter (15.1%) and Easter (12.6%) holiday periods.

Accommodation statistics are another important statistical source, but are not without their limitations – it can be difficult to separate visitors from other travellers, and domestic from inbound visitors for example. However, they can provide a proxy measure for domestic tourism, and the number of nights spent is a good indicator of the magnitude of travel within the country as it not only reflects the visit itself but also the length of stay. Accommodation statistics also provide information on the distribution of domestic tourism across the territory. This will be discussed further in the following section.

Distribution of tourism by market, region and state

Accommodation arrival and overnight data provide information on the different destination and visitation patterns and the spread of international and domestic tourists across the territory, with international demand in particular concentrated in a number of destinations. Two thirds of international tourists stayed in sun-sea-sand destinations in 2012, compared with just under a third (31%) of domestic tourists. International visitors counted for the majority of visitors to Cancún, the Riviera Maya and Los Cabos, while domestic visitors accounted for a much higher share of visitors to Acapulco and Veracruz-Boca del Río, for example.

Figure 1.11. Domestic and international arrivals in hotels by region, 2014

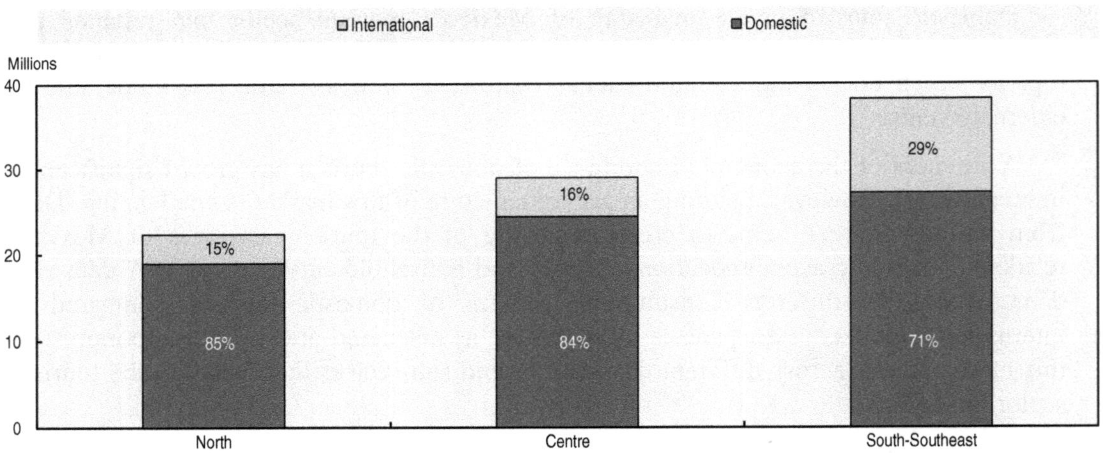

Source: DATATUR, Compendium, extract May 2016.

International tourists accounted for 19% of arrivals in hotels, but almost double the share of overnights (33.1%), as they stayed longer than domestic visitors (3.72 nights, compared with 1.77 nights). international visitors were also more likely to stay in 5 star hotels (62.5% of arrivals and 74.7% of nights in the five star category, compared to 21.9% and 29.3% for domestic tourists).

International tourism is heavily concentrated in the South-southeast region, which accounts for 58% of international arrivals and two thirds of overnights (66.6%) (up from 42.8% and 57% in 2005). A further 24% of international arrivals and 18.7% of overnights are recorded in the Centre region. The North region accounts for 18% of arrivals and 14.8% of overnights, reflecting the shorter stay of border tourists.

Figure 1.12. Domestic and international nights in hotels by region, 2014

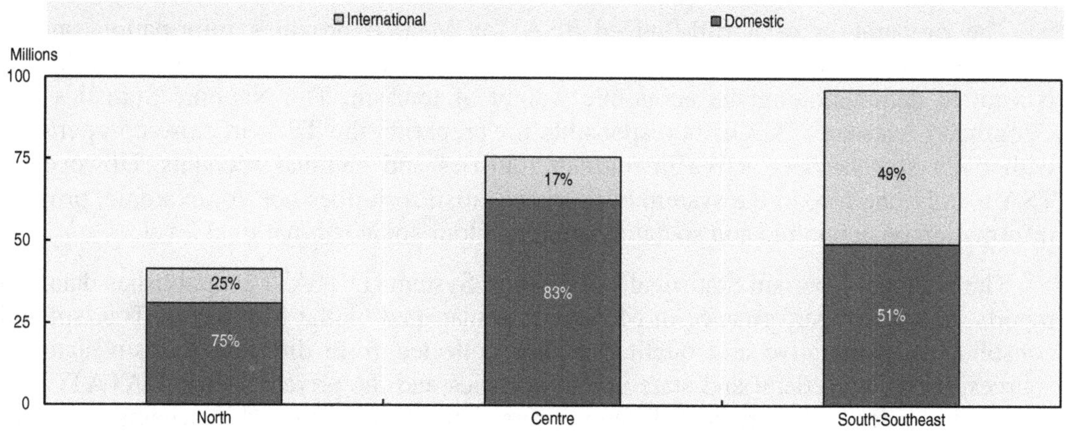

Source: DATATUR, Compendium, extract May 2016.

Three quarters of international arrivals (77.3%) are concentrated in six states - Quintana Roo in the South-southeast region alone accounts for almost half of all international arrivals (47.5%), followed by Mexico City (10.6%) and Jalisco (5.7%) in the Centre, and Baja California (4.5%) and Baja California Sur (5.6%) in the North. This concentration is even more marked when it comes to overnights. Almost nine out of ten international overnights (86.6%) are concentrated in five states – Quintana Roo in the South-southeast region alone accounts for almost two thirds of all international overnights in Mexico (62%), followed by Baja California Sur (8.3%) in the North, and Mexico City (6.2%), Jalisco (5.2%) and Nayarit (5%).

Domestic arrivals accounted for four out of every five hotel arrivals (81%) and two in every three overnights (66.9%), demonstrating the shorter stay of domestic tourists. These are more evenly spread across the territory: the Centre region accounts for 42.9% of arrivals and 43.8% of overnights, the South-southeast region accounts for 33.6% of arrivals and 34.5% of overnights, while the North region accounts for 23.5% of arrivals and 21.7% of overnights. The highest concentration of domestic arrivals and overnights is in Mexico City (11.2% and 10.3%) and Jalisco (7.6% and 10.2%), followed by Guerrero (6.8% and 7.7%) and Veracruz (6.9% and 5.8%). In contrast with the heavy international concentration in Quintana Roo, the domestic market accounts for 4% of arrivals and 5.7% of overnights in this state.

On average, visitors stay 2.14 nights in hotel accommodation in 2014, with international visitors staying longer (3.72 nights) than domestic visitors (1.77 nights). While the average length of stay has remained largely stable for the domestic market, is has risen from 3.1 nights in 2005 for the international market. International visitors stayed longest in Baja California Sur (5.51 nights) and Nayarit (5.47), followed by Quintana Roo (4.85). Baja California Sur also recorded the longest length of stay for domestic visitors (four nights). The South-southeast region accounted for just under half of all overnights (45.1%) in 2014. This is slightly higher than the share room stock in the region, reflecting the longer average stay of visitors to this region.

Strengthening the tourism statistics and intelligence structure

The purpose of this review was not to do an in-depth review of tourism statistics in Mexico. However, it has highlighted gaps in information and ways to improve the statistical information on tourism to better drive business and policy decision-making.

The preparation of a full-fledged TSA for Mexico provides information on the economic significance of tourism and its role in Mexico's economy at national level. This is vital in demonstrating the economic weight of tourism. The National Statistics and Geography Institute (INEGI) is responsible for preparing the TSA, in close co-operation with other stakeholders active in tourism statistics and national accounts. However, a TSA is only one tool in the system of tourism statistics. It does not, for example, provide information on economic and social dynamics of tourism at sub-national level.

The National Tourism Statistical Information System (DATATUR) publishes data and reports on tourism performance in Mexico. It is managed by the Ministry of Tourism and consolidates quantitative and qualitative data collected from different tourism statistics sources, including federal and state public agencies and the private sector. DATATUR is designed to cater to the needs of different users, from those interested in accessing general data trends to more advanced statistical users interested in conducting more in-depth analysis. The website includes a digital library with analysis of key tourism indicator trends, survey results and impacts of tourism policies and programmes in Mexico.

A large amount of data is available through DATATUR and time series are generally complete with limited data gaps. The Compendium on Tourism Statistics is well done and a useful tool for end-users. It provides official historical data and is updated and published annually. This data does not necessarily align with data tables published online, which are updated on a more regular basis (monthly/quarterly/weekly). Tourism information is highly fragmented, as data is disseminated across a number of different platforms with limited integration. This is confusing from an end-user perspective and makes accessing data difficult. Timeliness and consistency also continue to be a challenge. More in-depth analysis and understanding of the drivers behind data trends, and the implications for policy, would further support evidence-based decision making.

Demand-side information on tourism is particularly lacking. The Bank of Mexico provides data on inbound people and monetary flows, while the Ministry of the Interior's Migration Policy Unit provides data on air passenger arrivals by nationality and country of residence. However, there is a dearth of information on the background and characteristics of these visitors, their travel and consumption patterns, and their expectations and satisfaction with different aspects of their trip to Mexico. These weaknesses could be addressed by a visitor survey, complemented by in-depth market research and analysis of Mexico's competitive position in key source markets.

Given the size and significance of domestic tourism, information on this segment would also benefit from improvements. Partial information on this important market makes any evaluation of tourism difficult and incomplete. There is thus a need to build on recent efforts (e.g. origin-destination surveys) and expand work and analysis on domestic tourism consumption. Ongoing work to strengthen tourism statistics in other areas (e.g. investment, employment, competitiveness, sustainability) and to harness the potential of Big Data and other alternative and technology-based data sources will also help to fill the information gaps, and strengthen the data infrastructure supporting tourism, subject to budgetary limitations.

A range of public and private stakeholders play an important role in providing and disseminating key information on tourism at national and sub-national level. Strengthening co-operation between the producers and end-users of tourism statistics would improve the robustness, credibility and quality of this information. This in turn will enhance the use of tourism statistics and support more evidence-based policy and business decision-making.

Efforts should focus on building a modern system of tourism statistics that provides timely and reliable information on both the production and consumption aspects of tourism. The primary focus should be on quantitative data, but a good knowledge of tourism demand also requires qualitative information. A strategic view with clear priorities and strong partnerships across all levels of government and with the private sector needs to be established to implement a national statistical system. This applies to all countries, including Mexico.

References

Bentancor A. and V. Robano (2014) The Part-time Premium Enigma: an Assessment of the Chilean Case, Economia, Spring 2014, Vol. 14, Number 2, pp29-54

CNET. (Consejo Nacional Empresarial Turístico) (2016). Panorama de la Actividad Turística en México No. 17, http://www.cnet.org.mx/panorama_17.pdf

DATATUR. (2016). Results of Tourism Activity Mexico 2015. http://www.datatur.beta.sectur.gob.mx/RAT/RAT-2015-12(EN).pdf

INEGI. (2015). Cuenta Satélite del Turismo de México 2014, Bolétin de Prensa Núm. 516/15, 2 de diciembre de 2015 http://www.datatur.sectur.gob.mx/SitePages/ProductoDestacado3.aspx

OECD. (2016a). *OECD Economic Outlook*, OECD Publishing, Paris. DOI: http://dx.doi.org/10.1787/eco_outlook-v2016-1-en

OECD. (2016b). *OECD Tourism Trends and Policies 2016*, OECD Publishing, Paris. DOI: http://dx.doi.org/10.1787/tour-2016-en

OECD. (2015a). *OECD Economic Surveys: Mexico*, OECD Publishing, Paris http://dx.doi.org/10.1787/eco_surveys-mex-2015-en

OECD. (2015b). *OECD Employment Outlook 2015*, OECD Publishing, Paris. DOI: http://dx.doi.org/10.1787/empl_outlook-2015-en

SECTUR. (2013). Encuesta Nacional de Gasto Turístico en los Hogares, SECTUR, http://www.datatur.sectur.gob.mx/Documentos%20Publicaciones/ENGATURH_2013.pdf

UNWTO. (2016a). World Tourism Barometer, Vol. 14 May 2016, http://cf.cdn.unwto.org/sites/all/files/pdf/unwto_barom16_03_may_excerpt_.pdf

UNWTO. (2016b). World Tourism Barometer, Vol. 14 July 2016, http://www.e-unwto.org/doi/abs/10.18111/wtobarometereng.2016.14.4.1

Annex
Statistical tables

Table A.1. Direct contribution of tourism to the Mexican economy, 2005-14

	2005	2006	2007	2008	2009	2010	2011	2012	2013	2014	% change	Annual Growth Rate
	Million MXN, current price										2005-14	2005-14
National GVA	9 028 899	10 120 003	10 962 144	11 941 199	11 568 456	12 723 475	14 021 257	15 116 998	15 444 778	16 311 337	80.7	6.8
Tourism GDP	836 245	917 595	974 834	1 028 907	1 029 399	1 105 479	1 171 476	1 267 939	1 335 295	1 394 210	66.7	5.8
Agriculture[1]	288 107	323 355	360 285	392 984	387 015	425 590	448 103	505 675	506 394	537 245	86.5	7.2
Mining	694 981	794 968	901 739	1 054 691	786 997	966 823	1 298 146	1 315 847	1 176 101	1 168 070	68.1	5.9
Construction	730 041	848 233	923 691	1 030 710	991 397	1 040 901	1 152 544	1 236 784	1 166 705	1 229 139	68.4	6
Manufacturing industries	1 559 631	1 832 579	1 905 965	2 027 255	1 928 312	2 199 445	2 393 798	2 703 787	2 715 436	2 887 563	85.1	7.1
Trade	1 352 744	1 505 533	1 627 935	1 785 940	1 661 552	1 894 386	2 172 857	2 354 947	2 483 002	2 666 530	97.1	7.8
Transport and warehousing	558 195	622 037	666 691	700 557	691 371	796 765	860 889	945 708	1 001 762	1 061 946	90.2	7.4
Insurance and financial services	278 230	301 573	356 249	390 550	409 416	439 976	452 489	472 716	535 440	569 440	104.7	8.3
Real estate services[2]	1 143 565	1 248 268	1 337 494	1 448 376	1 502 829	1 592 103	1 686 555	1 768 489	1 839 112	1 907 465	66.8	5.8
	Million MXN, constant price										2005-14	2005-14
National GVA	10 870 105	11 410 946	11 778 878	11 941 199	11 374 630	11 965 979	12 435 058	12 937 094	13 119 492	13 401 295	23.3	2.4
Tourism GDP	914 477	970 637	996 120	1 028 907	982 398	1 004 935	1 033 969	1 081 057	1 089 216	1 112 911	21.7	2.2
Agriculture[1]	351 456	373 045	390 308	392 984	377 848	390 856	366 831	397 118	407 434	421 848	20	2
Mining	1 119 429	1 111 413	1 095 487	1 054 691	1 012 072	1 020 993	1 017 204	1 026 049	1 024 518	1 009 054	-9.9	-1.1
Construction	872 476	948 296	992 914	1 030 710	968 200	975 507	1 015 099	1 039 974	990 336	1 010 226	15.8	1.6
Manufacturing industries	1 941 123	2 028 482	2 047 910	2 027 255	1 857 907	2 016 704	2 109 315	2 196 097	2 222 750	2 314 583	19.2	2
Trade	1 602 195	1 713 187	1 783 203	1 785 940	1 563 520	1 749 038	1 919 062	2 010 579	2 055 659	2 120 001	32.3	3.2
Transport and warehousing	650 555	677 734	701 085	700 557	650 008	700 120	728 423	758 002	776 371	801 530	23.2	2.3
Insurance and financial services	245 337	283 784	320 270	390 550	403 945	488 618	523 318	563 367	621 971	616 548	151.3	10.8
Real estate services[2]	1 303 086	1 357 266	1 402 417	1 448 376	1 464 031	1 504 544	1 548 510	1 587 152	1 603 059	1 635 670	25.5	2.6

Base year 2008.

1. Including animal husbandry and exploitation, forestry use, fishing and hunting.

2. Including rental of equipment and intangibles.

Source: INEGI, extract May 2016.

Table A.2. Travel-related exports, 2005-15

	2005	2006	2007	2008	2009	2010	2011	2012	2013	2014	2015	% change	Annual Growth Rate
	Million MXN, current price											2005-15	2005-15
Tourism exports[1]	129 256	132 852	141 341	148 829	156 401	151 522	147 665	167 501	178 162	215 830	276 665	114.0	7.9
Goods exports	2 332 364	2 726 130	2 970 531	3 216 396	3 094 171	3 768 880	4 346 796	4 879 187	4 855 367	5 283 880	6 038 972	158.9	10.0
Services exports	175 989	177 724	192 801	203 045	205 095	198 691	202 168	222 210	267 253	291 415	358 319	103.6	7.4
Total exports	2 508 352	2 903 854	3 163 332	3 419 442	3 299 265	3 967 571	4 548 965	5 101 397	5 122 620	5 575 295	6 397 291	155.0	9.8
Tourism share in services exports	73.4	74.8	73.3	73.3	76.3	76.3	73.0	75.4	66.7	74.1	77.2		
Tourism share in total exports	5.2	4.6	4.5	4.4	4.7	3.8	3.2	3.3	3.5	3.9	4.3		
	Million MXN, constant price											2005-15	2005-15
Tourism exports[1]	144 318	143 199	147 129	148 829	149 145	138 043	129 283	141 124	144 504	167 080	207 770	44.0	3.7
Goods exports	2 906 532	3 152 039	3 263 911	3 216 396	2 820 464	3 450 267	3 754 422	3 974 337	4 043 480	4 331 612	4 683 915	61.2	4.9
Services exports	199 501	192 177	202 256	203 045	196 115	186 114	180 719	190 586	220 031	228 267	276 863	38.8	3.3
Total exports	3 106 033	3 344 215	3 466 167	3 419 442	3 016 579	3 636 382	3 935 141	4 164 923	4 263 510	4 559 880	4 960 778	59.7	4.8
Tourism share in services exports	72.3	74.5	72.7	73.3	76.0	74.2	71.5	74.0	65.7	73.2	75.0		
Tourism share in total exports	4.6	4.3	4.2	4.4	4.9	3.8	3.3	3.4	3.4	3.7	4.2		

Base year 2008.

1. Expenditure by tourists and same-day visitors.

Source: INEGI and OECD calculations.

Table A.3. Tourism contribution to balance of payments, 2005-15

	2005	2006	2007	2008	2009	2010	2011	2012	2013	2014	2015	% change	Annual Growth Rate
	Million USD											2005-15	2005-15
Tourism balance	4 203	4 068	4 457	4 802	4 305	4 737	4 037	4 291	4 827	6 603	7 357	75	5.8
Oil balance	14 541	19 380	17 545	14 978	10 369	11 482	13 739	11 817	8 614	880	-10 115	-169.6	-3.6
Manufacture balance	-22 771	-24 712	-26 198	-28 354	-14 802	-14 476	-14 729	-12 775	-12 046	-7 534	-9 672	57.5	-8.2

Source: Bank of Mexico, extract May 2016.

Table A.4. Internal tourism consumption by type of tourism and product, 2014

	Domestic tourism consumption	Inbound tourism consumption	Internal tourism consumption
	Million MXN, current price		
Total	..	..	..
Consumption products	1 846 685	254 592	2 101 277
Tourism characteristic products	1 332 107	219 301	1 551 408
Accommodation services for visitors	131 019	57 680	188 699
Food and beverage serving services	202 068	71 680	273 748
Passenger transport services	449 602	29 963	479 565
Air passenger transport services	..	..	..
Railways passenger transport services	..	..	..
Road passenger transport services	..	..	..
Water passenger transport services	..	..	..
Passenger transport supporting services	..	..	..
Transport equipment rental services	..	..	..
Travel agencies and other reservation services	20 625	2 827	23 452
Cultural services	4 024	3 687	7 711
Sports and recreation services[1]	15 204	14 817	30 020
Country-specific tourism characteristic goods	509 566	38 648	548 213
Country-specific tourism characteristic services	..	..	..
Other consumption products	514 578	35 291	549 869
Tourism connected products	..	..	..
Non-tourism related consumption products	..	..	..
Non-consumption products	..	..	..

1. Includes cultural services, sports and entertainment activities.

Source: INEGI,Tourism Satellite Account 2014.

Table A.5. Number of people[1] employed in tourism, 2005-15

	2005	2006	2007	2008	2009	2010	2011	2012	2013	2014	2015	% change	Annual Growth Rate
												2006-15	2006-15
Total employment	37 844 912	38 785 911	39 853 294	40 056 906	41 082 034	41 214 377	42 888 986	43 930 472	44 710 784	45 015 097	46 568 093	20.1	2.1
Total tourism employment	..	3 006 141	3 078 628	3 186 444	3 280 242	3 324 620	3 409 804	3 536 686	3 628 195	3 640 970	3 803 442	26.5	2.6

1. Data refers to self-employed workers, subordinates and paid workers in quarter 4.
Source: DATATUR based on Encuesta Nacional de Occupación y Empleo (ENOE) INEGI.

Table A.6. Number of paid jobs in tourism, 2005-14

	2005	2006	2007	2008	2009	2010	2011	2012	2013	2014	% change	Annual Growth Rate
											2005-14	2005-14
Total tourism employment (direct)	2 199 392	2 221 001	2 255 546	2 254 038	2 202 369	2 236 388	2 215 389	2 265 940	2 298 513	2 300 472	4.6	0.5
Tourism industries	1 654 218	1 653 101	1 665 478	1 657 925	1 613 291	1 659 756	1 644 854	1 684 695	1 715 578	1 719 335	3.9	0.4
Accommodation services for visitors	142 010	141 418	142 411	142 011	134 247	140 431	136 144	134 455	138 687	142 488	0.3	0
Hotels and similar establishments	..	..	..	..	..	..	..	..	..	..	..	..
Food and beverage serving industry	773 878	769 703	770 581	780 803	772 522	775 165	777 970	814 234	839 378	827 964	7	0.8
Passenger transport	350 999	350 968	360 669	359 260	354 404	357 462	359 468	360 557	363 109	373 698	6.5	0.7
Air passenger transport	..	..	..	..	..	..	..	..	..	..	..	..
Railways passenger transport	..	..	..	..	..	..	..	..	..	..	..	..
Road passenger transport	..	..	..	..	..	..	..	..	..	..	..	..
Water passenger transport	..	..	..	..	..	..	..	..	..	..	..	..
Passenger transport supporting services	..	..	..	..	..	..	..	..	..	..	..	..
Transport equipment rental	..	..	..	..	..	..	..	..	..	..	..	..
Travel agencies and other reservation services industry	17 977	18 337	19 162	19 517	17 968	17 844	18 146	19 036	19 224	20 083	11.7	1.2
Cultural industry	11 770	11 661	11 528	11 353	11 584	11 537	11 249	11 791	11 656	11 521	-2.1	-0.2
Sports and recreation industry[1]	38 621	39 507	40 059	40 717	39 679	41 018	40 976	41 412	42 252	41 722	8	0.9
Retail trade of country-specific tourism characteristic goods	318 963	321 507	321 068	304 264	282 887	316 299	300 901	303 210	301 272	301 859	-5.4	-0.6
Other country-specific tourism industries	..	..	..	..	..	..	..	..	..	..	..	..
Other industries	545 174	567 900	590 068	596 113	589 078	576 632	570 535	581 245	582 935	581 137	6.6	0.7

1. Includes cultural services, sports and entertainment activities.
Source: INEGI, Tourism Satellite Account 2014.

Table A.7. Inbound visitor arrivals, 2005-15

	2005	2006	2007	2008	2009	2010	2011	2012	2013	2014	2015	% change		Annual Growth Rate
	000 arrivals											2005-15	2014-15	2005-15
Visitors	103 146	97 701	93 582	92 948	88 044	81 953	75 732	76 749	78 100	81 042	87 221	-15.4	7.6	-1.7
Tourists	21 915	21 353	21 606	22 931	22 346	23 290	23 403	23 403	24 151	29 346	32 145	46.7	9.5	3.9
Non-border tourists	12 534	12 608	13 041	13 425	12 501	13 327	13 237	13 665	14 562	16 000	18 350	46.4	14.7	3.9
Border tourists	9 381	8 745	8 565	9 505	9 845	9 962	10 166	9 738	9 589	13 346	13 795	47	3.4	3.9
Same-day visitors (excursionists)	81 231	76 348	71 976	70 017	65 698	58 664	52 329	53 346	53 950	51 696	55 076	-32.2	6.5	-3.8
Border excursionists	74 524	69 832	65 034	63 526	59 997	52 615	47 039	48 148	49 394	45 911	48 962	-34.3	6.6	-4.1
Cruise passengers	6 707	6 516	6 943	6 491	5 701	6 048	5 289	5 199	4 555	5 785	6 115	-8.8	5.7	-0.9

Source: Bank of Mexico, DATATUR, Compendium, May 2016.

Table A.8. Contribution of international visitors to foreign currency earnings, 2005-15

	2005	2006	2007	2008	2009	2010	2011	2012	2013	2014	2015	% change		Annual Growth Rate
	Million MXN, current price											2005-15	2014-15	2005-15
International visitors	129 256	132 852	141 341	148 829	156 401	151 522	147 665	167 501	178 162	215 830	276 665	114	28.2	7.9
International tourists	100 159	104 297	113 420	120 897	128 118	126 240	124 493	141 559	151 401	190 684	246 083	145.7	29.1	9.4
Non-border tourists	93 108	97 699	106 530	113 014	119 916	119 315	117 553	134 094	144 475	180 830	233 547	150.8	29.2	9.6
Border tourists	7 051	6 599	6 890	7 882	8 201	6 924	6 941	7 466	6 925	9 855	12 535	77.8	27.2	5.9
Same-day visitors (excursionists)	29 097	28 554	27 921	27 931	28 283	25 283	23 172	25 941	26 761	25 146	30 582	5.1	21.6	0.5
Border excursionists	24 141	23 554	22 469	22 555	22 117	18 600	17 215	20 150	22 187	19 570	23 934	-0.9	22.3	-0.1
Cruise passengers	4 956	5 000	5 453	5 377	6 166	6 682	5 957	5 792	4 574	5 576	6 648	34.1	19.2	3

Source: Bank of Mexico, DATATUR, Compendium, extract May 2016.

Table A.9. Source markets based on air arrivals by country residence, 2012-15

	2012		2014	2015		Share in total arrivals	% change	Annual Growth Rate
	Rank	Volume	Volume	Rank	Volume	2015	2012-15	2012-15
United States	1	6 061 766	7 348 503	1	8 604 578	58.6	42	12
Canada	2	1 547 641	1 646 158	2	1 707 798	11.6	10	3
United Kingdom	3	339 071	432 305	3	477 284	3.3	41	12
Colombia	10	128 691	292 441	4	363 159	2.5	182	41
Argentina	6	227 892	218 378	5	309 625	2.1	36	11
Brasil	5	233 931	300 919	6	286 807	2	23	7
Spain	4	239 742	256 350	7	265 031	1.8	11	3
Germany	8	151 982	185 305	8	197 172	1.3	30	9
France	7	179 268	186 048	9	188 941	1.3	5	2
Perú	13	74 326	120 690	10	142 073	1	91	24
Italy	9	133 605	141 237	11	138 310	0.9	4	1
Chile	12	81 092	101 591	12	123 884	0.8	53	15
Venezuela	11	103 403	146 816	13	93 143	0.6	-10	-3
Japan	14	65 009	80 859	14	85 886	0.6	32	10
Costa Rica	16	55 873	63 187	15	82 556	0.6	48	14
Guatemala	17	48 102	56 085	16	82 206	0.6	71	20
Australia	18	44 908	61 056	17	68 976	0.5	54	15
Korea	21	31 710	52 810	18	67 855	0.5	114	29
China	23	25 972	43 854	19	55 659	0.4	114	29
Panama	20	32 826	42 748	20	55 324	0.4	69	19
Ecuador	22	27 846	45 012	21	54 137	0.4	94	25
Netherlands	15	56 320	50 357	22	51 501	0.4	-9	-3
Switzerland	19	33 132	40 560	23	40 854	0.3	23	7
Cuba	25	9 767	19 495	24	25 932	0.2	166	38
India	24	11 559	14 697	25	16 659	0.1	44	13
Other contries		21 567	39 297		29 565	0.2	37	11
Total		10 826 326	12 958 514		14 677 627	100	36	11

Source: Migration Policy Unit, SEGOB, extract May 2016.

Table A.10. Exchange rates, 2005-15

	2005	2006	2007	2008	2009	2010	2011	2012	2013	2014	2015
MXN per USD	10.9	10.9	10.9	11.1	13.5	12.6	12.4	13.2	12.8	13.3	15.8
MXN per EUR	13.6	13.7	15	16.3	18.8	16.7	17.3	16.9	17	17.6	17.6

Source: OECD Database, extract May 2016.

Table A.11. Number of domestic tourist arrivals and nights in hotels, 2005-14

	2005	2006	2007	2008	2009	2010	2011	2012	2013	2014
Number of tourist arrivals										
North	10 587 291	10 387 057	11 665 561	16 572 529	15 027 651	15 611 910	16 093 405	16 673 497	17 814 775	18 938 956
Centre	14 197 077	15 091 677	16 132 750	21 403 441	19 425 619	20 261 220	21 027 614	21 538 348	23 203 819	24 383 081
South-Southeast	19 140 156	19 997 574	23 446 122	23 872 038	23 233 545	23 686 703	23 236 059	24 960 578	26 099 414	27 156 008
Number of tourist nights										
North	19 034 640	19 684 909	21 164 523	27 521 242	25 351 444	25 236 754	26 776 910	29 051 934	29 123 772	31 014 193
Centre	46 779 656	48 250 342	48 003 156	49 177 368	46 251 744	50 015 183	56 181 638	57 756 081	59 040 128	62 649 752
South-Southeast	32 907 235	33 512 712	37 179 304	36 627 704	35 189 369	37 616 241	38 426 939	40 125 458	41 192 486	49 370 856

Source: DATATUR, extract June 2016.

Table A.12. Number of international tourist arrivals and nights in hotels, 2005-14

	2005	2006	2007	2008	2009	2010	2011	2012	2013	2014
Number of tourist arrivals										
North	4 197 486	4 442 628	4 407 240	4 047 506	3 394 365	3 085 780	3 027 594	3 134 881	3 222 854	3 419 640
Centre	5 200 401	5 695 493	4 791 958	5 701 987	4 165 609	4 452 345	4 087 412	4 078 880	4 120 759	4 559 646
South-Southeast	7 020 959	6 580 927	7 571 006	8 265 237	7 038 363	7 506 000	7 708 401	8 228 879	9 759 516	11 008 328
Number of tourist nights										
North	10 585 804	11 469 356	11 172 973	10 072 726	9 295 667	9 339 598	9 254 112	9 421 433	9 423 485	10 436 528
Centre	12 897 370	15 983 088	12 927 223	15 567 937	11 216 308	12 600 771	10 721 634	10 546 543	10 376 406	13 205 171
South-Southeast	31 148 709	29 917 689	35 139 122	36 391 195	29 158 688	33 712 818	34 575 290	37 559 218	43 964 768	47 075 898

Source: DATATUR, extract June 2016.

Chapter 2
Towards an integrated approach to tourism policy in Mexico

Tourism is high on the policy agenda in Mexico. The country has a remarkable range of well-articulated tourism plans and programmes which aim to spur investment and economic growth, promote balanced regional development and stimulate more productive, inclusive and sustainable growth. Ensuring these plans and programmes are effectively co-ordinated and implemented will be vital to realising Mexico's tourism development potential, and delivering on these objectives. This chapter examines the tourism policy making environment and reviews the main plans, strategies and initiatives. It reviews the institutional arrangements and governance framework for tourism policy, and considers the mechanisms to support coherent and co-ordinated tourism policy development.

Introduction

Tourism policy in Mexico aims to spur investment and economic growth, promote balanced regional development and stimulate more productive, inclusive and sustainable growth across the territory. Effective and integrated public policies are needed to achieve this. Tourism policy development is increasingly complex and addressing the challenges faced by the tourism sector demands an integrated approach across many government departments, at different levels of government, and with the close involvement of the private sector.

A strong institutional framework is important to achieve this and to support a competitive tourism sector with a diversified range of services and destinations in Mexico. Effective governance practices that reflect the changing business and policy environment can help to facilitate an integrated, whole-of-government approach to tourism and support more sustainable and inclusive tourism growth. OECD work on governance has identified a number of important considerations in any policy response to improve the supporting framework for effective tourism governance (Box 2.1).

This chapter examines the tourism policy making environment in Mexico. Tourism policy priorities and key plans, strategies and tourism-related policy initiatives are discussed, along with the institutional arrangements and governance framework. The chapter examines how tourism policies are developed, implemented and enforced, and identifies areas for further consideration to facilitate the coherent and co-ordinated development of tourism in Mexico.

Strategic vision, policy framework and implementation of tourism policy

Tourism is high on the policy agenda in Mexico. Each new administration publishes a National Development Plan setting out government policy and strategy for the coming six years. Sectoral plans are then prepared for individual economic sectors, including tourism. Successive administrations have recognised tourism's potential to boost economic growth, job creation and service exports. During the last four decades, the Federal Government has played a central role in planning, developing and financing the expansion of tourism in Mexico, notably through an integrated resort development model in coastal destinations.

Tourism has been identified by the current Administration as a priority economic sector, to promote a more prosperous and inclusive Mexico, generating economic, social and employment benefits across the country. Reflecting this, tourism has a central role to play in economic policy in Mexico and tourism policy is an integral part of national development strategies, policies and programmes. This marks an enhanced recognition of tourism as a vibrant export-oriented sector within the wider Mexican economy.

The tourism dimensions of these plans are ambitious and wide-ranging, covering key tourism development issues and providing the overall policy framework for tourism in Mexico. Ensuring these plans and actions are effectively co-ordinated and implemented will be vital to realising Mexico's tourism development potential and delivering on these ambitions. Clearer articulation of a strategic vision for the sector, prioritisation of the challenges, and actions to address these, would strengthen tourism development in Mexico. This includes greater detail on the roles and responsibilities of different actors in delivering on these priorities, and measureable milestones to evaluate progress. Effective implementation will also require an improvement in governance and institutional capacity, and sufficient funding.

Box 2.1. Improving the tourism policy governance framework

- A clear definition of the roles of various levels of government in tourism, and the roles and functions of the various organisations involved in tourism policy. In some countries these roles are being specified in law.
- At national level, there is a trend to the development of one peak industry association which may be comprised of organisations representing different sectors. At a sub-national level, a variety of different organisations may represent sectors or branches of national representative organisations.
- A tourism strategy is a commonly used tool for engaging and co-ordinating government, industry, destination communities and other stakeholders. A common problem with a tourism strategy is the need to provide sufficient funding for its implementation. Communication is an important element of successful implementation of a strategy.
- Tourism policy governance across multiple levels of government requires competent local actors. A variety of tools exist for capacity building at the national and sub-national level, but it is important to tailor training to deliver the skills required. Involvement and capacity building of tourism operators and local government may be enhanced by active learning-by-doing programmes.
- Destination Management Organisations (DMOs) are an important component of effective governance at the sub-national level. Their boundaries should reflect both economies of scale in marketing and organisation, and be based on the travel patterns of travellers. DMOs also provide a sub-national focus for policy development and capacity building and a focus for communication with private sector actors.
- In developing policy and responses to crises it is important for governments to include tourism representatives in decisions due to the horizontal characteristics of the tourism sector.
- It is therefore important to ensure that relevant data and analysis are available which in turn may require additional resources and competencies in tourism organisations. It is also important to ensure that policy decision-making is longer-term, transparent and that outcomes are evaluated.

Source: OECD (2012).

Key strategies, policies and programmes supporting tourism

National Development Plan 2013-18

Mexico's National Development Plan 2013-18 (*Plan Nacional de Desarollo* – PND) explicitly recognises tourism as a strategic sector in the economy, with high capacity to create jobs, stimulate regional development, compete in global markets, contribute to growth in other economic sectors, and generate value through integration in domestic production chains. The potential to grow markets in which SMEs operate, and to preserve Mexico's natural and cultural wealth, which are key tourism assets, is also recognised.

In order to leverage this potential and take advantage of sustained growth in tourism at the global level, the Plan acknowledges the need for a more sustainable tourism development model. It also recognises the need for active policies to better integrate tourism into domestic and global value chains, spread the economic and social benefits to help reduce poverty and increase social inclusion, and preserve natural and cultural resources. The need to improve the value added of the tourism offer and attract visitors from high value tourism markets is also recognised, including emerging markets in Russia, China, Korea and Latin America. Mexico is well-positioned in the sun-sea-sand segment, but opportunities exist to generate economic flows from alternative tourism segments related to Mexico's diverse tourism asset base. The domestic market also offers strong potential.

Under the Prosperous Mexico pillar *(Próspero)*, the Plan sets out four strategies to modernise and reposition Mexico's tourism sector globally, and harness Mexico's tourism potential to generate greater economic benefit in the country. These strategies cover four broad areas of governance, innovation and competitiveness, investment, and sustainability (Box 2.2). The Plan seeks to raise the profile of tourism and clearly recognises the need to promote horizontal and vertical policy co-ordination, improve the value added of the tourism offer, tap into emerging tourism markets, offer a more diverse range of quality products, and facilitate access to finance in order to foster innovation and investment.

Box 2.2. Tourism strategies in the National Development Plan 2013-18

- **Boosting planning and transformation of the tourism sector.** Strategic actions: update the regulatory and institutional framework, better align tourism policy and actions of Federal and State governments, improve budgetary and programmatic co-ordination and mainstream government actions, in line with national tourism policy.
- **Encouraging supply-side innovation and enhancing tourism competitiveness.** Strategic actions: strengthen the infrastructure and quality of tourism services and products, diversify and innovate the product and destination offer, complement sun-sea-sand destinations with alternative offering (cultural tourism, ecotourism, adventure tourism, MICE etc.), develop a National Quality Assurance Certification System, develop competitiveness agendas for destinations, foster greater collaboration and co-ordination with the private sector, local governments and service providers.
- **Fostering greater investment and financing flows, and effectively promoting destinations.** Strategic actions: foster and promote financing schemes with the development banks; develop a comprehensive international tourism promotion strategy and develop new tourism products to stimulate and consolidate the domestic market, supporting the efforts of the private sector.
- **Promoting sustainability and social benefit from tourism.** Strategic actions: create instruments to help tourism be a clean industry, strengthen the tourism model based on economic, social and environmental sustainability, and promote the conservation and preservation of cultural historical and natural heritage (e.g. responsible wastewater management, sewage and wastewater treatment, drinking water quality).

In addition to recognising tourism's economic potential, the National Development Plan 2013-18 also recognises the role tourism can play as part of Mexico's wide strategy of engagement in the international community. Tourism is playing an important "economic diplomacy" role in other OECD countries also. This is most evident in Australia and France, where primary responsibility for tourism has been moved to sit within the ministries responsible for foreign affairs.

To deliver on this vision, the Plan recognises the need for and is supplemented by a sectoral strategy for tourism.

Sectoral Programme for Tourism 2013-18

Derived from the National Development Plan 2013-18, the Sectoral Programme for Tourism 2013-18 (*Programa Sectorial de Turismo* – PROSECTUR) sets out Mexico's tourism policy objectives, and the strategies and actions to achieve these. Five national tourism policy objectives are set out: to enhance co-operation and transform the sector to take advantage of Mexico's tourism potential, strengthen the competitive advantages of tourism in the country, facilitate financing and public-private investment projects with tourism potential, boost tourism promotion to contribute to market diversification, and promote more inclusive and sustainable tourism development (Box 2.3).

Box 2.3. Policy objectives, strategic actions in the Sectoral Programme for Tourism 2013-18

Transform the tourism sector and strengthen co-operation to take advantage of the tourism potential. Strategic actions: strengthen institutional capacities; promote horizontal and vertical co-ordination across government to align policies, actions and resources; and strengthen consultation with the private sector, civil society and academia.

Strengthen the competitive advantages of tourism. Strategic actions: generate information, research and knowledge about destinations and products; encourage innovation, diversification and consolidation of tourism products by region and destination; promote high quality service standards; stimulate the professionalisation of tourism service providers; and promote a comprehensive security policy for tourists.

Facilitate financing and public-private investment projects with tourism potential. Strategic actions: expand access to credit and financial instruments; promote greater levels of private sector investment for entrepreneurs; provide financial management training and technical assistance for tourism projects; promoting funding and targeted investment for integrally planned resorts (*Centros Integramente Planeados* – CIP); and strengthen investment attraction mechanisms.

Boost tourism promotion to contribute to market diversification and the development and growth of the sector. Strategic actions: promote Mexico as a quality tourism destination offering a variety of attractive and unique experiences; develop and promote the domestic market; and encourage market diversification.

Promote sustainable development of tourism destinations and expand the social and economic benefits for local communities. Strategic actions: tourism planning to identify the potential of natural and cultural capital; design sustainable instruments to combat climate change and support a cleaner, more resilient tourism industry; strengthen the contribution of tourism to the conservation and sustainable use of heritage; promote broad and fair distribution of economic and social benefits to local communities; and create instruments to make tourism accessible to more Mexicans.

In addition to the five sectoral objectives, and in line with the National Development Plan 2013-18, the Programme also sets out cross-cutting agendas on productivity and gender to strengthen the competitiveness of tourism and increase tourism's development impact. The productivity agenda aims to target programmes and spending to raise productivity, improve labour market functioning and create more paid and formal employment. The gender agenda seeks to support women's rights and equality of opportunity, increase labour market participation of women and promote female leadership and participation in decision-making.

The Sectoral Programme for Tourism 2013-18 is a comprehensive and ambitious multi-year plan to stimulate tourism in Mexico. It is directly derived from and closely aligned with the National Development Plan 2013-18, and in turn provides the policy framework for state and municipal level tourism plans and programmes. The existence of such a long term tourism strategy approved at the highest level of government can play a key role in engaging public and private sector stakeholders toward a common vision for the sector and can be a useful mechanism to support a whole-of-government approach to tourism development.

The importance of long term planning to develop tourism and support good governance is increasing recognised across OECD countries. A longer-term approach fosters the development of the sector, rather than simply seeking to stabilise, adjust or re-orientate to new market opportunities. Economic conditions, the political context and other factors can make such long term planning challenging. Current budgetary realities are impacting on Mexico's ability to deliver on this programme, while the wider context makes it difficult to develop and implement a longer-term vision for the tourism sector beyond the term of each administration.

National Infrastructure Plan 2014-18

Also derived from the National Development Plan 2013-18 is the National Infrastructure Plan 2014-18 (*Programa Nacional de Infraestructura* – PNI), which significantly includes a dedicated section on tourism for the first time. Infrastructure performs a vital role for the functioning of the economy, and well-allocated infrastructure investment can contribute to raising growth and social welfare. The Plan recognises the need for tourism to be taken into account in infrastructure planning and has the express aim of developing competitive infrastructure to, among other things, promote tourism as a strategic axis of regional economic development and well-being.

Tourism development relies on the existence of adequate network infrastructure (energy, water, transport, telecommunications) to support tourism businesses and handle people flows to and around the destination. The lack of a comprehensive infrastructure investment strategy which takes into consideration the transversal nature of tourism has impacted the sector's development. To address this, the Plan envisages an integrated tourism infrastructure policy to use public investment from the three levels of government to improve tourism attractions and destinations, and encourage private investment to strengthen and consolidate the tourism offer.

Two areas of infrastructure are targeted: tourism-supporting investment in major "public good" infrastructure on which tourism depends, and tourism-specific investment in new tourism centres, based on the integrated resort development model in priority destinations identified in the Sectoral Programme for Tourism 2013-18. A range of projects aim to improve the infrastructure and facilities in major tourism destinations, diversify supply and create new tourism products, attractions and destinations, promote tourism competitiveness and co-ordinate infrastructure development with transport, environment, urban development and other policies (Box 2.4).

Box 2.4. Tourism infrastructure projects in the National Infrastructure Plan 2014-18

Improve infrastructure and facilities in major tourism destinations (6.1): to consolidate tourism destinations, diversify tourism products and strengthen the economic impact of the Magic Towns, colonial towns and regions.

Strategies include: regenerate historic urban districts and heritage-based destinations, including Magic Towns (monuments, colonial buildings and archaeological sites, craft and food centres); renovate and develop tourism infrastructure and facilities in tourism sites of interest (lighting, access and services, marinas, museums, trams, parks, convention centres etc.); strengthen the maintenance and operation of integrally planned resorts; beach reclamation and protection from erosion; support Magic Towns.

Promote the creation of new tourism infrastructure to diversify supply (6.2): including the construction of tourism attractions, new destinations and products (sun and beach, nature, culture, cruise, luxury, sport, congress and conventions, other).

Strategies include: construction of convention centres (Aguascalientes, Torreón, Córdoba), new tourism attractions in established centres (Nuevo Acapulco), and public beach parks, investment to strengthen infrastructure in Magic Towns and other areas of tourism interest, develop segments and products with strong regional development potential (consolidation of Mesoamerican heritage in Chichén Itzá, Palenque, Calakmul, Teotihuacán).

Promote co-ordinated infrastructure development with policies aimed at promoting the competitiveness of tourism (6.3): based on criteria of productivity, accessibility, diversity and specialisation.

Strategies include: construction of infrastructure to improve mobility (Friendly airports, modernisation of tourism ports, new road access), create more sustainable tourism destinations (water sanitation, solid waste), improve the facilities and urban image of historic centres to develop cultural tourism (underground cabling) and encourage tourism to protected natural areas.

In total, an investment portfolio of MXN 181.2 billion is foreseen over the five-year period to directly support tourism (2.3% of the total investment under the Plan) by developing new, and improving the existing, infrastructure in destinations. Public investment was originally envisaged to amount to MXN 69 billion (MXN 41.9 billion from the Federal budget, MXN 19.3 billion in subsidies and MXN 7.9 billion in state investment), with the balance of the investment (61.9%) coming from the private sector, the highest share of private investment anticipated under the Plan.

The tourism sector also stands to benefit from wider infrastructure development, notably under the communication and transport and urban development pillars which include projects to improve passenger mobility and develop modern, safe, sustainable and integrated transport infrastructure, and support universal internet access. These projects are likely to be particularly important in using tourism as a vehicle for regional and local development, helping to open up access to and supporting smaller-scale tourism development in communities and areas across the territory.

Investment in infrastructure is a strategic and priority matter to generate economic growth and development in Mexico. Infrastructure deficits are recognised to limit the potential for more sustainable and inclusive tourism development in the country. Delivery of these infrastructure developments will help to strengthen Mexico's tourism offer, and support the attractiveness and competitiveness of Mexico as a tourism destination. A number of high profile projects have been postponed or cancelled since the Plan was launched, while recent budget cuts have also impacted on investment in tourism-supporting and tourism-specific infrastructure development.

Regional Development Programmes 2014-18

Tourism's capacity to stimulate regional economies and support local communities is recognised in Mexico. Tourism is identified as an engine of regional development in the National Development Plan 2013-18 and the Sectoral Programme for Tourism 2013-18. The National Infrastructure Plan 2014-18 also outlines an integrated vision for regional development, with strategic regional tourism projects complemented by national and inter-regional projects.

Individual Regional Development Programmes 2014-18 for the North, Centre and South-southeast regions contain tourism development plans and projects to complement national tourism policy, with initiatives to attract tourism investment, develop ecotourism and other opportunities to take advantage of regional assets, create region-wide tourism routes, design and offer new tourism products and professionalise human resources for tourism. The current tourism offering, nature of tourism assets and opportunities for tourism development differ across the regions, and this is reflected in the individual regional development programmes.

The importance of tourism varies at regional level. The sector is particularly important to the economy in the south-southeast region, which is also identified as having the greatest potential to develop and benefit from further tourism development (Box 2.5). Economic growth in the region is limited by the complex geography, low population density (outside Puebla, Veracruz and Tabasco), and weak transport links, with the states bordering the Pacific less developed. High levels of marginalisation and poverty are also a feature.

The Regional Development Programme for the South-southeast 2014-18 includes a specific section on tourism development, with projects to modernise and extend the road network, air and sea terminals, equipment and urban image, signage and maintenance of tourism attractions. The need to support businesses and promote training and skills development is also noted, and the programme also seeks to develop local suppliers in the tourism market to generate greater local benefit.

Greater clarity is needed on how these plans fit together, as part of a shared strategic policy approach to tourism. In the absence of this, the variety of plans makes for a complex policy making environment. There is a lack of precision on the connections between the various strategies and plans, and on how the different levels of government and agencies work together to align the actions foreseen, communicate with each other on what they are trying to achieve and best use available resources to help meet shared economic priorities.

A clearer articulation of a strategic vision for tourism in Mexico, and a prioritisation of the actions to address these, would help engage public and private sector stakeholders toward a common vision for the sector, support a whole-of-government approach, foster the development of the industry and enhance the impact of tourism at national and local level. This would help to move beyond policy "silos" and build consensus on the most important cross-cutting issues which need to be worked on together to achieve real economic growth and inclusion (OECD, 2010). It would also provide a framework to monitor and assess progress in implementing tourism policy, which remains a challenge.

Box 2.5. Tourism and regional development in Mexico

South-south east region: Tourism makes an important contribution to the south-south east regional economy, and is an important source of employment. The south-southeast region accounts for around 54% of total tourism GDP in Mexico, 38% of tourists (based on arrivals in hotels) and around 39% of the country's hotel offer, with an average occupancy rate of 51.2% (slightly lower than the national occupancy level of 53%). Within the region, an important share of tourism activity is concentrated in Guerrero (Acapulco) and Quintana Roo (Cancún and Riviera Maya). Aside from the sun-sea-sand product, new tourism products like eco and cultural tourism are recognised to provide opportunities in Chiapas, Campeche, Veracruz and Yucatán. The region has the greatest endowment of natural and cultural assets in the country, including the Mesoamerican Corridor which is recognised for its diversity. However, the National Infrastructure Plan 2014-18 notes that a more strategic approach to development is needed to facilitate mobility and strengthen projects to expand the impact of tourism beyond the peninsula. The Regional Development Programme for the South-southeast 2014-18 includes plan to attract and maintain investment, develop region-wide tourism routes, design and offer new tourism products, and professionalise human resources for tourism.

Northern region: Tourism in the north is linked with industrial activity and border trade, highlighting the need to strengthen the attractiveness of the tourism offer and develop tourism niches in the region. The Regional Development Programme for the North Region 2014-18 highlights the limited development of the tourism and hotel offer away from traditional sun-sea-sand destinations, and need for investment in a multi-modal transport network to improve connectivity to and between destinations, in order to more efficiently exploit the region's natural and cultural assets.

Centre region: The centre region has considerable infrastructure, hotel and room capacity, and serves to move tourism between north and south. Mexico's two biggest airports in terms of passenger movement are located in the region, Mexico City and Guadalajara, and are attractive to domestic visitors due to their proximity to the main tourism destinations in the region. The National Infrastructure Plan 2014-18 notes that maintaining the attractiveness and dynamism of this region requires innovation and infrastructure development, while the Regional Development Programme for the Central Region 2014-18 notes the need to support the development of industrial and tourism clusters in the region.

Effective implementation is essential to deliver on Mexico's ambitious tourism policy objectives. This requires strong governance and institutional capacity to make the most of tourism policies and programmes, as well as mechanisms to monitor progress and evaluate outcomes. The evaluation of policy outcomes closes the circle between action and result and can lead to the continual improvement of tourism competitiveness. Tourism is a constantly evolving sector and regular monitoring and evaluation is essential to measure the performance of public spending on tourism and to ensure that policies are effective and fit for purpose.

There is evidence that Mexico would benefit from a stronger focus on implementation and on monitoring and evaluating the success of policy measures over time. Limited information is available to assess the extent to which Mexico's remarkable range of well-articulated tourism plans, programmes and initiatives are prioritised and implemented, the outcomes measured, and learnings drawn to inform more effective future policy. The resource constraints facing policy makers in Mexico makes this situation more challenging, but also more necessary. A proper implementation framework would provide a clear roadmap for how shared policy objectives are to be achieved, including detailed agreements on joint actions, budgets and timescales.

Legal and regulatory framework for tourism development

The General Tourism Law 2009 provides the legal framework for tourism development in Mexico, and creates the basis for tourism policy, planning and programming throughout the national territory. The Law sets out the respective roles and responsibilities of the three levels of government in Mexico, and establishes the basis for co-ordination between the federal, state and municipal authorities, and participation of the private and civil sectors. It also sets out the legal framework for the conservation, protection, improvement, promotion and use of national tourism resources, including natural and cultural assets, while creating and developing new tourism attractions.

Under the Law, the Federal Ministry for Tourism (SECTUR) is tasked with developing and leading national tourism policy, planning and development, in accordance with criteria to promote competitiveness and deliver sustainable, balanced development. The Ministry is required to develop a Sectoral Programme for Tourism aligned with the National Development Plan, specifying national tourism policies, objectives and priorities. It is also charged with leading tourism development programmes, including tourism territorial planning and sustainable tourism development zones. The Ministry is required to register tourism service providers, organise and publish tourism-related statistics, and conclude international agreements to promote foreign investment in tourism. The Law also sets out the legal framework under which the parastatal bodies under the responsibility of the Ministry operate, and their functions, namely the Mexico Tourism Board and the National Fund for Tourism Development (FONATUR).

The Law requires that the Federal Ministry for Tourism co-ordinates with other federal agencies and institutions on matters materially relevant to tourism, and works with other levels of government, the private sector and civil society to boost tourism development. It provides for an inter-ministerial Executive Tourism Commission, led by the Ministry of Tourism, to address issues which fall under the responsibility of two or more federal institutions and serve as a consultative body on tourism matters. It also provides for a consultative Tourism Advisory Council at federal level to propose strategies and co-ordinate the activities of federal agencies and institutions on tourism matters, in addition to Local Tourism Advisory Councils at state level. In each instance, there is provision to invite representatives of the private sector, civil society and academia to participate.

Finally, the Law sets out the framework to verify compliance with the Law, its regulations and the official tourism standards in Mexico, either by the Federal Ministry of Tourism, or through the state and municipal governments.

Tourism is impacted by a diverse range of regulatory provisions in Mexico and operates within a complex environment. Mexico's main regulatory instruments are the Official Mexican Norms, which are compulsory product, process and service standards. Seven official norms specifically apply to tourism and relate to: minimum safety standards for dive operators, safety requirements for campsites, liability insurance requirements, service levels for general tourism or cultural guides, service standards for specialised activity guides, consumer protection rules and contracts between service providers and users, and safety requirements for adventure tourism service providers. In addition to regulations linked with the tourism sector (destinations, service providers, tourists), regulations in other areas also have an influence (e.g. migration, transport, safety, environment, culture, business).

Tourism is also covered by environmental legislation, including the recent General Wildlife Law 60 TER amendment which prohibits tourism projects which affect the natural carry capacity of the ecosystem and in particular the mangrove forests in coastal destinations.

Legal and regulatory reform

Mexico has been engaging in a bold package of structural reforms to break free from three decades of slow growth, low productivity, pervasive labour market informality and high income inequality. Major structural measures have been legislated to improve competition, education, energy, the financial sector, labour, infrastructure, telecommunications and the tax system, among many, and implementation has started in earnest (OECD, 2015).

As part of this wider legal and regulatory reform agenda, Mexico has taken steps to strengthen the legal and institutional framework for tourism, and improve the environment in which the sector operates. The Ministry of Tourism has identified five major reforms within the tourism sector. Two internal reforms have involved an internal restructuring of the Ministry of Tourism, to better respond to the changing tourism demands and harness the sector's potential to stimulate economic growth and development, and the introduction of new rules of procedure, both of which were accomplished in 2014. The Ministry is currently undergoing a further restructuring process, linked with the constrained budgetary environment. This process is expected to be completed by the end of 2016.

The Ministry of Tourism is a large ministry with wide ranging competences and responsibilities and a complex structure. These reforms should focus on modernising and streamlining the organisation of the Ministry, and enhance the linkages between the planning and implementation functions within the Ministry, and with the Mexico Tourism Board and FONATUR. In particular, the reforms should seek to simplify the institutional framework for tourism and clearly set out the roles, responsibilities and linkages within the Ministry of Tourism, and the mechanisms for engaging with public and private actors.

Three external reforms relate to the legal and regulatory framework within which tourism operates, notably in relation to the General Tourism Law 2009, and its regulations, and the Federal Public Administration Law. While the General Tourism Law 2009 is relatively new, several changes to it and the related regulations have been identified as necessary to respond to the dynamically changing environment. Mexico has therefore opted to carry out a comprehensive review of the Law, to better support tourism development. The regulations under the General Tourism Law were revised and published in the official journal in 2015. The Ministry of Tourism also made a proposal to reform Article 42 of the Federal Public Administration Law to update the regulatory framework under the Ministry, which had not been substantially reformed in over 30 years.

The Ministry of Tourism is also participating in the wider regulatory reform agenda led by the Ministry of Economy's Federal Commission for Regulatory Improvement (COFEMER). A federal review identified, classified and prioritised a total of 246 regulatory procedures directly or indirectly linked with the tourism sector, and the Ministry of Tourism and COFEMER made simplification proposals. A quarter of the procedures analysed were included in the Regulatory Improvement Programme 2015-16. The Ministry of Tourism can also identify and propose secondary regulations for modification, simplification or elimination, as part of the wider horizontal regulatory agenda (see Chapter 5 for further discussion on the reforms to facilitate the creation of new tourism businesses through the Rapid Start Business System).

Institutional arrangements and governance

The Mexican government consists of three levels: federal, state and municipal. This multi-level governance framework has implications for the governance of tourism, and the co-ordination and implementation of tourism policy. Central government plays a vital role in developing cohesive, effective tourism policy in this context, while subnational levels of government also play a significant role, as full competence for tourism does not lie with the central government. Due to its cross-cutting and fragmented nature, tourism requires both horizontal and vertical co-ordination, within government, and with the private sector.

The Sectoral Programme for Tourism 2013-18 identified the need for an integrated vision around which actors can work together to deliver common outcomes, along with a fundamental change in the institutional framework in Mexico to support the effective implementation of national tourism policy which aims to stimulate productivity, innovation and creativity; create a more stable business environment; secure the required infrastructure; ensure environmental sustainability, quality standards and human resources for tourism.

The multiplicity of stakeholders active on tourism in Mexico represents a significant challenge in terms of organisation and governance, and for the implementation of a coherent and efficient national tourism strategy. There is a need to better connect national tourism policy development with regional tourism policy development, and to bring the different players around a shared vision.

Structure and functions of the Federal tourism administration

At national level, the Federal Ministry for Tourism is the lead government agency with responsibility for tourism policy, planning and development. Its mission is to design and implement policies to strengthen tourism development, promote innovation, improve quality and competitiveness, encourage mainstream strategies to co-ordinate actions of government, the private sector and civil society, and contribute to sustainable and inclusive growth.

It is responsible for: developing and leading national tourism policy; promoting domestic and international tourism; regulating tourism planning, programming, promotion and development; encouraging the development of tourism-supporting infrastructure; and co-ordinating the actions of federal, state and municipal authorities. Other activities include implementing environmental policy instruments, participating in emergency and disaster prevention and response programmes, conducting research and building knowledge on tourism in Mexico, and promoting legal and regulatory compliance. The Ministry may enter into agreements with state and municipal authorities to design and implement tourism development programmes, and to manage and monitor sustainable tourism development zones.

Figure 2.1. Organisational structure of Mexico's Federal Ministry of Tourism[1]

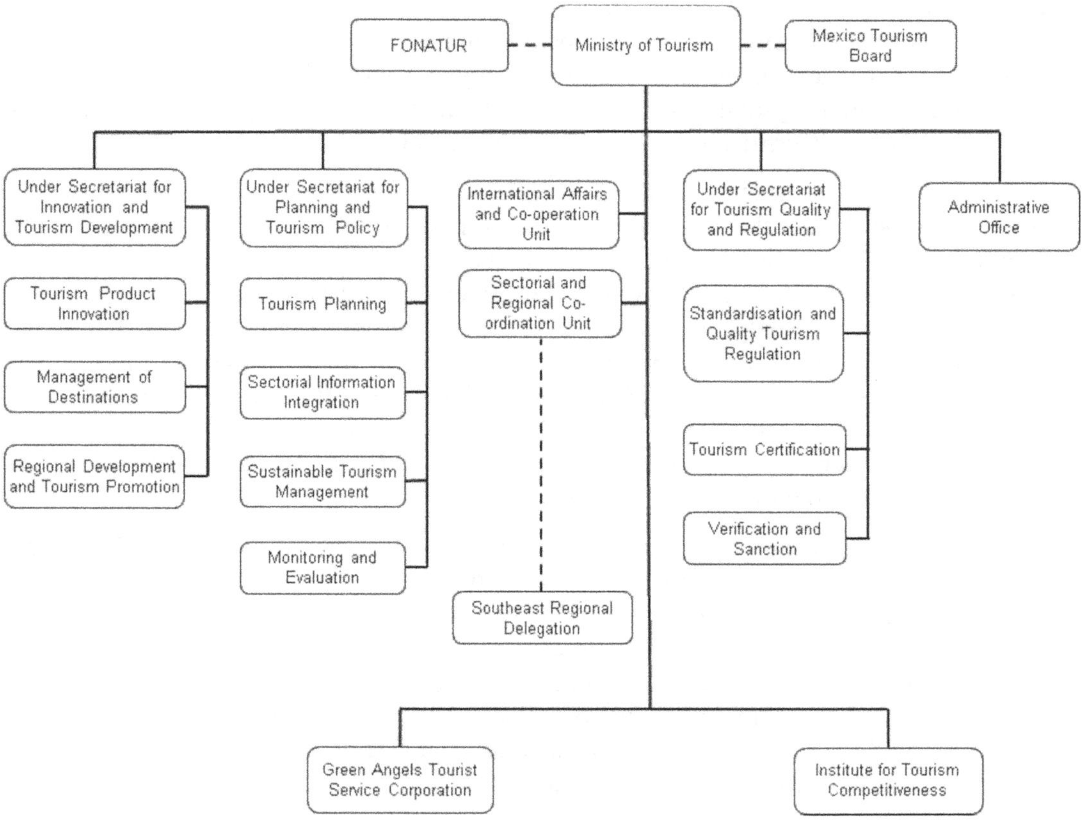

1. Other tourism bodies active on tourism include the state and municipal governments, the tourism industry and non-governmental organisations, universities and civil society.

Source: OECD, adapted from the Ministry of Tourism, 2016.

The Ministry is composed of three under-secretariats, with responsibility for Innovation and Tourism Development, Planning and Tourism Policy and Tourism and Quality Regulation.

The Under-Secretariat for Innovation and Tourism Development is responsible for stimulating innovation, encouraging the development and diversification of competitive tourism products, promoting public and private investment and financing, and supporting the sustainable management and development of tourism in destinations and regions. It co-ordinates the actions of the three levels of government, the private sector and civil society, and is composed of four directorates: Tourism Product Innovation, Destination Management, Regional and Tourism Development and Tourism Investment and Financing.

The Under-Secretariat for Planning and Tourism Policy is responsible for strategic planning and implementation, monitoring and evaluation of national tourism policy. It collates and disseminates knowledge and information, and proposes local tourism management schemes and co-ordination strategies and mechanisms to support the design of effective plans, programmes and priority projects. This includes the General Territorial Tourism Planning Programme, and the designation of sustainable tourism development zones. Four directorates sit within the under-secretariat and focus on: Planning, Integrated Sector Information, Sustainable Tourism System, and Monitoring and Evaluation.

A new Under-Secretariat for Tourism and Quality Regulation was established under the 2014 restructure, to increase the quality of tourism services and boost the competitiveness of tourism in Mexico. It focuses on regulation and standard-setting and is responsible for developing and managing the National Tourism Register and the National Tourism Certification System. It is composed of three directorates: Quality and Standards Regulation, Tourism Certification, and Verification and Compliance.

Under the 2014 restructure, a new Sectoral and Regional Co-ordination Unit may be created to co-ordinate the activities of the various units within the Ministry, its decentralised and parastatal bodies, as well as the Federal Tourism Cabinet. It was also intended to lead the Ministry's regional implementation strategy and co-ordinate the activities of the five newly created regional offices the Northeast, Northwest, Centre, Southeast and Southwest to promote the effective implementation of tourism development programmes. The intention was that each office would represent the Ministry on regional issues in its dealings with federal, state and municipal authorities, along with chambers of commerce, industry associations, local committees and civil organisations within their respective region.

Under the current reorganisation, the Sectoral and Regional Co-ordination Unit may be disbanded and its responsibilities allocated to other divisions within the Ministry. The regional offices have also been disbanded, as part of the 2016 restructuring process. It is not yet clear how the essential horizontal and vertical co-ordination functions envisaged for the Sectoral and Regional Co-ordination Unit will be assured within the new organisational structure. Strengthening co-ordination and collaboration with each level of government, and the private sector, remains a key challenge for effective tourism policy development and implementation in Mexico.

A major focus of the current leadership of the Ministry of Tourism is to enhance the strategic and effective co-ordination between federal government agencies, international development organisations, and state and municipal authorities, as well as the private sector, to share information, align policy objectives and more effectively implement the ambitious targets of the National Development Plan and the Sectoral Programme for Tourism. The aim is to co-ordinate the efforts of the federal and local government, private sector and non-tourism partners to transform Mexican destinations into innovative host communities which offer high-value experiences to domestic and international tourists, enhance the natural and cultural heritage, and strengthen local economic and social development.

The Ministry has responsibility for two decentralised bodies – the Green Angels and the Institute of Tourism Competitiveness.

Green Angels is a decentralised corporation responsible for designing policies and strategies to promote safety and provide information, support and assistance to tourists. The programme seeks to strengthen the image of Mexico as a safe and attractive destination for both domestic and international visitors. It does this by providing information, guidance and support to tourists, including road-side mechanical and accident assistance, and in response to emergencies and disasters.

The Institute of Tourism Competitiveness (ICTUR) is a centre of knowledge and applied research aimed at strengthening the competitiveness of the tourism sector in Mexico. Formerly the Centre for Advanced Studies in Tourism, the Institute was renamed to reflect the new focus on competitiveness. The Institute works closely with universities and researchers to generate and disseminate information, and train and professionalise human resources in the sector, to promote innovation and critical thinking, support better decision-making and improve tourism management and policy. It does this by providing funding for applied research on priority issues, encouraging knowledge and technology transfer, delivering training and cultural awareness programmes, and providing innovation and technical assistance. This is the main mechanism through which the Ministry engages with academia on matters of tourism policy.

The Ministry of Tourism is also responsible for and co-ordinates the activities of two parastatal organisations.

The Mexico Tourism Board (CPTM) implements marketing and promotion policy. It co-ordinates, designs and develops tourism promotion strategies for the domestic and international market, and promotes Mexico's destinations, activities and natural and cultural offering. It is a public-private body and works in partnership with tourism industry stakeholders and operates through 23 global offices in 14 countries (United States, Canada, Colombia, Brazil, Argentina, United Kingdom, France, Spain, Berlin, Italy, Russia, China, Korea and Japan). The Mexico Tourism Board employs 200 people, has an annual promotional budget of USD 165 million (Box 2.6).

Box 2.6. Innovative approach to financing tourism promotion in Mexico

Mexico has experimented with alternative finance sources to foster tourism promotion in a context of budgetary limitations, by channelling revenue from non-immigrant taxes towards strengthening the country's image around the world. On 31st December 1998, Mexican Congress approved the Non-Immigrant Tax (DNI), a flat rate of MXN 237, which should be directed to the monitoring and supervision of immigration-related activities. At the same time, tourism institutions in Mexico were facing budgetary limitations affecting tourism promotion. This situation exposed the need to find alternative ways to plan and finance promotion in order to attract international tourists. Consequently, Mexico's government developed a new strategy to finance and design promotion. In May of 1999, Mexico's government created the Mexico Tourism Board, as a State-Owned Enterprise, an organisation entrusted to co-ordinate, design and develop the national and international strategies for tourism promotion, working closely with local governments and the private sector. The Mexican government decided to support the board with revenue from the DNI. As of 2001, DNI's participation in the total budget was MXN 33 million, approximately 5.7% of the Board's total budget.

During the following years, a series of reforms to the Federal Duties Law, where the DNI is recognised, acknowledged the importance for promoting tourism for Mexico's government. Since 2002, a higher percentage of total DNI revenue was directed to the Board, 50% for migration issues and 50% for the Tourism Board. In 2007 it was established that only 20% of the total revenues would be directed to immigration activities, with the remaining 80% being be directed to tourism. 10% is allocated by law to the National Fund for Tourism Development, intended for research and infrastructure projects that improve destinations. By the end of 2011, DNI's participation in the total budget was almost MXN 1 649.5 million, approximately 60.7% of the total budget. In just one decade, the budget directed to promote country branding and strengthen Mexico's image around the world increased by nearly 5 000% from 2001 to 2011.

Source: OECD (2014b).

The National Fund for Tourism Development (FONATUR) is responsible for planning and programming tourism development and stimulating private and civic investment financing. Since its creation in 1974 by the Ministry of Finance and Public Credit (SHCP), it has acted as a facilitating instrument for foreign investors. Its mission is to identify, create and develop sustainable tourism projects to promote tourism investment, create jobs and stimulate economic and regional development.

To better align policy, product development and promotion activities, the Ministry has created product-focused working groups (Cultural Tourism and Gastronomy, Nature-based, MICE and Medical tourism) which jointly involving the Ministry of Tourism, FONATUR and the Mexico Tourism Board, as part of the current restructuring process. An Information and Trends Task Force has also been created to bring a stronger market-centred focus, resolve information gaps and strengthen results measurement.

FONATUR plays a key supply-side role and has extensive tourism planning and implementation knowledge and experience in a Mexico context, while the Mexico Tourism Board is active on the demand-side. Closely aligning these demand and supply side perspectives to share information and expertise will be critical to ensure the destination and product offer in Mexico moves with the market and is closely aligned with and caters to what consumers are looking for from their travel experience. This in turn is a fundamental pillar to inform policy that is close to the market and is focused on strategic and priority issues. The current reorganisation of the Ministry of Tourism should therefore look to further strengthen the relationship with and between the Mexico Tourism Board and FONATUR.

Role of State and municipal authorities and their tourism development powers

Under Mexico's federal government structure, certain tourism policy, planning and development responsibilities are in the charge of the state and municipal authorities which have a central role to play in implementing national tourism policy, as set out in the General Tourism Law 2009.

State authorities are responsible for tourism development issues which affect two or more municipalities and are tasked with developing, implementing and evaluating local tourism policy. Each state is required to develop a Local Tourism Programme, derived from and aligned with the National Development Plan and Sectoral Programme for Tourism, and validated with the Federal Ministry of Tourism. Municipal authorities are in turn responsible for developing a Municipal Tourism Programme.

This process helps to align local and municipal plans with national development and tourism strategies. Greater consultation between the different levels of government in developing their respective plans would further support this, enabling a more strategic approach to tourism at each level with a clearer understanding of the respective implementation roles in this. It is worth noting that the terms of offices and mandates of different levels of government do not always align. This has limitations for defining priorities and planning, as well as continuity between administrations on matters relating to tourism.

Each state is also required to establish a Local Tourism Advisory Council composed of local officials responsible for tourism. Representatives from relevant federal, state and municipal bodies, the private sector and civil society may also be invited to participate. Municipal authorities are in turn required to establish a Municipal Tourism Board to co-ordinate tourism development strategies and actions by public, private and civil sector actors. Both state and municipal authorities may also issue opinions to the Federal Ministry of Tourism on tourism-related matters. In the case of municipalities, this is limited to investment projects for tourism development or services in the municipality.

States are responsible for implementing tourism policy instruments and encouraging the development of tourism infrastructure, as well as assisting the Federal Ministry of Tourism with hotel classification and monitoring compliance with legal and regulatory provisions associated with the regulation. States also work with relevant municipalities to design, implement and evaluate local tourism and territorial planning programmes. They, along with municipalities, may propose areas to be declared sustainable tourism zones, and are responsible for managing and monitoring these zones. The three levels of government may intervene to stimulate tourism in these areas, and encourage investment, employment and proper territorial planning.

Other state activities include promoting tourism activities and destinations, supporting SMEs, participating in emergency and disaster prevention and response programmes, conducting research to support local tourism development and disseminating information, providing assistance to tourists and channelling complains to the competent authority. The municipal authorities are charged with assisting with these activities, and with implementing tourism policy instruments not expressly assigned to the federal or state authorities.

Effectively co-ordinating the policies and actions of three distinct and autonomous levels of government is a challenge in Mexico, but it is essential in the design and implementation of policies that are effective in boosting tourism and economic growth. Coherence and consistency between levels of government are necessary to ensure that tourism policies and implementation are mutually supportive and reinforcing. No institutionalised mechanism exists to support this type of co-ordination and meetings between the Ministry of Tourism and the state counterparts appear to take place on an *ad hoc* basis.

One of the main mechanisms through which the Ministry of Tourism co-ordinates with state and municipal authorities is within the context of specific programmes. Through the Programme for Sustainable Regional Tourism Development and Magic Towns (PRODERMAGICO) in particular, the Ministry works directly with state governments by providing economic resources to improve the tourism infrastructure in destinations and to develop sustainable tourism zones. FONATUR and the Mexico Tourism Board also engage with sub-national level governments in the performance of their respective activities.

The Ministry of Tourism also participates in a number of state-level committees and working groups related to the work of other federal ministries and agencies, on issues relevant to tourism. One example is the state-level Territorial Planning Committees led by the Ministry of Agrarian, Territorial and Urban Development (SEDATU). Other federal ministries also engage with state governments on tourism issues in the context of specific programmes and projects, such as the Ministry of Social Development's (SEDESOL) local community and employment plans and Fund for Social Infrastructure.

These examples indicate that co-ordination between the different levels of government is taking place. However, this appears to be largely at the technical rather than the strategic level, indicating that there is significant room for improvement. The reversal of the decision to create regional offices within the Federal Ministry of Tourism appears to have further weakened the capacity to co-ordinate vertically in the absence of other mechanisms. This is a challenge in the context of reduced budgetary resources, but essential for the development and implementation of efficient and effective tourism policies. Strengthening this type of co-ordination is thus something which needs to be prioritised.

Engagement of the private sector in policy making

Collaboration with the private sector is important in developing and implementing effective tourism policies and enabling destinations and the tourism industry to become more competitive and sustainable. The private sector plays a primary role in the provision of tourism services and is often best placed to identify tourism development opportunities and those areas where government policy interventions can be of most assistance.

With private sector participation in policy making increasingly seen as an essential element of good governance, strengthening the effectiveness and impact of tourism policy, governments are actively taking steps to ensure policy makers and industry work together effectively. The private sector needs to be actively involved at all stages of the process, from guiding policy and programme development to implementation and delivery, to ensure that programmes and policy interventions are appropriately aligned with and respond to the sector's needs, which are fast changing, continually evolving and increasingly complex.

Tourism policy making in Mexico would benefit from being more participative with a more regular, institutionalised relationship with the private sector. While the Sectoral Programme for Tourism 2013-18 refers to the need to work more closely with the private sector, and private sector participation has been instrumental in the development and implementation of certain projects (e.g. development of the National Tourism Certification System and the identification of air routes with tourism potential), no clear mechanism exists to work with the private sector in the development and delivery of policy objectives.

One of the challenges in seeking private sector level policy input in Mexico is the range of bodies that represent different types of businesses and branches in the sector. Because each of these groups of businesses have particular issues and problems it is difficult for tourism to speak with one voice.

A range of associations represent different branches of the industry in Mexico. The National Tourism Business Council (CNET) brings together a number of these associations, while the Confederation of National Chambers of Commerce – Services and Tourism (CONCANACO-SERVYTUR) represents SMEs in the tourism sector. However, consultations with the private sector highlighted the poor co-ordination and exchange of information between the various associations, and the absence a single organisation to draw together these different strands and provide industry leadership.

OECD work on governance points to a trend where peak tourism industry bodies are established to more effectively speak on behalf of the private sector as a whole. In Chile, the Federation of Tourism Enterprises was created to act as a single interlocutor with the government. The Portuguese Tourism Confederation plays a similar role in Portugal, and help to align private sector interest and gain critical mass.

Mexico may wish to consider working with the private sector to create a similar National Tourism Industry Council to act as the sector's main interlocutor for policy makers. This council may be composed of representatives from the various representative bodies for the different industry branches which are already in existence in Mexico.

Purpose of the Federal Tourism Cabinet and its working groups

Established in 2013, the Federal Tourism Cabinet is a high-level policy instrument intended to co-ordinate policies and actions to stimulate tourism and achieve national tourism policy objectives. This formal mechanism meets twice a year and is chaired by the President of Mexico. It is horizontal in nature and brings together federal ministries and agencies to agree and implement a common tourism development agenda. This agenda is linked with the four strategic pillars, programmes and actions of the Sectoral Plan for Tourism 2013-18, which in turn is aligned with the National Development Plan 2013-18. It seeks to strengthen tourism policy planning and implementation, and streamline and optimise the use of public resources.

The Cabinet is intended to be a strategic policy instrument focused on tourism policy priorities and provides a framework to support more integrated approach to tourism policy making across government at Federal level. It offers strong potential to valorise tourism and support the integration of tourism issues into other policy areas. It can help to drive the policy agenda and overcome the challenge of policy "silos", encourage ministries and agencies to work together towards commonly agreed policy objectives.

Figure 2.2. Structure of the Federal Tourism Cabinet and its working groups

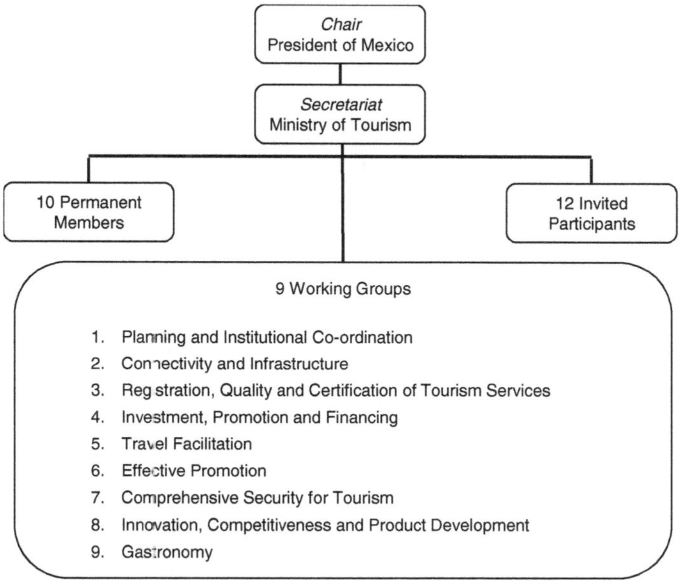

The Cabinet is comprised of ten permanent members representing ministries most relevant to tourism. A further 12 public agencies participate on an invited basis. The work of the Tourism Cabinet is organised through nine working groups (Figure 2.2). Each working group is responsible for setting the agenda and defining the scope of the group's activities. Participation and level of inter-government co-ordination varies across groups as a result, while some working groups have made more progress than others.

Building on a review of the first two years of operation of the Tourism Cabinet, less active working groups are being encouraged to strengthen their activities, while the public sector finance situation has also required some reprioritisation of activities (e.g. connectivity). The large number of working groups and limited progress made on some activities suggests that the Cabinet would benefit from focusing its energies and resources on developing solutions to a smaller number of core priority areas. This extends also to the activities within the working groups; prioritising these activities becomes all the more important given the current budgetary constraints in Mexico.

Other OECD countries have similarly created committees or working groups to co-ordinate tourism policy development, either on an ad hoc basis to address a particular policy issue, or on a more long-term basis focusing on a core number of issues. In the United Kingdom, for example, a new inter-ministerial group to facilitate tourism growth is focusing on five key areas, while the Tourism Policy Council in the United States is similarly organised around five themes.

As policy issues are addressed, priorities change and new ones emerge, the make-up and work of the Cabinet will also need to evolve, to keep the focus on strategic policy issues. Criteria have been established to prioritise the policy issues addressed by the Tourism Cabinet, ensure these are cross-cutting and strategic in nature, and bring together the relevant public actors to implement the projects. Stronger implementation of these criteria, along with closer monitoring of progress and advance planning for transitioning projects out of the Tourism Cabinet, would help enhance effectiveness and focus, and prevent the work of the Cabinet from getting bogged down in activities that are already happening or working well. Awareness of the impacts arising from the activities of the Cabinet will also be important to institutionalise the role of the Cabinet and ensure continuity through political cycles.

As a federal instrument to facilitate horizontal co-ordination, the Cabinet does not directly involve the state and municipal levels of government. Vertical co-ordination has rather focused on co-ordinating and aligning policies across the three levels of government, on a case-by-case basis. Consideration should also be given to identify ways to engage with sub-national levels of government, either within the framework of the Cabinet, or in parallel.

The effectiveness of the Cabinet as an active and strategic policy instrument would also be enhanced by strengthening the engagement with the private sector and civil society to improve the impact of policy. One of the objectives of the Cabinet is to incorporate the initiatives and opinions of the private sector and civil society, and provision is made for their participation in the Cabinet. However, engagement with industry and civil organisations does not take place on regular or systematic basis, although individual instances of successful co-ordination can be identified.

Beyond the Tourism Cabinet, the Federal Ministry of Tourism also participates in committees and working groups led by and related to the work of other federal ministries and agencies on issues relevant to tourism, to support the integration of tourism issues into other policy areas. These include the Specialised Technical Committee on Regional and Urban Development, managed by the National Institute of Statistics and Geography (INEGI) and the Monitoring Technical Group for the Regional Development Programmes, managed by the Ministry of Agrarian, Territorial and Urban Development. In some instances, joint committees have been established, such as the Joint Committee with the National Housing Commission to address housing issues for the local population in tourism destinations.

The Ministry of Tourism also engages directly with other federal ministries and agencies on specific issues and initiatives, either on an ad hoc or more formal basis. It has signed a formal co-operation agreement with the National Financial Institute (NAFIN) and FONATUR, for example, to co-ordinate financing efforts and support large and small businesses in the tourism value chain, at each stage in the business lifecycle.

Beyond the Ministry of Tourism, other ministries and agencies are actively developing smaller scale tourism and support tourism development in pursuit of wider policy objectives related to, for example, the environment, rural and community development and indigenous communities (e.g. Ministry of the Environment and Natural Resources (SEMARNAT), National Commission of Natural Protected Areas (CONANP), Ministry of Social Development (SEDESOL), National Financial Institute for Agricultural, Rural, Forestry and Fisheries Development (FND). These developments are taking place in parallel to the activities of the Ministry of Tourism.

Public funding for tourism development

The overall public budget for the Federal Tourism Administration is MXN 5.2 billion in 2016, of which MXN 4.1 billion is allocated to current spending and MXN 1.1 billion to investment. Of this, almost a third (MXN 1.6 billion or 30.2%) is current spending allocated to the Programme for Sustainable Regional Tourism Development and Magic Towns, to boost the tourism offer (MXN 1.2 billion) and develop diversified, sustainable and competitive destinations (MXN 0.4 billion).

Table 2.1. Tourism public expenditure at federal[1] level, 2016

Million MXN, constant price

Quality and Comprehensive Care Tourism Programme	205 682
Integrated planned resort conservation and maintenance	186 560
Promotion of Mexico as a tourist destination	867 279
Development and promotion of investment in the tourism sector	578 559
Development and promotion of sustainable tourism projects	89 556
Regulation and certification of tourist quality standards	48 168
Tourism infrastructure projects	1 000 700
Infrastructure maintenance	5 831
Pre-investment studies	74 307
Administrative support activities	254 950
Support activities to public service and good governance	56 296
Planning and conducting tourism policy	252 721
Boosting competitiveness of the tourism sector	19 122
Regional and Sustainable Tourism Development and Magic Towns Programme	1 571 714
Total	5 211 444

Base year 2010.

1. Supplemented by expenditure at state and municipal level.

Source: SECTUR.

The second biggest share (MXN 1 billion) is investment spending allocated to tourism infrastructure projects (19.2%), with a further 11.1% (MXN 0.6 billion) current spending assigned to promote investment in the sector. This expenditure is attributed to FONATUR, which accounts for MXN 1.9 billion or 37% of federal public expenditure when other spending is factored in, including the upkeep and maintenance of CIPs (MXN 0.2 billion).

The other main part of the federal tourism budget is current spending earmarked for the Mexico Tourism Board for marketing and promotion. In total, MXN 0.9 billion or 17.3% of direct federal tourism expenditure is apportioned to the Mexico Tourism Board. FONATUR and the Mexico Tourism Board exercise their budgetary resources independently of the Ministry of Tourism, as they are separate legal entities and have other assets and income sources, aside from public funding.

Following a steep rise in the level of public expenditure on tourism at federal level from MXN 1.8 billion in 2007 to MXN 3.4 billion in 2008 (85.6%), the overall trend over the following years was one of growth, peaking in 2015 at MXN 6.8 billion. More recently, the federal tourism budget has fallen by almost a quarter in 2016 (Figure 2.3). Despite this drop, federal tourism expenditure in 2016 is 120.6% higher than the 2007 level in real terms.

Figure 2.3. Federal expenditure for tourism sector development, 2007-16

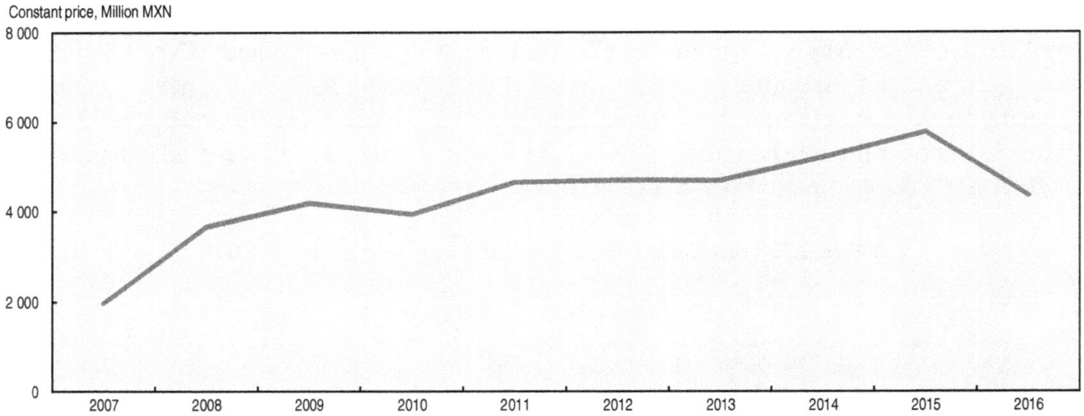

Base year 2010.

Source: SECTUR.

The recent reductions in public funding for tourism makes a long term integrated approach to planning, evaluation and performance management problematic. It has also led to a reduction in staff numbers and loss of expertise, impacting the capacity to develop effective jointed up tourism policy.

This data provides a magnitude of public tourism spending at federal level. This is supplemented by expenditure at state and municipal level. Compiling information at sub-national level is complex and time-consuming, as public tourism spending is not specifically identified in state level budgets, but rather is combined with spending on other economic activities.

Public spending in other policy areas also contributes to tourism development, through the provision of public goods and infrastructure. However, while visitors and the tourism sector may benefit from this expenditure, and tourism may contribute to the better use of these facilities, it is not considered to directly support tourism policy measures.

References

OECD. (2014), *OECD Tourism Trends and Policies 2014*, OECD Publishing, Paris. DOI: http://dx.doi.org/10.1787/tour-2014-en

OECD. (2012). *OECD Tourism Trends and Policies 2012*, OECD Publishing, Paris. DOI : http://dx.doi.org/10.1787/tour-2012-en

OECD. (2010). *Breaking Out of Policy Silos: Doing More with Less,* OECD Publications, Paris.
DOI: http://dx.doi.org/10.1787/9789264094987-en

Diario Oficial (2014) Manual on the Organisation of the Ministry of Tourism, http://www.dof.gob.mx/nota_detalle.php?codigo=5355113&fecha=05/08/2014

Diario Oficial (2013) Creation of the Tourism Cabinet, http://www.dof.gob.mx/nota_detalle.php?codigo=5321494&fecha=08/11/2013&print=true

Chapter 3
Connecting tourists with destinations in Mexico

The Mexican transport system has a vital role to play in moving domestic and international tourists from their place of residence to, and around, their final destination. Transport is a key enabler of tourism. Addressing the challenge of better connecting tourists with destinations, and on to various attractions, is necessary if Mexico is to diversify its tourism offer and source markets, strengthen tourism in regional areas, and better spread the benefits. This chapter describes the interaction between transport and tourism policies and identifies opportunities to better align tourism and transport development. It also examines connectivity strategies to improve traveller mobility, handle travel flows and link hubs with destinations.

Introduction

Connecting tourists with destinations is a challenge that can be seen under different lenses and scales. This challenge can be global, bringing tourists from countries that are nearby or on the other side of the world, and connecting Mexico with growing markets in Asia and elsewhere. At the country level, it can involve bringing tourist from their point of entry or place of residence to their ultimate destination, and beyond. It can also be very local, enabling tourists to reach a local attraction from their hotel. This variability of scale, combined with the federal structure of Mexico, means that connectivity cuts across all levels of government, be it national, state or municipal, and each stakeholder is important in order to ensure tourists enjoy a seamless transportation experience.

Transportation enables tourism, just as tourism enables transportation. Improved co-ordination between tourism and transport policies can help to improve visitor mobility and the tourism experience. The transport system has an impact on how people travel and their choice of holiday, destination and transport mode. Improving transportation, through better policies, seamless connectivity, quality services quality and lower fares, will improve the attractiveness of a destination, and making transport part of the visitor experience can be a source of competitive advantage. As the transport system serves both visitors and residents, improvements for one type of clientele can have positive implications on the other (OECD, 2016).

This chapter describes the interaction between transport and tourism policies in Mexico. It identifies key areas of transport policy that impact the achievement of tourism objectives, along with opportunities to better align tourism and transport development. It also examines connectivity strategies to improve traveller mobility, handle travel flows and link hubs with destinations.

Aligning transport and tourism policies

Transport and tourism policies and planning must be interlinked and coherent with each other, and with wider government priorities. Any misalignment will result in disequilibrium between demand and supply of transport services. It also risks yielding a less than optimal outcome for policy makers in both areas. A basic tenant of transport economics is that transport is the product of a derived demand. People do not seek mobility for the sake of mobility but rather to accomplish something else – in this case, tourism. Thus transport policies must be crafted in a way that aligns and supports tourism polices to better cater to the derived demand they will generate.

As transport is a derived demand, it is unsurprising that connectivity with Mexico's major international tourism markets such as the United States, Canada and Europe is concentrated in key coastal resorts including Cancún, Riviera Maya, Puerto Vallarta and Los Cabos. In contrast, domestic tourists looking for a sun-sea-sand experience are more likely to choose destinations like Acapulco, Veracruz-Boca del Río, Cancún and Mazatlán. This indicates that from a transport policy perspective, the connectivity needs of international tourists are different to those of domestic tourists, and they must almost be treated as two separate markets, with little possibility of synergies.

International tourists also favour the coast in practically the same proportions as Mexicans favour the interior. The result of this is clear when one observes, for example, how the intercity bus network is clearly designed for domestic tourists. If a goal of the tourism policy is to bring more international tourists away from the coast and into the interior to develop areas like cultural, gastronomy, medical and ecotourism, then Mexico will have to ensure that it has the proper transport policies in place to support that goal.

Recent tourism trends also have implications for transport. For example, the growing interest in secondary destinations will require the transportation system to adapt and ensure it offers proper connectivity to these smaller nodes of the network. This may not be a direct connection to international tourism market, as that may not be economically feasible. Therefore it requires connectivity to the international gateway in a way that is seamless for the tourist and provides an experience in itself, rather than simply a means to get from A to B. The part transport can play in the tourism experience can also be seen, for example, where tourists travel by bicycle in many destinations. Here, the attraction is as much the villages visited as the trip between them. However, for this type of tourism to be successful, it requires strategic alignment between transport and tourism policies to ensure tourists enjoy the best possible experience.

According to the Sectoral Programme for Tourism 2013-18, investments in transport infrastructure have been focused around areas of high population concentration. Many secondary tourism destinations are fragmented with no adequate transport systems to facilitate the mobility of tourists, making the area less attractive. Competing policy priorities are at play here for scarce infrastructure funding. Giving preference to projects in areas of high population concentration can be a very reasonable policy in itself, but decision makers need to be aware of the impact this has on tourism demand in more remote areas.

Aligning tourism and transport policies also requires a proper strategy regarding land-use. In most OECD countries, this is done through the use of transport plans which integrate land use and transport planning, but this is something that is lacking in Mexico. The Ministry of Agrarian, Territorial and Urban Development (SEDATU) has an important role to play here, providing the necessary spatial planning components to policy makers to ensure that transport and tourism develop within a broader strategic planning exercise. This includes having a clear outlook on where future tourism, population and employment centres will develop, ensuring that density is commensurate with the transport network's capacity to accommodate demand, and establishing clear roles and responsibilities for SEDATU, the Ministry of Tourism, and the Ministry of Communications and Transportation (SCT) in planning for future infrastructure and transport links.

A clear example of where this alignment seems to be challenging is with surface access to the new international airport in Mexico City. Two separate projects looking at this complex issue are currently underway – one by SEDATU, and another by SCT and the new airport authority. Meanwhile, the airport is being built without a formalised public transport access plan in place. OECD (2015a) recommended that since the development of the plan is behind schedule, new studies by SCT should leverage results already obtained by SEDATU. It also recommended SCT open up the tendering process to international experts, in addition to local firms, and that local transport authorities are formally included in developing the surface access plan. This situation clearly shows the need for more effective collaboration between various stakeholders and clear definitions on the roles and responsibilities for both.

Finally, aligning transport and tourism policies is not just about planning for growth, but also about planning for disasters. Mexico is located in a region where there are real hurricane and earthquake risks. Policy makers must therefore plan for the resiliency of the transport system and how to efficiently evacuate tourists prior to or quickly after a natural disaster.

Resiliency planning also includes the provision of logistical platforms to supply chain bringing food and medical necessities to tourist and local populations in disaster areas; and infrastructure recovery planning for the rebuilding of damaged but critical infrastructure, and the alternatives that exist until the damaged infrastructure can be fully operational.

The Tourism Cabinet Connectivity and Infrastructure group has or is in the process of delivering nine strategic projects including work to: identify possible new air routes to improve connectivity and guide future air services agreements negotiations; promote Mexico through better travel experiences; improve cruises at smaller cruise ports; and redevelop "Gate 75" in Terminal 2 of Mexico City International Airport at an estimated cost of MXN 140 million, to improve passenger processing and enhance regional connectivity.

Promoting an intermodal, user friendly transport system for tourism

The goal for any tourist is to safely get from origin to destination with an acceptable trade-off between speed, comfort and cost. In an ideal world, tourists could complete their travel in one easy step, using one mode of transport. However, this preference may not be compatible with the structure of the transport network. Tourists may have to add additional steps and introduce different modes to the transport chain. If the process seems too complicated, too expensive or unreliable, they may reconsider visiting a destination. The transport system should be user friendly, safe and secure, environmentally sustainable, efficient and affordable. Mobility services should be easy to use, affordable and combine multiple modes of transportation, and provide reliable and timely information and guidance through different devices and means new innovations and solutions (VTT, 2014).

The passenger transport sector is adept at moving tourists from origin to destination via strategic nodes, which are at the heart of the hub and spoke network. This is especially efficient when the entire transport chain is carried out by one company, or when several companies work together to provide a seamless experience. For example, airlines within the same alliance routinely carry passengers from their country of origin to coastal resort destinations, via a connection through Mexico City. Airlines have successfully expanded on this model, through interlining, code share, alliances and metal-neutral joint ventures, to offer a seamless transport experience across different carriers. As long as passengers travel on a single ticket and with airlines who work together, the system globally works relatively well, thanks to standardised practices and co-ordination between air carriers.

Where the transport system struggles more is when a modal transfer is required. While policy makers focus on transport systems, transport operators tend to be unimodal in their approach. Modal operators have good reasons for focusing on a single mode, but from a tourism perspective it is important to look at how linkages operate between modes for individual journeys, and the entire trip. Tourists are concerned with the transport chain from origin to destination, and will be as inconvenienced by an incident within a mode of transport as during the hand-off between two modes. Tour operators differ from traditional transport operators in that their focus is on transporting passengers from origin to destination, including synchronising flight arrivals and ground transfers. This ease of travel comes at the cost of flexibility, although increasingly tour operators are injecting some flexibility to cater to tourists seeking convenience and exploration off the beaten path.

This review found few if any examples of truly integrated intermodality for tourists in Mexico. This is a key issue for distributing the economic benefits of tourism beyond the main transport hubs and tourism centres. A seamless modal transfer integrated into a single ticket is probably the most desirable product to achieve this. However, more often than not, modal segments link together at one physical node, but operate completely independently. Buses help to connect the main airports with the surrounding areas, for example. Mexico City International Airport has two bus terminals which operate 24 hours a day, serving nearby cities including Puebla, Tlaxcala and Querétaro. Bus services also connect Cancún Airport with downtown Cancún and Ciudad del Carmen, as well as the hotel areas of Riviera Maya and Tulum.

One area for improvement could thus be in the area of integrated transport ticketing. Determining who should be responsible for ensuring this integration happens is a challenge, however. Airports are the physical nodes where the intermodal connection takes place. The air carriers and bus companies provide the modal transport services, but may not have compatible systems to offer integrated products. Also, international air carriers may not see much return in creating a niche product only for the Mexican market. This creates the opportunity to establish some type of neutral distribution portal which can offer travellers a one-stop shop where they can customise a trip across multiple service providers and tailor a package which includes flights, ground transportation and tourism services.

An interesting model of seamless transport is provided by how Germany's national carrier, Lufthansa, operates its regional feeder network in conjunction with Deutsche Bahn, the German national railway. The airline and rail operator have co-ordinated their schedules, ticketing and operations to provide the passenger with a seamless transportation experience. Passengers flying from Stuttgart to Mexico City via Frankfurt, for example, can choose to fly or take a train between Stuttgart and Frankfurt Airport. The rail option reduces the travel time, cost and carbon footprint, and enables the traveller to depart from the city centre which may be more convenient. The train has a Lufthansa flight number and if the passenger misses the onward connection due to delays, the airline will rebook them on the next available flight (or train).

In Mexico, there may be some potential to develop an integrated service between air carriers and bus operators serving airports with scheduled bus services. This would enable airlines to sell an integrated, multimodal ticket between a point on their network and a point on the intercity bus network. It could encourage travellers to venture beyond the major international gateway, such as Mexico City or Cancún, particularly if an appropriate level of marketing is used to support the secondary destination with some emphasis put on how easy it is to get there. This could provide a viable alternative transport option to destinations that could not otherwise economically sustain air services.

An integrated ticketing approach could extend to both the transport and tourism component of the journey. This could involve selling a single ticket providing access to public transport and major tourism sites. Such a ticketing system could force a rethink of fare collection on Mexican public transport, through the introduction of smart cards for example, which would improve the user experience for tourists and locals alike. Alternatively, transport operators could partner with tourism operators to market a ticket that combines bus travel and access to tourism attractions, or bus travel and accommodation. This type of integrating ticketing is used in other OECD countries and would make travel easier and more flexible, helping to encourage travellers to explore beyond the major tourism centres. Such a strategy could also prove useful in enhancing connectivity to Magic Towns such as Tecate in Baja California, which is located near

Tijuana and could attract cross-border tourists who may be more inclined to visit if offered a seamless tourism experience.

The user experience extends beyond making intermodal connections easier. At a primary level, a user friendly transport system installs a sense of confidence and safety in travellers who are able to navigate an unknown system in an unfamiliar place with ease. Communication with the user plays an important role here. This means easy access to information in a language the tourist understands to help tourists to plan their trip and manage their transport requirements in response to delays or other changes.

This makes multilingual information platforms essential to the user friendliness for international tourists, many of whom come from non-Spanish speaking countries. The websites of major Mexican intercity bus companies are only available in Spanish. This makes travel planning and ticket purchase more difficult, even if online translators or travel blogs in the language of the traveller can help to get around these issues. By comparison, Paris' public transport website (www.ratp.fr) is available in six languages, reflecting the important number of non-French speaking tourists to the city.

In addition, international tourists need to understand how the Mexican transport system works. Tourists may find it challenging to understand the intercity bus system in Mexico, for example. With so many bus companies operating in Mexico, some of which have dedicated bus stations, it may be difficult for travellers to know which company serves which route and where the bus departs from, as well as to compare prices between carriers. One website helping to address this challenge, www.busolinea.com, acts as an intercity bus ticket distributor and enables travellers to purchase tickets from 14 different bus companies in English, as well as car sharing services such as blablacar.

Box 3.1. Improving the transport user experience for women

Without safety, there is no mobility – when travellers feel that their welfare is being threatened it will negate any positive impact that a user friendly transportation system may have. Thus the perception of safety becomes paramount. Despite the great advances that have been accomplished in terms of gender equality, it remains an unfortunate fact that women can feel more vulnerable than men when using transport services, especially because of sexual harassment. Thomson Reuters (2014) quotes a YouGov poll that found that 64% of women using public transport in Mexico City had been groped or physically harassed, a level three times as high as that found in London. For this reason, some special measures have been put in place to improve the user experience and specifically target a women's sense of security. For example, during peak hours carriages at the front of the train on the Mexico City subway are reserved exclusively for women and children. Bus company ADO offers women travelling on their own the option to sit next to another woman in order to reduce potential harassment, a service that is likely to be particularly appreciated on long, overnight trips. These are measures that address the symptoms rather than the root cause, but they do enable women to feel safer using transport services and guard against loss of mobility. In the short term these types of solution can prove beneficial to increasing a women's sense of security when using the transport system. When combined with public awareness campaigns, more stringent enforcement by law enforcement, this can have long term beneficial effects.

New technologies can also help in providing users with meaningful information. The umbrella authority which oversees public transport in Mexico City, SETRAVI, has developed a new digital platform to collect, manage and analyse urban transport data through an open source platform, with assistance from the World Bank. This data has been made public, enabling other software developers to incorporate it into their applications. It makes it possible to use Google, for example, as a public transport planner, which solves a number of user friendliness issues and provides tourists with a platform they may already be very familiar with. It has also helped the city's transit agencies develop practical open tools, including a real-time tracking tool that informs users of disruptions in the system and provides route change options.

From visual signage to online trip planning to real-time information on the next arrival of buses, these are all elements which can be improved in Mexico and would encourage tourists to explore Mexico with a sense of ease, which also translates into a sense of security. Safety is particularly an issue for women when using public transport, and may limit their willingness to explore the country outside of the large destinations. It is thus important to make sure that gender issues are addressed and all users of the Mexican transport system, male or female, are safe and feel safe (Box 3.1).

A final aspect of the user experience is quality standards. Here, the Tourism Cabinet's working group on registration and quality is making important progress to provide tourists with higher and more consistent standards. For example, it has developed tools to enable service providers to display that they maintain certain quality standards, have increased consumer protection enforcement and has worked to certify car rental agencies meet certain standard levels. Reassuring tourists that service providers meet quality standards can encourage them to do business with these companies. However, travellers are increasingly turning to social media and peer review websites for travel information, like TripAdvisor, rather than official measures on quality standards. Thus governments should adopt a two-pronged approach, leveraging both official classification standards and educating stakeholders on the optimal use of social media review sites.

Air transport connectivity

Air transportation plays a key role in supporting Mexico's tourism sector and its overall economy, and developments in aviation can have major implications for the sector. Air transport provides vital connectivity between tourism generating areas and tourism destinations. It is the obvious modal choice for long haul and intercontinental travel, and 46.2% of international tourists arrived by air in 2014 (SECTUR, 2015a). This mode also plays as important role in domestic tourism and moving people around the country, supported by deregulation of the domestic air transport sector in Mexico combined with the emergence of low cost carriers such as Volaris and Interjet. Thus air connectivity has both international and domestic dimensions, as the country's vast geography and the long distances make air travel the ideal mode to transport tourists to and around the country.

Air travel has experienced strong growth in Mexico over the past quarter of a century with arriving passengers growing 4.9% per year on a compounded basis (Figure 3.1). Growth was slightly stronger for international passengers (+5.2% per year) than domestic passengers (+4.8% per year). In the first half of 2015, Mexico enjoyed strong connectivity growth as capacity on international flights grew 10.3%, going from 10.8 million to 11.9 million according to the Ministry of Tourism. The largest increase came from Colombia, on the heels of a decision by the Mexican government to remover visa requirements for nationals from that country as part of its goal to strengthen economic ties with other Pacific Alliance countries.

Figure 3.1. Air passenger arrivals, 1990-2015

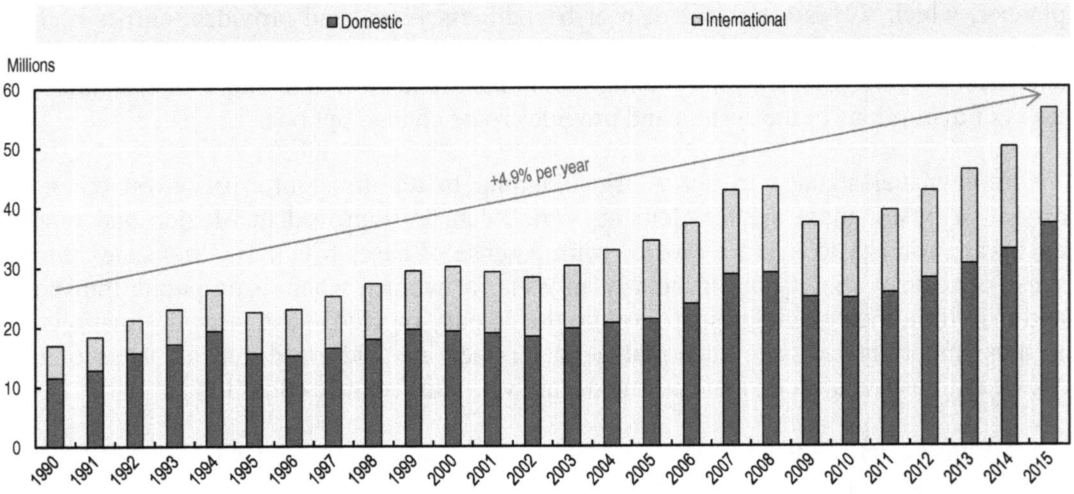

Source: SECTUR (2016).

Cancún is the busiest international airport in the country, welcoming 6.7 million passengers in 2015, ahead of 6.4 million in Mexico City. Together they account for over two thirds of international air traffic in Mexico (Figure 3.2). Only three other airports, Guadalajara, Los Cabos and Puerto Vallarta had over a million international passenger arrivals. However, Mexico City remains a far busier airport, having 4.2 times more domestic traffic in 2015. This is due to the fact that Mexico City is the economic and political centre of the country and Mexico City airport is a key hub connecting secondary airports with destinations in and outside Mexico. Cancún is primarily an origin-destination airport, with limited hub functionality.

Figure 3.3 shows that while Mexico City and Cancún have had similar international traffic for over a quarter of a century, domestic traffic has always been more concentrated in Mexico City and this the gap has been widening since about 2011. In the last decade, Cancún has seen domestic traffic triple with annual growth outpacing Mexico City by 11.7% compared to 5.3% for the national capital. However, in absolute numbers, Cancún added 2 million domestic passengers whereas Mexico City added 5 million.

In many countries, there is a convergence between business and leisure tourism markets enabling carriers to service both on the same routes. In Mexico, however, there is less overlap, aside from Cancún which has an important meetings, incentives, conference and events (MICE) sector. As a result, most non-North American operators focus on serving Mexico City, more geared to business tourism, and Cancún, with very limited direct long haul connectivity to other destinations, as shown in Table 3.1. North American carriers tend to offer two very distinct products: a year-round service to major business centres; and a more leisure oriented and seasonal service to coastal destinations.

Figure 3.2. International air passenger arrivals by major airport, 2015

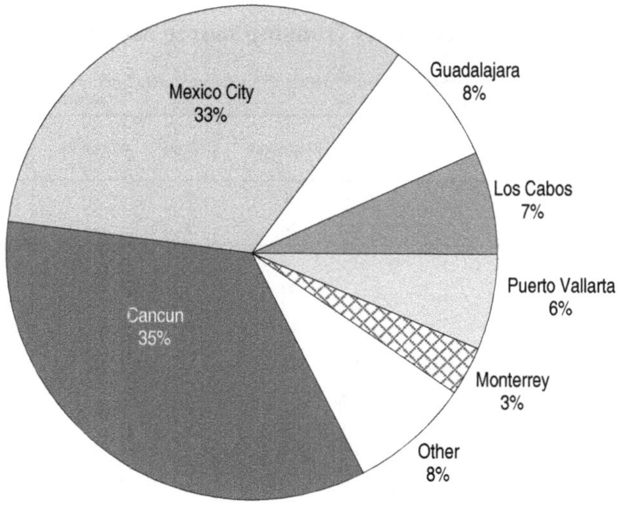

Source: SECTUR (2016).

Figure 3.3. Domestic and international air passenger arrivals to Cancún and Mexico City, 1990-2015

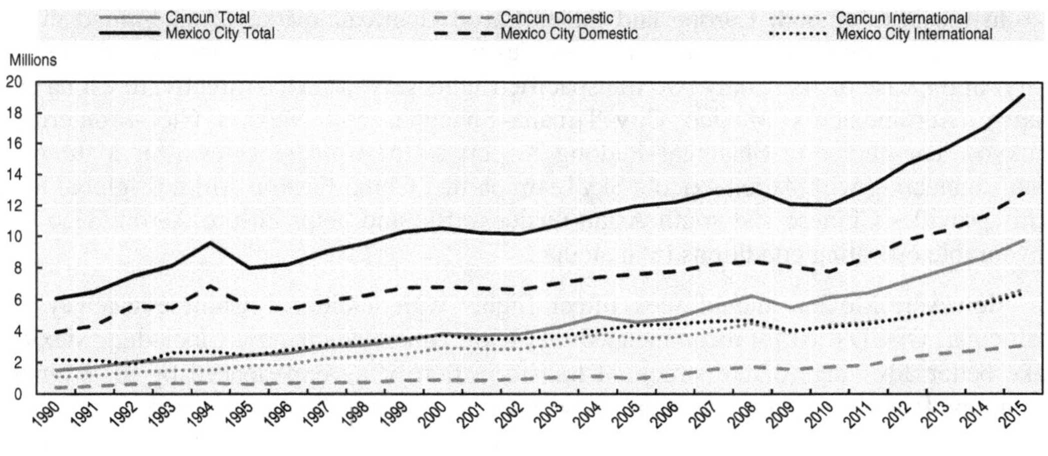

Source: SECTUR (2016).

International air connectivity

Mexico enjoys strong air connectivity with its largest source markets, but weaker connectivity with emerging markets (Table 3.1). Mexico's main international gateways all enjoy direct services to the United States and, to a lesser extent, Canada. However, nearly all services from other countries with direct service connectivity to Mexico are limited to the two main gateways of Mexico City and Cancún. The former, as the national hub could act as a transfer point to reach numerous inland and coastal destinations. However, the latter only serves Cancún and is the international gateway for the Riviera Maya and Yucatán Peninsula. The strong connectivity with North America explains why, on a nationality basis, visitors from the United States and Canada make-up 86.3% of arrivals, compared to 6.3% for Europeans and 4.4% for Latin Americans (UNWTO,

2016). Of course there is a two-way causality relationship at play here: air connectivity generates more tourism, and more tourism generates better air connectivity.

Table 3.1. Direct scheduled flight frequency from top source markets to Mexico's main airports

X At least a flight per week; - No service

	Cancún	Mexico City	Los Cabos	Puerto Vallarta	Guadalajara	Cozumel	Monterrey	Leon	Mazatlan	Zhuatanejo
United States	X	X	X	X	X	X	X	X	X	X
Canada	X	X	X	X	-	X	-	-	X	X
United Kingdom	X	X	-	X	-	-	-	-	-	-
Colombia	X	X	-	-	-	-	-	-	-	-
Argentina	X	X	-	-	-	-	-	-	-	-
Brazil	X	X	-	-	-	-	-	-	-	-
Spain	X	X	-	-	-	-	-	-	-	-
Germany	X	X	-	-	-	-	-	-	-	-
France	X	X	-	-	-	-	-	-	-	-
Peru	X	X	-	-	-	-	-	-	-	-
Italy	X	-	-	-	-	-	-	-	-	-
Chile	X	X	-	-	-	-	-	-	-	-
Japan	-	-	-	-	-	-	X	-	-	-

Source: SRS Schedules, 2015.

In the case of both Europe and major Latin American markets, the limited direct connectivity reduces the attractiveness of destinations other than Cancún and Mexico City. In the case of Asia, only two transpacific flights serve Mexico directly, to China and Japan (Aeroméxico's Mexico City–Tijuana–Shanghai and Mexico City–Monterrey–Tokyo). The choice of Shanghai–Pudong Airport as the Chinese gateway is a strategic one, connecting with Aeroméxico's SkyTeam partner China Eastern Airlines' global hub. This provides Chinese and south Asian feeder traffic and helps ensure Aeroméxico has favourable operating conditions in Shanghai.

However, Mexico should seek direct flights with additional Chinese gateways in particular. OECD (2015b) recommended that Latin American countries, including Mexico, take better advantage of the structural transformation being experienced by the Chinese economy. Part of this transformation has seen Chinese society being more oriented towards leisure tourism. However, Latin America captured less than 1% of the total Chinese market outbound market in 2013, and Mexico, only a fraction of this. There is potential for robust growth in the coming years that would not only require a tourism product adapted to Chinese preferences, but also far better and broader air connectivity, bringing Chinese tourists directly from where they live to where they want to spend their vacation, offering a similar level of service to that already offered to North American tourists.

Lack of direct air connectivity between key international markets outside of North America and Mexican cities – outside of Mexico City and Cancún – represents an impediment for tourism development. There are reasons for this lack of connectivity tied to geography, history, culture and economic development. However, if Mexico's policy goal is to diversify away from its North America Free Trade Agreement (NAFTA) partners as source markets, it will need to explore new and promising markets, and ensure it has the proper air connectivity to support these markets.

Analysis of air connectivity between 2000-13 found that connectivity was highest in the country's three largest cities – Mexico City, Guadalajara and Monterrey – and beach destinations such as Acapulco, Cancún, Puerto Vallarta and San José del Cabo, as well as Tijuana, likely due to it being adjacent to the US border (SECTUR, 2015b). This is consistent with what is observed today and is clearly shown in traffic statistics.

The Ministry of Tourism further analysed connectivity across the network, looking at the number of connections a passenger would have to make for travelling between any two random points. In interpreting these results, it is important to keep in mind that no weighting is done on actual demand. In 2000, they found that 7% of city pairs enjoyed direct flights, while 71.9% required one connection and 19.6% required two connections. In 2013, the number of airports in the study grew from 127 to 155 and the analysis showed a small drop in direct connections (5.7%), and an increase in single (72.4%) and double (21.2%) connections. Overall, this indicates slightly more connected hubs, but increasingly supported by a second hub.

When large centres are excluded, the analysis shows a greatly improved situation, with 93.5% requiring one or two connections in 2013, compared with 58% in 2000. This shows that the network had restructured to significantly increase the connectivity of hubs and, indirectly, smaller centres of population. The low level of direct connectivity for smaller destinations (5.8%) does not reflect limitations created by policies, but rather routes which air carriers choose not to operate as they believe it would not be the most profitable use for their asset.

Domestic air connectivity

From Mexico City, the following table shows the capacity and number of flights for the ten busiest domestic destinations served by Aeroméxico, which likely offers the best connectivity with international flights. After Cancún, Monterrey and Guadalajara, connectivity quickly falls off and is usually higher in the winter than in the summer, with Cancún and Guadalajara being notable exceptions to that trend.

Table 3.2. Weekly flight capacity from Mexico City with Aeroméxico, 2013

Destination	Summer		Winter	
	Flights	Seats	Flights	Seats
Cancun	111	15 337	80	11 812
Monterrey	104	12 036	107	13 704
Guadalajara	121	12 196	110	11 452
Tijuana	39	5 464	37	5 359
Merida	39	3 715	49	5 551
Villahermosa	38	3 631	44	5 127
Veracruz	56	3 800	62	4 271
Hermosillo	27	3 600	27	3 636
Acapulco	43	3 574	35	3 134
Puerto Vallarta	30	2 558	32	3 715

Source: SRS, 2015.

Domestically, the air transport market is deregulated from a price and capacity perspective, which has enabled low cost carriers like Volaris, Interjet and VivaAerobus to establish themselves in addition to regional carriers like TAR Aerolineas and Aeroméxico, the country's largest air carrier. The domestic network now reflects what carriers believe is economically optimal, while taking into account the lack of capacity at Mexico City. Carriers are structured in a hub and spoke system with hubs in major Mexican cities (Mexico City/Toluca, Guadalajara, Monterrey, Tijuana and Culiacan) which means that travellers between two medium or small Mexican cities are usually required to connect through a hub, making them less well connected, thus reducing their attractiveness for tourists already in a medium or small destination. However, this is a market issue and not a policy issue.

Bilateral air service agreements

Regulatory systems that impede entry and discriminate amongst suppliers have been shown to reduce the volume of overall passengers and tourists in particular, while liberalising air transport can help build up a stronger tourism industry (Zhang et al., 2014). This is consistent with empirical evidence gathered over nearly four decades of progressive liberalisation, where removing restrictions have at worse a neutral impact on demand and at best a strongly positive one. However, this requires prioritising the development of tourism over the protection on incumbent carriers, who will be forced to adapt to new entries and greater competition. It is thus germane to keep in mind that while aviation is an important sector of the Mexican economy, contributing around 3% to the national GDP in direct, indirect and induced effects, tourism contributed 8.5% to Mexico's GDP in 2014.

Mexico recognises the importance of air connectivity to its tourism sector and has taken steps to address this, through more liberal air services agreements, with the United States and Canada for example, as well as the construction of a new airport in Mexico City (OECD, 2016). This will provide the infrastructure required for Mexico City to become an important gateway to Latin America and improve its global connectivity. However, Mexico's approach to air services agreements seeks to balance the needs of the tourism industry with the needs of its airlines, consumers and freight transporters. This can lead to an outcome that is less than optimal under a purely tourism lens and has delayed some liberalisation efforts, particularly with the United States. To date, Mexico has no true open skies agreements with unlimited first to fifth freedom. In contrast, the United States has these types of agreements in place with 119 countries (US Department of State, 2016) and Canada with 44 countries (Transport Canada, 2015), at time of writing.

The new and expanded air services agreement between Mexico and the United States is a very important step forward in liberalising the air transport market between Mexico and its largest tourism source market. The agreement calls for unlimited third and fourth freedoms between any points in both countries, and places no limits on multiple designations (US Department of State, 2015). It removed limits on carriers and routes which had prevented leisure carriers to fully exploit this market. However, the agreement is not an Open Skies in the standard definition of the term as fifth freedoms for passenger services (allowing connectivity to or from a third country) are constrained and prescribed.

The results of these restrictions are two-fold. First, these restrictions protect some specific markets for home carriers, in effect limiting competition and traffic growth on those routes. Second, the agreement may pose a challenge to the proposed joint venture between Delta and Aeroméxico, as US policy makes the granting of anti-trust immunity conditional on having a full open skies agreement. Mexico's competition regulator, COFECE, approved the joint venture in May 2016, provided Aeroméxico surrender eight slot pairs at Mexico City Airport. The USD 1.5 billion joint venture would benefit both carriers as they face new competition in the market and would likely stimulate traffic between both countries.

Table 3.3: Status of air services agreement negotiations

In negotiation (6)	Awaiting signature (21)			Signed (7)	Awaiting ratification (7)
China	Bahrain	Jordan	Russia	Brazil	Canada
Ecuador	Belize	Kenya	South Africa	Indonesia	Cuba
Finland	Colombia	Latvia	Spain	Italy	Italy
Luxemburg	El Salvador	Netherlands	Switzerland	Kuwait	Indonesia
Panama	Guatemala	Nicaragua	Trinidad	Portugal	Turkey
Scandinavia	Honduras	Peru	Venezuela	Qatar	United Arab Emirates
	Iceland	Philippines	United Kingdom	Saudi Arabia	United States

Source: SECTUR, 2016.

Mexico is currently negotiating air service agreements with six countries, with a further 21 agreements awaiting signature, while seven each have been signed and are awaiting ratification (Table 3.3). Box 3.2 shows an example of how Morocco removed restrictions in its aviation market with the European Union, allowing some of the largest carriers in the world to compete with its own airlines and the positive effect that has had on tourism there.

It is important to distinguish between national aviation policy with respect to air service agreements, and airlines making business decisions. Restrictive air service agreements impede the development of air connectivity at secondary airports, especially in cases where airlines are limited to pre-determined routes or a ceiling on frequency which they prefer to use in busier markets, such as Mexico City or Cancún. It also reduces connectivity for those large markets when incumbent carriers prefer a situation of limited traffic rights to contain competition and maintain their market shares. However, airlines may have strategic reasons to limit the connectivity they offer. For example, it makes perfect sense for Aeroméxico to choose to only serve Shanghai and rely on feed from China Eastern Airlines to flow passengers from China and eastern Asia. This results in greater indirect connectivity at the expense of direct connectivity. This is not a policy issue but a strategic issue by a private carrier in how it wishes to structure the passenger flows over the North-Pacific.

Mexico's relatively liberal and open air service agreements with the United States and Canada do not restrict the establishment of routes between those countries and secondary destinations. Therefore, when Mexican communities do not enjoy the direct air connectivity they think their local tourism market warrants, the issue at hand is a business decision and not a national policy. In effect, airlines have decided that the best use of a scarce and capital-intensive resource such as an aircraft is on a route which does not connect to the community in question.

In such situations, local communities could adopt some local policies that would encourage airlines to reconsider their decisions. There are many options available to communities but the approach that usually proves more effective is to provide some marketing support to stimulate a higher, sustainable level of demand. Other strategies, such as providing financial incentives to carriers have shown more problematic results, with airlines often suspending services once funding has ended. Thus any local policy to stimulate growth in air transport connectivity should, at a minimum:

- have clear and transparent guidelines,
- be open and accessible to all carriers,
- demonstrate measurable results to show value for taxpayer money,
- aim to develop the long term tourism market rather than simply provide funds for immediate route start-up,
- be structured in a way that reduces public contributions over time as the service becomes financially viable.

Box 3.2. Promoting tourism through aviation liberalisation and better connectivity in Morocco

While culturally extremely different, there are strong parallels between the tourism markets of Mexico and Morocco. Both countries enjoy a strong domestic tourism market and have their largest tourism generating market only a couple of hours flight away - the United States for Mexico and the European Union for Morocco,. Both countries also have a mixed tourism offer, be it sun and beach, culture or gastronomy. In the case of Morocco, the ambitious Vision 2010 tourism grew into Vision 2020 which aims to quintuple tourist arrivals in 20 years (ITF, 2015). With the European Union generating about 80% of its international visitors, achieving such ambitious goals would require far greater connectivity with the European Union. To that effect, in 2006, it signed a very liberal air service agreement with the European Union that provided unlimited third and fourth freedom traffic rights, and in the second phase a limited fifth freedom opportunities to sixteen countries mainly bordering the Mediterranean for EU carriers and to other EU countries for Moroccan carriers, excluding in both cases cabotage.

The immediate impact of this air service agreement was the creation of new connectivity between secondary European airports and Morocco. The number of routes grew from 57 in January 2005 to 118 by January 2012, with the establishment of 70 new routes and the discontinuation of 9 existing routes. The number of EU airports with direct air services to Morocco grew from 65 in 2005 to 77 in 2010, and tourist arrivals nearly doubled between 2000 and 2010 to reach over 9 million. Traffic between Morocco and the European Union grew by two thirds between 2006 and 2010, going from 6.6 million to 11 million and the nature of tourism changed, with the entry of low cost carriers creating new demand for week-end excursions. In opening up its markets, Morocco witnessed that the overall market share of its carriers declined, although their volume of passengers actually increased. This was to be expected, considering the significantly larger size of EU carriers and a bias by passengers to fly airlines from their own country when possible. From a transportation or tourism policy perspective, the Moroccan approach can be deemed to be successful as it significantly increased the number of tourists from, and improved connectivity with, the European Union, and even lowered fares through the introduction of low cost carriers. As for Moroccan carriers, while their market share decreased, the increase in size in the overall market has enabled them to remain highly competitive with the much larger EU carriers.

The National Chamber of Aviation, CANAERO, which represents the air transport sector in Mexico, has frequent consultations with the Mexican government. In addition to identifying new routes, promoting new destinations and reducing airport taxes and fees, one of their objectives is to establish subsidies to develop new air routes. This last item can be quite challenging for policy makers. The previous discussion on subsidies should serve as guidance to policy makers in ensuring that public monies only be spent for a limited time and on routes with a strong development potential.

Air transport infrastructure

The lack of runway capacity at the existing airport in Mexico City translates in some pent up demand which may not be met until late 2020 when the new airport is expected to open. Mexico City's Benito Juárez International Airport has been operating at capacity for about a decade. The main issue is that the proximity of the two parallel runways which prevents using them independently, limiting actual capacity to 61 movements per hour, equivalent to 1.5 runways. The runways are fully saturated and the airport is operating above its theoretical capacity of 32 million passengers per year, with about 38.5 million passengers in 2015. Operating at or over capacity has created some pent-up demand for airport access.

The Mexican Government is building a new international airport in Texcoco, slightly east of the existing airport. In its first phase, the new airport will have nearly 50% more capacity than the existing airport, a proportion expected to rise to 250% when all phases of construction will be completed in 2050. By then the airport should have a capacity of 120 million passengers per annum. The aim of this new airport is to sustain the development of tourism and to enable Mexico to become a true Latin American hub, connecting Asia, Europe and North America to Mexico and points in Central and South America. The International Air Transport Association (IATA), an airline trade body advising the planning of the new airport, sees the new airport as a way for Mexico to become a transfer point between Asia and South America. This would imply significantly better connectivity between Mexico and these two markets, which, in turn, would make it easier for tourists from either market to come visit Mexico. Thus one can see a convergence of interests being accommodated by the new airport, to serve both passengers flying to and around Mexico. Increased international connectivity would likely be accompanied by increased domestic connectivity to ensure that all these new tourists can easily reach their final destination in Mexico.

While waiting for the new airport to open, options are rather limited to expand capacity, considering the existing airport is slated to be closed and demolished when the new airport opens. It also creates resiliency issues as delays can rapidly grow and accumulate since there is no spare capacity to absorb them. Thus any solution must be relatively low cost and quick to implement during the last four operational years of the airport. A simulation of ways to increase the utilisation of the airport shows that while operational improvements are possible at the airport, the lack of runway capacity risks negating much of the benefits flowing from these improvements (Mendoza-Dorantes et al, 2015). That being said, while the airport remains operational, anything that can improve the passenger experience would certainly be a positive. However, these would likely be low impact measures that would not have a material impact on the airport's overused capacity.

Cancún International Airport has also been experiencing capacity constraints, and has taken appropriate measures to rectify the situation. Cancún is a hub for low cost carriers Volaris and VivaAerobus but these carriers do little or no interline with foreign carriers, meaning that tourists from abroad wanting to connect via Cancún must self-connect, which is not always very timely. The airport has been experiencing a series of terminal expansions, first at Terminal 2 in 2014 and then Terminal 3 in 2015, raising that terminal's capacity from 6 million passengers per year to 10 million passengers. Overall, the airport's capacity is about 23 million passengers per year. A new, fourth terminal is also being developed and is tentatively expected to be operational by 2017 (Asur, 2014).

Other airports across the country do not show any notable capacity constraints. However, these airports have been unable to attract international flights from outside North America on a regular basis, due to commercial rather than policy reasons. These tourism destinations would likely have a very high proportion of leisure travellers, meaning the market may have a yield too low for some network carriers. However, they may show potential to leisure carriers and tour operators, particularly from Europe, who already operate flights to and from the Caribbean. Pursuing these markets may require Mexico to adopt a more liberal approach, at least for airports outside of Mexico City and Cancún. Australia provides a very good example of how to liberalise secondary destinations, to achieve the policy goals of promoting tourism and connectivity, while balancing the goal of supporting the national carrier. It adopted a unilateral open sky regime for all but its most popular destinations, encouraging foreign carriers to establish services there.

Sea transport connectivity

The sea mode is essentially cruising. Mexico plays an important role in global cruise industry, representing about a third of the cruising market. The cruise industry is an important generator of visitors to Mexico. In 2015, Mexico received 5.9 million cruise passengers through 18 ports along the Caribbean and Pacific Coast, up 6.4% on 2014.

Table 3.4. Cruise passenger traffic in Mexico's main cruise ports, 2000-15

Rank 2015	Port	2000	2005	2010	2015	% change 2000-15	% change 2010-15
	Mexico total	3 189 365	6 537 783	6 663 297	5 920 927	86%	-11%
1	Cozumel	1 504 603	2 519 179	2 919 221	3 397 169	126%	16%
2	Ensenada	336 593	592 981	362 285	684 716	103%	89%
3	Majahual	0	650 263	655 189	425 102	..	-35%
4	Cabo San Lucas	263 557	619 503	699 871	383 729	46%	-45%
5	Progreso	22 676	191 745	284 611	329 269	1 352%	16%
6	Puerto Vallarta	237 381	543 518	553 514	322 471	36%	-42%
7	Mazatlán	225 804	472 826	526 294	195 033	-14%	-63%
8	Huatulco	16 486	84 196	133 857	47 089	186%	-65%
9	Chiapas	0	0	25 720	35 306	..	37%
10	Pichilingue	0	24 101	15 719	27 508	..	75%

Source: SECTUR (2016).

Following an extended period of dynamic expansion, growth has stalled over the last decade and Mexico's cruising industry has struggled to regain momentum (Figure 3.4, Table 3.3). Passenger traffic in 2015 was 11% off the peak recorded in 2010 (6.7 million), while the number of ports of call was also down on peak levels (by 33% from 3 267 in 2005). At the same time, ship size has been steadily growing and the average number of passengers per ship call more than doubled between 2000 and 2015 (Figure 3.5).

Cozumel is by far the largest cruise port in Mexico, and the second most important cruise destination in the world in terms of passenger traffic, and fifth overall when including turnaround ports. Despite stagnating ship calls, passenger traffic to the port has continued to grow. Cozumel handled 3.4 million passengers in 2015 and has the highest number of passengers per call in the country. It expects to receive close to 1 100 ships in 2016, with a capacity of 3.2 million passengers. The port has capacity for seven cruise ships in three terminals, following a USD 20 million investment by Carnival Cruise Line in its exclusive-use Puerta Maya terminal in 2015.

Figure 3.4. Cruise passengers and ship calls, Mexico and selected ports, 1985-2015

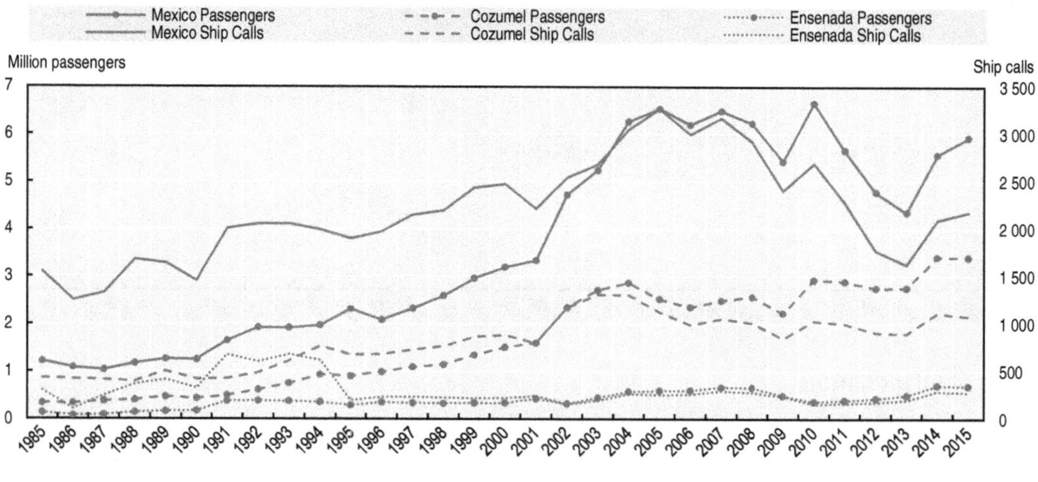

Source: SECTUR (2016).

Traffic at many other ports, however, has remained unchanged or declined during the past decade. Cabo San Lucas, Mazatlán and Puerto Vallarta on the Pacific Coast have all experienced significant declines in traffic, as have Acapulco, Manzanillo and Zihuatanejo. This has led to a concentration of cruising activity in a smaller number of ports. In 2005, around 80% of passenger traffic was found in the top 6 ports; by 2015, that same proportion was generated by the top 4 ports – Cozumel, Ensenada, Majahual and Cabo San Lucas.

Ensenada is a notable exception to the general decline in cruising on the Pacific coast in recent years, likely due to its close proximity to the United States. Stopping in Ensenada enables non-US registered cruise ships to operate a cruise along the California coast or Catalina while respecting the Jones Act and not being considered cabotage. Ensenada is also the only port in Mexico where cruise ship turnaround, likely due to its relative proximity to San Diego.

The economic benefits and environmental impacts from cruising tend to be very localised. Cruises can provide a significant economic activity for sightseeing and shopping in close proximity to cruise ports, but have a more limited impact on the hospitality sector, or in inland destinations particularly when they are more than two hours away by road. Cruise passengers only have a limited time in port, with accommodation and meals provided on board. This limits the expenditure impact on the local economy, and further afield. In Cozumel, Carnival Cruise Line's Puerta Maya terminal includes a well-developed shopping and dining offer, which increases the port's attractiveness as a cruise destination, but competes with local tourism services for passenger and crew spending. Also, most cruise ship calls in Mexico are simply stops on a longer itinerary, with the limited exception of Ensenada where turnarounds procure a larger economic impact.

Figure 3.5. Passengers per ship call, 1985-2015

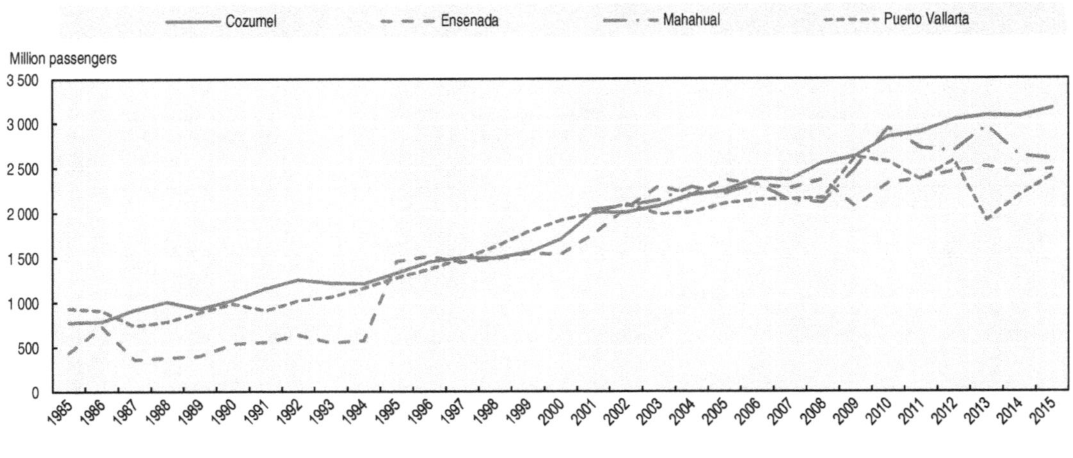

Source: SECTUR (2016).

An average cruise ship passenger on a Mexican port of call will spend about USD 72 per day in 2014, compared to USD 79 per day in 2013. This situation is significantly better in Cozumel where average daily passenger expenditure can reach USD 100. Analysis by the Florida Caribbean Cruise Association (2012) indicates that Mexico's performance is significantly below the Caribbean average (USD 95), in part because Mexican prices are relatively lower than destinations such as Saint Martin (USD 185 daily expenditure) or San Juan (USD 110 daily expenditure). While the difference of USD 23 per passenger between Mexico and the Caribbean average may seem small, when multiplied across 5.6 million cruise passengers in 2014 alone, this can become a significant missed economic opportunity.

Infrastructure and connectivity remain issues for cruising in Mexico. As part of the National Infrastructure Programme 2014-18, the Mexican government expects to invest MXN 700 million to build a new cruise terminal in Puerto Vallarta, as current infrastructure only provides berthing for three ships. There is also a project to build a turnaround port at Puerto Peñasco, Sonora, at an estimated cost of MXN 1.4 billion. Located on the Sea of Cortes, this could be Mexico's second home port after Ensenada. The project has experienced several setbacks but the tourism promotion board of Sonora, COFETUR, expects it to generate MXN 115 million in economic activity when completed. The location of Puerto Peñasco as a home port is facilitated by the close road proximity to Arizona in the United States, but is hampered by a lack of connectivity at the newly built Mar de Cortés International Airport.

The land transport interface with cruise ships is particularly important, to bring cruise passengers and crew from the cruise ship to attractions within reasonable distance from the cruise port. This is an important challenge which can enhance the cruise visitor experience and help spread the economic benefits more widely. Cruise companies currently make extensive use of pre-arranged tours, and the presence of an extensive Mexican bus industry ensures that chartering buses to run tours is not an issue.

Land transport is particularly challenging for passengers wishing to make their own travel arrangements while in port. This is usually significantly cheaper than taking a tour booked through the cruise ship, and generates direct spending in the local economy, but entails a degree of risk for the passenger. Cruise ships guarantee that the ship will not leave before all cruise tours return to the ship. However, the same is not true for independent travellers who must ensure they return back to the ship on-time. Passengers need to be confident local transport services will have them back on time. The availability of clear information and the confidence that the timetable would be respected are therefore important. This means local transport operators should tailor their products to those specific needs, particularly that of reliability, in order to encourage independent travellers to venture beyond the port city.

Developing the proper infrastructure and connectivity to enable Mexican cruise ports to be a gateway to a variety of easy to access inland and coastal attractions which are unique to Mexico will make these ports more attractive to cruise passengers and cruise lines, and offer repeat cruisers different experiences every time they visit. There also seems to be some strong development or redevelopment potential for cruising activity along the Pacific Coast and in the Gulf of Cortes, but this will require commensurate infrastructure to connect ports in those regions with inland attractions.

Ground transport connectivity

Road infrastructure and performance

The road network in Mexico constitutes the backbone of the transport system, and provides much of the connectivity to bring tourists to and beyond the country's main tourism centres. At over 377 000 km in length as of 2012, Mexico has the most extensive national road network in Latin America, and is ranked nineteenth in the world. Over 115 000 km of the network is paved (CIA, 2015) and close to 50 000 km is part of the federal network. Mexico's road network is articulated around 14 strategic transport corridors, crossing the country from north to south, and from the Pacific to the Atlantic coast (SCT, 2014). Mexico's highway network has dramatically expanded in the past three decades and covers the whole country, with a core network of major highways fanning out from Mexico City to major tourism hubs, such as Cancún, Veracruz and Acapulco, and further north to the US border states, where the road network caters to US tourists from areas close to the border travelling to destinations in northern Mexico, or visiting friends and relatives.

The National Infrastructure Plan 2013-18 includes significant allocations for road transportation. It calls for the investment of MXN 493 billion to add or upgrade 72 520 km of roadway using both traditional public funding and public-private partnerships. The plan also calls for a 1 647 km long network of eight backbone highways, which offer superior performance to traditional highways. This comes on top of the previous six year plan which saw public and private investments in Mexico's road network topping MXN 290 billion. Some road projects have carried over from the previous presidential term. Opened in late 2013, for example, the Durango-Mazatlán highway connects the centre of the country with the Pacific coast and involved building 63 tunnels and one of the world's tallest suspension bridges (Baluarte Bridge) at a cost USD 2.2 billion. The Jantetelco–El Higuerón section of the Siglo XXI highway created a direct link between Morelos and Puebla and was completed in 2014 at a cost of MXN 900 million.

The road network in Mexico is better developed in the north than in the south, reflecting the country's economic centre of gravity. Remote locations are also predictably less well served than major centres. Addressing these infrastructure gaps would help develop tourism in regions like Campeche, Chiapas and Oaxaca. It would also provide socio-economic opportunities for these underserved regions and make use of the comparative advantages these regions have to offer. For example, areas of tourism development Mexico wants to promote, such as gastronomy, culture and archaeology are more prevalent in the southern regions of the country but are also, ironically, the least easy accessible. This could be an area where several ministries, including the ministries of Tourism, Agrarian, Territorial and Urban Development, and Communications and Transport, co-operate in encouraging state and local governments to address these infrastructure gaps. However, the current state of public finances in Mexico could make some of these projects unaffordable at present.

Mexico has actively encouraged the private sector to get involved in road construction through public-private partnerships and toll concessions. Much of the need for on-going investment is linked to persistent infrastructure deficiencies, especially for roads at the state and local levels where quality has significantly deteriorated. The World Economic Forum's Global Competitiveness Report 2014-15 ranks Mexico 27th out of OECD countries, and 57th amongst 144 economies, for the quality of its road infrastructure.

Road transport is not only about infrastructure but also about performance. An important challenge to tourism development is ensuring tourists can access attractions of interest, safely and with ease, in a country the size of Mexico with an area of nearly two million square kilometres, and only two major international gateway airports. This is particularly an issue for non-gateway destinations, and for leisure tourists with the time to explore and who are in search of new and different experiences. Smaller communities with significant tourism assets must ensure they enjoy good connectivity to the closest international gateway or transport hub.

Self-drive touring itineraries are a viable option and are common in many OECD countries. However, abundant congestion especially around urban areas and on alternative roads to toll highways makes driving in Mexico challenging for tourists. Mexico's poor road safety record is also a serious impediment to such an approach and may deter tourists from driving. At 14.7 road traffic deaths per 100 000 inhabitants in 2010, Mexico has the highest road fatality rate in the OECD, and ranked second only to the much larger United States for total number of road deaths. One of the issues is a rather lax regime for granting drivers licences, with some states only requiring drivers to attend a class or pay a fee rather than pass a driving test. Drink-driving, texting or using a mobile phone while driving are also common.

Road safety has shown signs of improvements since 2010, with a drop in the number of crashes and fatalities despite an increase in the number of registered vehicles (OECD, 2016b). Improving safety on Mexico's roads requires a strategy involving better training, public outreach and better enforcement. There must also be far greater emphasis on prevention and road safety awareness than what currently exists. The Green Angels initiative is a good example of offering valuable service to road users in their time of need, but there is still much work to be done to bring Mexican roads to the safety levels of other OECD countries (Box 3.3).

Tourists also need clear directions and signage in order to get to their destination. Thematic signage through the use of tourism roads with their own brand identity is a way to draw tourists away from major sights and better spread the economic benefit of tourism. Mexico established the National Tourism Signage Programme (Programa de Señalización Turística Nacional) which designed a branding for two popular tourism routes on federal highways: the Pyramids route and the Monarch Butterflies route. There are also eight different state routes throughout the Yucatán peninsula each with its own theme, such as culinary, archaeology or Puuc (Mayan hills).

Box 3.3. Improving road safety for tourists with Green Angels initiative

The Green Angels Tourist Services Corporation, or *Angeles Verdes*, is an administrative agency under the Ministry of Tourism charged with patrolling toll roads across Mexico and providing assistance to motorists. *Angeles Verdes* was established in 1960. It operates about 300 vehicles equipped with basic mechanical spare parts, supplies and first aid necessities and capable of providing towing services. It provides a number of services such as mechanical assistance, assistance in case of accidents and tourist information. Staff is certified mechanics that are able to do light automotive repairs by the side of the road. They can also administer CPR and first aid. This free service provides a greater sense of safety to motorists, particularly tourists. The service is very popular, reporting over 117 000 service calls in the last 2 weeks of July 2015 (SECTUR, 2015). In the first seven months of 2015, *Angeles Verdes* served over 1.2 million clients and travelled over 10 million kilometres on Mexican roads. The Green Angels programme provides an important service to road travellers and encourages tourists to more widely explore Mexico. As such, this is a best practice that could inspire other countries looking to improve safety on their roads and offer some basic assistance services to motorists.

Guided tours are an alternative option to self-drive itineraries, and are plentiful in large tourism destinations such as Cancún. For tourism promoters, the challenge here is to have the tour stop in the tourism destination. Even if it does, local spending will likely be at a minimum and consist mostly of entry fees or souvenir shopping. For smaller destinations, a more interesting proposal is if the tourist could spend a night or two in the area, which would significantly increase its contribution to the local economy because of the need to purchase accommodations and other hospitality services. This may be facilitated by the intercity bus services.

Intercity bus network

Mexico enjoys a well-developed intercity bus network with high quality vehicles and services offering wide coverage of destinations. As the industry is deregulated, services are available where economically viable and the network covers most of the country. It also extends into the United States, where the largest intercity bus company, Greyhound Lines, has services to Tijuana, Monterrey and Nuevo Laredo which connect to the rest of the continental network. Greyhound also has a marketing agreement to sell tickets for one of the largest bus companies in Mexico, Grupo Estrella Blanca, at several Greyhound bus terminals in Texas, thus facilitating connections between both networks. However, significantly longer travel times compared to air travel make this option less attractive, especially for tourists not from areas bordering Mexico or wishing to travel further south.

Mexican intercity bus companies offer three classes of service, with luxury and first class buses offering services as good if not better than what is found across OECD countries. In fact, luxury buses in Mexico offer probably the best level of service and comfort in North America. Over 20 different intercity bus companies operate in Mexico, providing a range of route and service options to suit the needs of tourists. Some companies are umbrella groups operating under multiple brands. Most bus companies operate in only a few regions or a few routes, with some overlap. There is no national intercity bus company covering the entire country, or offering a bus travel pass as Greyhound does in Canada or the United States.

While it encourages competition, this fragmentation of the industry makes it challenging for tourists trying to plan their travel and find the right bus company for their desired itinerary. For example, there is no easy way for unfamiliar tourists to find out which company serves which routes. A system map could provide tourists with greater insights into how routes are organised and the various options available. In addition, complex itineraries involving multiple bus companies may not be possible to book online on the website of a given company. To alleviate this, websites such as www.busbud.com enable users to book bus tickets as long as the itinerary is offered by the same company. When direct services are not offered, tourists may have to purchase two different tickets on two different websites.

Language remains an important barrier for non-Spanish speaking tourists, as the websites of the major bus companies are only available in Spanish. The Mexico Tourism Board's website (www.visitmexico.com) offers tourism information in nine languages, but directs visitors to a Spanish-only website for information on intercity buses (www.miescape.mx). The website also contains information in English for each Magic Town, but only provides information on how to get to these towns for tourists travelling by car. No information is provided either for travelling by intercity bus or about circuits that could combine several destinations over a few days through a chartered bus.

Tourists wishing to travel by bus may end up limited to choices offered by tour companies, which may focus on more popular attractions and bypass other places of interest in the Maya World and elsewhere. Naturally, tour operators should feel free to construct itineraries that they believe are best suited for their clientele. This places the onus on the attractions themselves, and those who market them, to offer tourists clear transport options and indications for people not travelling by car.

An additional challenge for tourists is that a city may have multiple bus terminals. For example, Mexico City has four different bus terminals for the four cardinal points. This has the advantage of reducing bus travel times since buses do not need to cross the city. However, it adds a level of complexity for tourists looking for the right bus terminal, or connecting through Mexico City as they must transfer from one bus terminal to another. In other cases, such as Acapulco, there is both a multi-tenant bus terminal, Terminal de Autobuses Acapulco Centro, and at least three bus terminals belonging to individual carriers (Estrella de Oro, Estrella Roja and Estrella Blanca). This can make it more difficult for tourists to find the right bus terminal, and makes connections between bus lines more challenging.

Mexico would benefit from a more strategic vision to entice tourists to use Mexico's well-developed intercity bus network. Most products are presented as point-to-point services. There do not appear to be products such as travel passes for tourists to hop from one route to another, or itineraries which enable tourists to visit several interesting attractions on a pre-set circuit (e.g. 7-day or 14-day Mexico bus pass). Similarly, there is no ticket allowing travel on a combination of companies across regions, which would help bridge the market fragmentation. Likewise, there appears to be no co-ordination with other modes of transport to offer a seamless, multimodal product for tourists, especially air transport.

The piecemeal approach limits the attractiveness of this mode of transport, especially for international visitors are not as familiar as domestic tourists with how intercity buses operate in Mexico. Since intercity bus transport is a private and deregulated undertaking, the policy role here for the federal and state governments could be to promote the benefits of an integrated approach to motor coach operators and provide a neutral platform to foster co-operation between intercity bus companies, air carriers and tourism stakeholders.

Finally, accessibility remains an important issue and discourages tourists with mobility challenges to use this mode of transport (Box 3.4). To comply with national law, intercity buses have seating reserved for disabled passengers, but there is often no way to load a wheelchair onto the bus. Increasing accessibility of intercity buses must be planned in a holistic fashion, taking into account both the motor coach and the need for the bus terminal and other infrastructure to be accessible.

Box 3.4: Greying travellers and their accessible transport needs

All the major Mexican tourism generating markets, be it in North America, Europe or Japan, are experiencing a phenomenon of an ageing population with increasingly more disposable income willing to be invested in tourism. This so-called grey tourism market will be an important driver for tourism growth in the decades ahead and tourism destinations who which to capitalise on this market will have to ensure that they are able to meet their specific needs. While it is true that today's seniors are healthier and more mobile than at any time in human history, they do have special needs related to accessibility that could dictate which destinations to favour and which to shun. Assistive devices, a category which encapsulates wheelchairs, scooters, canes, crutches, and walkers can be effective tools to help seniors, and the mobility challenged, to regain some mobility independence. However, their use requires a transportation system able to adapt to these devices. This means that for Mexico to attract this important and growing market, it must examine its transportation system under a barrier-free paradigm. The obvious starting point is at the international gateway, ensuring that airports are fully accessible, barrier free and easy to navigate. However, the true challenge for Mexico is transportation beyond the airport. If the policy's aim is to draw tourists away from the capital and the resorts, then it must ensure that inland transportation is accessible and that tourists can clearly see in advance that accessibility will not be an issue. This means not only offering accessible transportation services but also making sure that tourists understand in their own language the services that are offered.

Other ground transport

Public transport

Urban transport systems in large Mexican cities are designed with the local population in mind, and there is little consideration or expectation that tourists will use these systems. This results in an important imbalance in modal choice, as tourists are often directed towards less environmentally sustainable modal choices for reasons of convenience and safety. This is forgetting the habits of tourists in their own countries, where people of all income brackets use public transport. This represents a missed opportunity to offer tourists more mobility options and encourage them to explore the city, especially in cities like Mexico City, Cancún, and Los Cabos. Improving public transport for tourists would also generate positive benefits to local population.

Mexico enjoys a rather developed public transport system, relative to other Latin American countries (Figure 3.6). Mexico is second only to Brazil for the subway network, reflecting the Mexico City subway network. Otherwise, there is limited dedicated mass transit infrastructure across the country, with conventional buses being by far the most popular and often the only public transport option, outside of Mexico City, Guadalajara and Monterrey.

The modal share of public transport and active transportation (walking or cycling) in major Mexican cities is also relatively high at around 70%, similar to levels seen in Barcelona, Prague or Vienna. By Latin American standards, large Mexican metropolitan areas ranked slightly below some of their counterparts in this area (Figure 3.7).

Figure 3.6. Mass transit infrastructure in selected Latin American countries, 2011

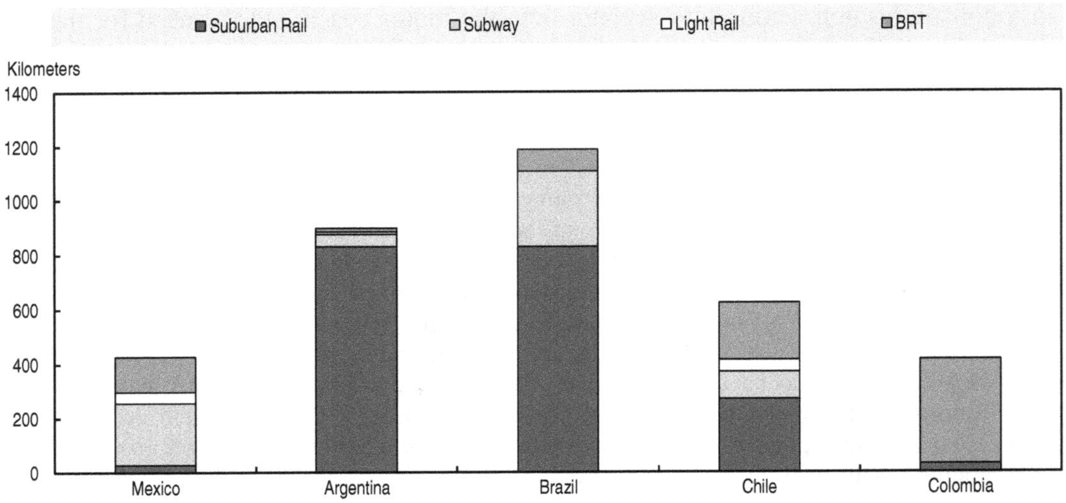

BRT: Bus Rapid Transit.

Source: Hidalgo et al. (2011).

Making public transport easier to navigate is helpful to tourists and the local population alike. Ease of navigation implies a combination of measures meant to inform travellers. This includes clear signage, maps, schedules, public announcements, apps for smart phones and interactive displays. It also means promoting public transport as a means of conveyance for tourists who often are frequent users of public transport at home. There is no reason to believe they would not pursue this sustainable transport choice, if given the opportunity. For the system to be tourist-friendly, it must be designed for a first-time user with limited Spanish language skills. This means favouring pictograms, colours and numbers over text, multilingual displays, announcements, websites and applications and tourist-oriented information when public transport services are adjacent to tourism attractions.

A number of major metropolitan areas around the world have taken steps to make their public transport systems friendlier for tourists and thus make more of the metropolitan area within easy reach of visitors. Cities like Paris have adopted a multilingual communication strategy on parts of the network most used by tourists, while Tokyo makes extensive use of English language signage, as well as number-coding each station. These are good examples of where tourists routinely make use of the extensive public transport systems available in these cities.

The public transport authorities may want to re-examine their user communication strategy and incorporate elements articulated around tourist needs and make Mexico's public transport system friendlier to tourists. Going about this can be relatively low cost and include measures such as multilingual signage, making public transport maps available in hotels and tourist information venues and creating visitor cards, like the *Paris Visite* or London pass which can combine access to major tourist sites with a public transport pass. Adapting public transport to tourists also requires a rethink of the role of public transport.

Figure 3.7. Public and active transport share in selected Latin American cities, 2007

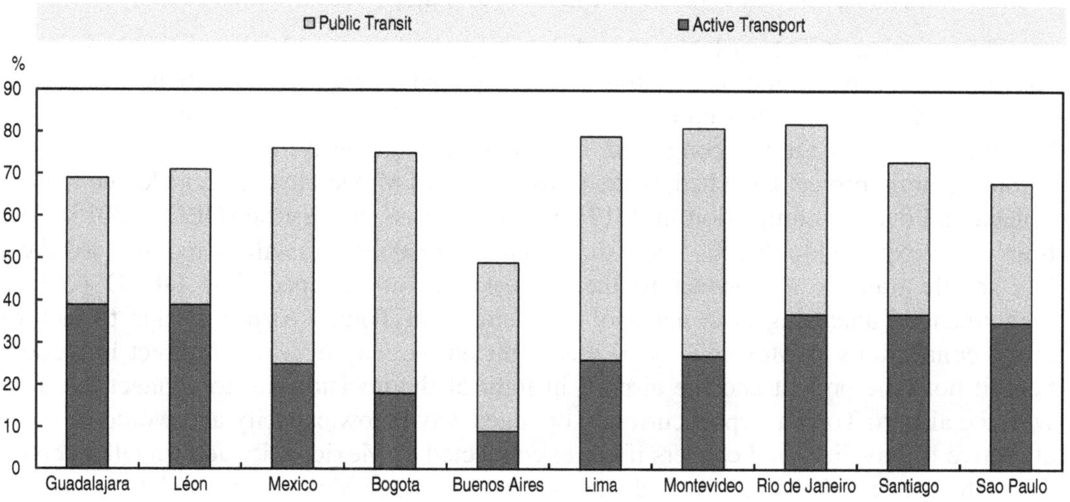

Source: Hidalgo et al. (2011).

While this chapter will not cover every public transport system in Mexico, there may be value in taking a closer look at the country's most heavily travelled, Mexico City. The transport system in Mexico City caters to a population of over 20 million people and is made up of conventional buses, the Metro Collective Transport System (subway) and the more modern Metrobus rapid bus system which uses dedicated lanes and stations on heavily travelled routes. Mexico City's subway system alone carries over 1.6 billion passengers a year, ranking it eight in the world and fourth among subway systems in OECD countries.

However, these services are often disconnected from each other and the public transport system remains challenging for the average tourist to use. Limited information on the network and the lack of modal integration between the subway, bus rapid transit and conventional buses makes navigating the public transport in Mexico City difficult. Subway stations provide no indications as to which buses serve the station, there are no maps showing all transit modes together and no integrating ticketing system. However, one website, www.viadf.com.mx does provide an integrated and multimodal view of public transport in the Mexico City metropolitan area.

Tourists may first experience the subway system at Mexico City's Benito Juárez International Airport. The Terminal Aérea station is located adjacent to the Terminal 1 but is not clearly indicated. The station is not designed with first time visitors or travellers carrying luggage in mind, as one must negotiate over 110 steps to reach the platform leading towards the city centre, and at least one transfer is required to reach the main hotel zones in the city. This is symptomatic of the entire Mexico City subway system where very few stations are fully accessible, making it challenging for passengers carrying luggage to navigate through the station.

The subway network itself is relatively easy to navigate, with the use of pictograms in addition to station names to ensure illiteracy is not an impediment to mobility. This can be helpful not only to the local population but also for travellers from countries that do not use the Latin alphabet or who may find Spanish difficult to read. However, with little or no English signage it can sometimes be a bit daunting for non-Spanish speaking tourists. The airport is also connected to the city's historical centre by the more tourist-friendly Metrobus, but this is far from where most major hotels are located.

The situation at Toluca International Airport, which is used by low cost-carriers and has higher concentration of leisure tourists, is also challenging. Located about 60 km west of Mexico City, Toluca has no public transport connection to Mexico City and can only be accessed by car via the congested Toluca–Mexico highway. A new MXN 38 billion commuter train project launched by the Government of Mexico to connect Mexico City to Toluca and due for completion in 2017 should help ease congestion (OECD, 2015). The train is not expected to directly serve the airport, and passengers will be required to take a bus shuttle transfer to connect to the nearest stop at Metepec. The OECD (2015a) recommended analysing how much of the demand at Toluca Airport is due to lack of direct connections to Mexico City to shed light on the way in which a direct link could benefit both the project and the airport, in light of the decision not to connect the train with the airport. Toluca airport currently operates way below capacity and would be more attractive to travellers and carriers if better connected to Mexico City and travellers could avoid the congested and relatively dangerous road between Mexico City and Toluca.

The OECD also recommended studying the possibility of extending this line to the new international airport in Mexico City (Box 3.5). The train line is now planned to terminate at the Observatorio metro station in the western part of Mexico City. There are plans to extend this line as far east as the new International Airport in Texcoco, and passing through the hotel area of Polanco and the business district. The choice of Observatorio as a terminal station is somewhat problematic for tourists. While it does facilitate the transfer to Metro line 1 and the western bus terminal (Terminal Central de Autobuses del Poniente), the station itself would not be the most favourable transit point for tourists arriving in the city. Clearly, some major improvements should be made to that station if it is to become a gateway to the city for domestic or international tourism.

Taxis

Taxi cabs are plentiful and offer affordable point-to-point transportation for tourists in Mexico's largest cities. However, two key related issues impact on the user experience for tourists: security and prices. Security in taxi cabs across Mexico is a real and serious concern. While much progress has been made, there is still at least a perception that the level of security can vary depending on the type of taxicab used. Tourists are frequently advised to use the more expensive hotel and *sitio* taxis. These warnings steer tourists away from legitimate, honest taxi drivers that do not use regulated taxi stands and undermines confidence in Mexico's taxi system. It also reinforces a feeling of insecurity which could encourage tourists to choose another country for their vacation.

Across all modes of transport, service providers should compete on service and price but not on safety or security. Mexico should take the necessary steps to make all marked taxis as safe and secure as hotel and *sitio* taxis, with the latter competing on level of service (e.g. quality of the car, English-speaking driver), rather than on passenger security. This includes more stringent screening (e.g. background checks), better enforcement of existing regulations, clear identification of taxi drivers, clear displays showing passengers how fares should be calculated and a dedicated bilingual (Spanish/English) helpline to receive and act on complaints about taxi drivers. Taxi regulators may want to look at New York City, London or Madrid as role models of high standards for the taxi industry.

Box 3.5. Public transport access for the new Mexico City Airport

The construction of a new Mexico City international airport to replace the existing one provides a once in a generation opportunity for Mexico to improve public transport access to the airport. The new international airport presents an opportunity for Mexico City to leap forward and become a role model for efficient and sustainable airport access. However, early indications are that this opportunity is not being fully utilised as there is still no clear airport access plan, except for road transport by the already heavily congested network. With the rapid growth in traffic expected in the first few years of the airport's opening, as pent-up demand for air travel can finally be met, one would expect worsening traffic conditions which may put into question some of the ambitious goals of this project, especially with respect to sustainability. Elsewhere in OECD countries, airport development has gone hand in hand with surface transportation planning to ensure that growth of aviation traffic does not lead to increase road congestion for all users.

Due to the very tight timelines involved in building the new airport, a solid, multimodal transport access plan has yet to be developed, which has raised a number of concerns around increased congestion, deteriorating air quality and lack of proper access (OECD, 2015a). Adding an additional complexity is that construction of the airport is already on the way, without a surface access plan beyond road access. This means that by the time a formal plan is developed and approved, it may require some costly retrofitting to adapt new infrastructure to that plan. One can thus see a significant risk in the airport opening with a surface transportation plan only partially implemented, which will reduce mobility options for tourists and likely lead to road congestion for all travellers. Thus, the Ministry of Tourism should work with both the Ministry of Agrarian, Territorial and Urban Development and the Ministry of Communications and Transport in helping them develop a surface transportation plan, ensuring that it takes into account the mobility needs of domestic and foreign tourists.

Ridesharing

Mexico has been a leading country in Latin America for the development of transportation network companies (TNC) such as Uber and Cabify, both of which are present in Mexico City. Uber is also present in Guadalajara, Monterrey, Puebla, Querétaro and Tijuana. At of time of writing, TNCs are not present in major tourism destinations such as Acapulco, Cancún or Puerto Vallarta. The absence of TNCs in Magic Towns (unless it is part of a larger metropolitan, such as Santiago) is likely due to the fact that these services tend to establish themselves in larger cities. Mexico City was the first city in Latin America to set down official regulations for TNC services. Platforms are charged a fee of MXN 4 000 per year on top of a 1.5% licence fee. There is also a vehicle permit fee of MXN 3 500 per year. Fees collected by the municipality are reinvested in a mobility fund to improve public transportation in the city. Puebla and the State of Mexico are also developing TNC regulations.

TNCs have the potential to facilitate mobility for tourists already familiar with TNC-type services at home, as tourists do not have to figure out how to use public transport or find a local taxi stand. As drivers are subject to security screenings and background checks, as well as client reviews and vehicle tracking through the driver's cell phone, a reasonable case can be made that these services offer a higher level of perceived safety than conventional taxis, whose drivers do not face a commensurate level of testing or any post-ride reviews.

Safety, actual and perceived, is an important consideration in discretionary travel decisions. Tourists who believe they can safely and easily travel within a city are more likely to explore secondary attractions. Services like Uber are increasingly popular among middle- and upper-class Mexicans, as they provide a safer and cost-competitive service compared to conventional taxis, while providing a higher level of service (The Guardian, 2015). Existing Uber clients would likely enjoy the convenience of using a familiar app to manage their ground transportation in Mexico as they do in their home country, with the added feeling of security provided by a cashless transaction system they already trust. In the case of business travellers, TNCs which enable the use of global corporate accounts also simplify transport management and expenses claims for business travellers. They can also better meet heightened security requirements and help provide a more seamless transportation experience, for example between the airport and the city.

The presence of TNC in Mexico has not been without difficulty. Protests by taxi drivers in Mexico City have demanded the government repeal the regulations allowing TNC and put an end to this type of service. This is not unlike the situation seen in other locations around the world. There is a predictable degree of opposition from incumbent taxi drivers, who are faced with a new, and far more agile, competitor. The challenges for governments is not to find ways to impede the progress of technology or the emergence of new business models, but rather foster their entry into the market to provide consumers, including tourists, with more mobility options while ensuring that the social consequences of these new entrants of incumbent stakeholders can be managed in a way that is fair and allows for traditional business models to evolve and better compete against new and emerging ones.

Rail transport

Rail transportation in Mexico is very developed for freight, reflecting the important trade that takes place between Mexico and its NAFTA partners, and the long distances where rail becomes competitive. Mexico currently has 26 727 km of tracks, including nearly 18 000 km of trunk lines (SCT, 2014). On the passenger side, however, little rail transportation takes place in Mexico. Aside from light rail services almost exclusively serving commuters in Mexico City and Monterrey, Mexico has three scenic tourist trains: the Chepe Copper Canyon train between Chihuahua and Los Mochis; the Jose Cuervo Express between Guadalajara and Tequila; and the Tren a Tecate other between Tijuana and Tecate. The first two services carried 200 000 passengers in 2012, up 5.8% in a year (SCT, 2014).

Under the current administrations plan to reinstate intercity rail travel in Mexico, there has been a MXN 43.6 billion project planned to create a rail link between Mexico City and Querétaro (210 km away), with further extension to Guadalajara. A second project plans to build a trans-peninsular train the Yucatán would link Mérida and Cancún (336 km away) at a cost of MXN 18 billion. However, both projects are currently on hold due to, among other things, a lack of financial capabilities. The new rail line between Mexico City and Toluca will also facilitate greater ground connectivity between these cities, and more importantly from a tourism perspective, between Toluca International Airport and Mexico City, albeit with limitation discussed previously.

Passenger rail transport in Mexico has the potential to target different types of traveller needs, including tourism. Rail connectivity between major urban centres could provide a cheaper and more environmentally friendly alternative to aviation. It would also bring passengers from one city core to the other, thus being more convenient than having to travel from and to the airport. However, for this type of service to offer a reasonable level of service, it would have to operate on dedicated tracks, separated from the much slower freight trains that criss-cross the country.

Considering the very high cost of building rail infrastructure, it will need to serve a variety of travellers, including business and leisure tourists, and people doing day trips between both cities. Good examples to look at here would be a European service such as Thalys, TGV, DB ICE, AVE or Eurostar, the Acela train in the United States or VIA Rail Canada's Quebec-Windsor corridor service. In all cases, these are relatively quick services, enabling same-day return and catering to a variety of different travellers. With the exception of the Canadian example, all these services operate at high speed and on dedicated passenger tracks.

Visitor arrivals experience

From a tourist's perspective, the transport experience covers the entire journey from origin to destination. As part of that journey, international tourists must go through customs and immigration inspection.

For visitors arriving by air, the inspection process begins in flight as customs and immigration forms are distributed to be filled out by passengers. Alternatively, visitors can download and complete the forms electronically in advance of travel, but must bring a print copy for inspection on arrival. The extent of the information required as well as the duplication of information requested present an opportunity to further streamline the process, in line with the Government's efforts at red tape reduction. A bigger issue is waiting time for processing on arrival. There are problems with waiting time on arrival at both major international gateways, Mexico City and Cancún. In Mexico City, the issue seems to be linked with a lack of staff and space, whereas in Cancún the issue is clearly a lack of sufficient areas to build more counters. Mexico is investigating ways to reduce wait time at both immigration and customs, within budgetary constraints.

In addition, Mexico employs a rather unique, random sampling method to determine which bags should be subject to secondary inspections. Passengers must press a button before exiting the customs area – a green light clears them to exit, a red light means they must submit to a secondary examination. This creates a funnel effect during busy periods as passengers waiting their turn. The fact this type of system is rather unique raises questions on how other OECD countries are able to obtain a commensurate level of national security without creating the line-ups that the current system generates.

Mexico has shown an ability to innovate with a number of different programmes to streamline and expedite entry, especially since the new immigration law came into force in 2012. Preferential measures include: electronic pre-authorisations for visitors from Russia, Turkey and Ukraine; multi-trip visas for business travellers from APEC economies; visa waivers for permanent residents of Canada, Japan, the United Kingdom, the United States and the Schengen area; and separate programmes facilitating entry for citizens of Guatemala and Belize travelling to the southern states of Mexico.

While the idea of these different programmes is excellent, they do not translate into expedited treatment at the airport and with the recent strong growth of international air arrivals, the current system seems to have exceeded its limits. Recent efforts to modernise and streamline customs and entry processes are a move in the right direction. This includes the introduction of the Trusted Traveller Programme (*Programa Viajero Confiable*) in Mexico, linked with the US Global Entry programme which expedites clearance for pre-approved, low risk travellers who can use dedicated lanes at Mexico City, Cancún and Los Cabos airports is a move in this direction. In 2015 this programme was extended to other airports with a high flow of international arrivals: Cozumel, Guadalajara, Léon, Mazatlán, Monterrey, Morelia, Puerto Vallarta, Queretaro, Toluca and Zihuatanejo. Work is also underway to permit international passengers to electronically complete and submit customs and immigration forms via their mobile device.

This situation presents the Mexican government with an opportunity to review its customs inspection process and seek ways to increase its fluidity. It should be noted that the entry process both for Mexico's NAFTA partners and the Schengen area are significantly more efficient, indicating that a high level of national security is possible while keeping processing times lower. There are opportunities here to make greater use of technology, through self-service kiosks for example and to expedite customs inspection for lower risk travellers.

For visitors arriving by road, there are 47 road border crossings along Mexico's 3 150 km northern border with the United States, with a further 11 border crossings along the shorter 1 121 km southern border with Guatemala and Belize. Excluding commuters, 62.7 million visitors arrived in Mexico across these land borders in 2015, of which 13.8 million were overnight visitors.

The Mexico-US border is the busiest in the world in terms of the number of people crossing, with about 173 million in each direction in 2014 (US Bureau of Transport Statistics, 2015). About three-quarters of the people cross by car, while less than a quarter cross by foot mainly in areas with major towns on either side of the border. The busiest border crossings include Tijuana–San Diego (San Ysidro), Juárez–El Paso and Mexicali–Calexico. Pedestrian traffic is made up mostly of day-trippers and cross-border commuter traffic. International bus service is rather limited with the Nuevo Laredo–Laredo and Tijuana–San Diego crossings accounting for about half the 2.8 million passengers crossing in each direction. There is no cross-border passenger rail service.

Excluding commuters and same-day visitors, traffic crossing the Mexico-US border can be broadly classified into three categories: visitors of friends and relatives, leisure and business travellers. This tourist traffic accounts for over 13 million, or around 7% of northern border crossings. While small compared with commuter and same-day visitors, US tourists crossing the northern land border represent over 40% of all international tourist arrivals to Mexico, which makes the effectiveness of the border process important for both commuters and the tourism sector.

A smooth and efficient border crossing can make the difference between travelling or not, especially in the case of US residents coming to Mexico for a short trip, either to shop or visit friends and relatives. The border entry process on the Mexico-US border is more fluid southbound than northbound. Any programme to facilitate re-entry into the United States from Mexico could help alleviate reticence by travellers to cross the border and would help make travel more fluid. Thus, Mexican tourism benefits not just from Mexican policies and programmes but, maybe even more so, by US policies.

To that effect, the Tijuana–San Ysidro border crossing recently received a USD 741 million expansion in September 2014 that enables it to have two inspection booths for each of its 25 lanes. This has significantly cut waiting times and increased traffic. In fact, the first quarter with an expanded customs facility (Q4 2015) saw a 25% increase in passengers crossing by vehicle compared to the same quarter in 2014, reversing the 1% year on year drop witnessed in the previous quarter (BTS, 2015).

There are several ways travellers can expedite their crossing of the Mexico–US border. Medical tourists in Tijuana may obtain a Fast Pass from the medical establishment or hotel they are patronising. This single-use pass allows tourists driving a car with either a US or Canadian licence plate and who have visited participating establishments in Baja to access a reserved lane that allows them bypass much of the congestion leading up to the San Ysidro border crossing. However, once there, the US border inspection is the same as for non-pass holders.

A second programme called Ready Lane is available at over a dozen northbound crossings in Arizona, California and Texas. This enables Americans with an RFID-enabled identification, such as a passport, enhanced drivers licence, permanent resident or border crossing cards, to access reserved lanes and reduce wait times at the border. A member of the Secure Electronic Network for Travellers Rapid Inspection or SENTRI trusted traveller programme can use dedicated SENTRI lanes to enter the United States at a number of designated border points, in addition to the Ready Lanes. Using a SENTRI lane requires that the vehicle and all of its occupants be already registered in the programme. SENTRI members can also use Global Entry kiosks and are eligible for expedited airport security checks in the United States, making the programme even more attractive.

One Mexican programme of note is the Paisano programme, which aims to facilitate visits to Mexico by Mexican's residing in the United States. Started in 1989, the programme deploys staff to the busiest southbound border crossings to facilitate processing, protect against corruption and provide travellers with information, particularly during the busy travel periods around Easter (*Semana Santa*), Christmas and the summer holidays. Under the programme, the value of goods which returning Mexican's can bring across the border is raised during heavy travel weeks. It also organises convoys to enable returning Mexicans to travel in greater safety, in co-operation with the Green Angels programme. In 2014 alone, about 11 million travellers made use of this programme, which is run by the Intersecretarial Commission (*Comisión Intersecretarial)* in conjunction with 17 government agencies. The programme also recognises the importance of strengthening cultural and social links and economic ties with Mexico's diaspora in the United States and Canada.

To help better manage the flow of tourists crossing the border on either side, there may be some value in exploring virtual queuing technologies that enable travellers to schedule appointments to cross the border rather than show up and wait. This concept is not new. It has been put in place by Go Swift at a border crossing between Russia and Estonia and won the 2015 International Transport Forum Transport Achievement Award. The concept also exists in trucking, for example between Lithuania and Belarus, or in a number of ports around the world (including Antwerp, Montreal, New Orleans, Vancouver), where trucks make appointments to access marine terminals. Even major theme parks, such as Disneyworld use a system of reservations to access rides through a fast pass that enables users to skip the queuing lines. The use of a reservation system with a dedicated lane could help alleviate wait times and encourage more day-trips by US residents into Mexico.

References

Asur. (2014) *3rd Quarter 2014 Earnings Call Transcript.* Online. October 23. http://www.asur.com.mx/assets/files/es/inversionistas/informacion-financiera/trimestral/2014/ASUR-Airports-Investor-Relations-Transcript-14Q3.pdf accessed on February 19 2016.

CIA. (2015). The World Factbook – Mexico. Central Intelligence Agency. https://www.cia.gov/library/publications/resources/the-world-factbook/geos/mx.html accessed on August 4 2015.

Cruise TT. (2016), Schedule for the Port of Cozumel. Available from http://ports.cruisett.com/schedule/Mexico/155-Cozumel/January_2016

Diario Oficial. (2013). Programa Sectorial de Turismo 2013-2018. Online. Available from http://www.sectur.gob.mx/PDF/PlaneacionTuristica/Prosectur_2013_2018.pdf

Florida–Caribbean Cruise Association. (2012). Economic Contribution of Cruise Tourism to the Destination Economies. Prepared by Business Research & Economic Advisors. September 2012. Exton.

Hidalgo, D., Huizenga,C. (2013) Implementation of Sustainable Urban Transport in Latin America. Research in Transportation Economics 40 (2013) 66-77.

International Association of Public Transport. (2015). Mobility in Cities Database. Synthesis Report. http://www.uitp.org/sites/default/files/cck-focus-papers-files/MCD_2015_synthesis_web.pdf accessed on July 31 2015. June 2015. Brussels.

IATA. (2007).Economic Benefits from Air Transport in Mexico. October. Online. Available from https://www.iata.org/whatwedo/Documents/economics/air_transport_mexico.pdf

ITF. (2015). Liberalisation of Air Transport. http://www.internationaltransportforum.org/Pub/resreports.html

Mexico Daily News. (2015) The train that budget cuts have not stopped. March 21 http://mexiconewsdaily.com/news/train-budget-cuts-not-stopped/ accessed August 5th 2015.

Mendoza-Dorantes, E.E, Alcaraz, C.Z., Motal, M.M., Delahaye, D. (2015). *Simulating Airport Capacity: Mexico City Airport* Cas. Online. Available from http://www.lr.tudelft.nl/fileadmin/Faculteit/LR/Organisatie/Afdelingen_en_Leerstoelen/Afdeling_C_O/Aerospace_Management_and_Operations/ATOS/Papers/2015/CATO2015_3_1_2.pdf

OECD. (2007). OECD Economic Surveys: Mexico 2007. OECD Publishing, Paris DOI: http://dx.doi.org/10.1787/eco_surveys-mex-2007-en

OECD. (2015a). *OECD Territorial Reviews: Valle De México,* Mexico. OECD Publishing, Paris.
DOI: http://dx.doi.org/10.1787/9789264245174-en

OECD/CAF/ECLAC. (2015b), Latin American Economic Outlook 2016: Towards a New Partnership with China, OECD Publishing, Paris.
DOI: http://dx.doi.org/10.1787/9789264246218-en

OECD. (2015c), Effective Delivery of Large Infrastructure Projects: The Case of the New International Airport of Mexico City, OECD Public Governance Reviews, OECD Publishing, Paris. http://dx.doi.org/10.1787/9789264248335-en

OECD. (2016). *Tourism Trends and Policies 2016*, OECD Publishing, Paris. http://dx.doi.org/10.1787/tour-2016-en

OECD. (2016a). Value Added and its Components by Activity, CITI rev 4. OECD Stat.

OECD. (2016b). « Mexico », dans *Road Safety Annual Report 2016*, Éditions OCDE, Paris.
DOI: http://dx.doi.org/10.1787/irtad-2016-31-en

O'Toole, R. (2009). High-Speed Rail Is No Solution. Cato Institute. May 4, 2009.

Page, S., Lumsdon, L.(2004) *Tourism and Transport: Issues and Agenda for the New Millennium.* Elsevier, Boston.

Perceptive Travel (2015). How to Navigate the quirky Mexico City Airport http://perceptivetravel.com/blog/2015/01/28/how-to-navigate-the-quirky-mexico-city-airport/ Tim Leffell. January 28 2015.

SCT. (2014) National Infrastructure Programme. Communications and Transportation Sector 2013-2018. Annex A. June 1, 2014.

SECTUR. (2015). Ángeles Verdes ha brindado más de 189 mil servicios de atención a turistas, en lo que va del Periodo Vacacional. Bulletin 137. August 9 2015. Press release 137/2015

SECTUR. (2015a) Results of Tourism Activity Mexico, 2014. February 18 2015. Mexico City.

SECTUR. (2015b). Evolucion De La Conectividad En La Red Aerea Mexicana Y El Crecimiento Del Tourismo Nacional. February. Online. Available from http://www.datatur.sectur.gob.mx/Documentos%20Publicaciones/2015_2_DocInvs.pdf

SECTUR. (2016) Results of Tourism Activity Mexico, 2015. February 15 2016. Mexico City.

The Guardian. (2015). Uber drivers attacked outside Mexico City airport as taxi drivers demonstrate. http://www.theguardian.com/technology/2015/jul/30/uber-drivers-attacked-outside-mexico-city-airport-as-taxi-drivers-demonstrate accessed on August 18th 2015. July 30 2015.

Thomson Reuters. (2014). Exclusive Poll: Latin American Women Disgusted by Sex Pests on Public Transport. Anastasia Moloney.
http://www.trust.org/item/20141029000109-cgbre/?source=spotlight October 29 2014.

Transport Canada. (2015), Blue Skies Policy, Made in Canada For Canada. https://www.tc.gc.ca/eng/policy/air-bluesky-menu-2989.htm accessed on June 16 2016.

World Bank. (2013) Mexico City Open Database Improves Transit Efficiency, Helps Commuters. News. November 5th 2013. Washington

World Economic Forum. (2014). The Global Competitiveness Report 2014–2015: Full Data Edition. Geneva.

UNWTO. (2015). Tourism Highlights 2015. http://www.e-unwto.org/doi/pdf/10.18111/9789284416899

UNWTO. (2016). Yearbook of Tourism Statistics, 2010-2014. Madrid.

US Bureau of Transportation Statistics. (2015). Border Crossing/Entry Data: Query Detailed Statistics.Online. Available from http://transborder.bts.gov/programmes/international/transborder/TBDR_BC/TBDR_BCQ.html

US Department of Homeland Security. (2013). SENTRI Fact Sheet. http://www.cbp.gov/sites/default/files/documents/sentri_fact_2.pdf. May 2013.

US Department of State .(2015). Air Transport Agreement between the Government of the United States of America and the Government of the United Mexican States. http://www.state.gov/e/eb/rls/othr/ata/m/mx/250782.htm. December 18.

US Department of State. (2016). Open Skies Partner. http://www.state.gov/e/eb/rls/othr/ata/114805.htm. June 14.

VTT Technical Research Centre of Finland. (2014). Smart Sustainable Mobility. http://www.vtt.fi/inf/pdf/visions/2014/V5.pdf . Espoo.World Travel; and Toursim Council (WTTC, 2014). Travel & Tourism Economic Impact - Mexico. Online. Available from http://www.wttc.org/-/media/files/reports/economic%20impact%20research/country%20reports/mexico2014.pdf. London.

Zhang, Y., Findlay, C. (2014) Air Transport Policy and its Impacts on Passenger Traffic and Tourist Flows. Journal of Air Transport Management 34, 42-48.

Chapter 4
Inclusive tourism development in Mexico

Mexico's well-established model of tourism development has benefited from significant public investment to successfully leverage the country's natural climate and coastline endowment over the last four decades. This model is now maturing, and is vulnerable to challenge from changing consumer demand patterns, environmental considerations and competitiveness issues. It is also unlikely that this model can support tourism policy objectives to promote more inclusive and sustainable growth. This chapter considers a future growth path for tourism in Mexico and focuses on destination development and product diversification. It examines strategies to better spread the benefits of tourism, improve the overall tourism offer, promote regional development and widen employment opportunities.

Introduction

Mexico is currently engaged in a process of reappraisal to reconsider and reimagine the country's tourism product offering. The well-established resort-based sun-sea-sand product has been successful in destinations like Cancún and Los Cabos in recent decades, where it has delivered in terms of attracting international tourism to the country. However, performance has been more mixed in other destinations, and has had limited success in supporting wider economic and social development. In its development over recent decades, this model of large scale integrated resort development has benefited to a considerable extent from the expertise and investment made available through state and federal government structures.

In considering tourism growth in the longer term, the resort-based sun-sea-sand product is vulnerable to challenge in a number of areas, including changing consumer patterns, environmental considerations, and competitiveness issues. Given that it is a focus of government policy to promote a greater regional spread of tourism, and to secure the greater economic and social inclusivity this can generate, it is now important to identify and support new and different models of tourism destination development. Mexico has an opportunity to build on this to develop a more competitive and sustainable tourism sector which responds to wider tourism trends and caters to a more diversified market.

This is not to suggest an abrupt move away from the existing tourism model in Mexico. New tourism paradigms take time to evolve and develop. It is to suggest however that a tourism sector capable of supporting both growth and inclusivity is likely to be based on a more diversified portfolio of tourism products and destinations. It could for example include new destination clusters offering unique and differentiated tourism experiences. It could also involve a refresh of the existing resort model, and a consideration of how that model could in future offer more value for the consumer, and more economic and social benefit for the local community.

This chapter considers a future growth path for the tourism industry in Mexico, and looks to understand how this growth can be secured having regard to the fullest possible implementation of inclusive tourism development and business practices. It focuses on tourism destination and product development that can be undertaken in a manner that is more sustainable and inclusive. It examines strategies to better spread the benefits of tourism, improve the overall tourism offer, and widen employment opportunities.

Aligning policies to support more inclusive tourism development

A commitment to more sustainable and inclusive tourism development is underscored in the National Development Plan 2013-18, which has as one of its key tourism strategies the encouragement of supply-side innovation to modernise and reposition Mexico's tourism industry globally and generate greater economic benefit for the country. The need to strengthen the tourism model based on economic, social and environmental sustainability and to conserve and preserve cultural and natural resources is also recognised.

Delivering on this pledge requires active and well-resourced policies to strengthen tourism-supporting infrastructure, enhance the quality of tourism services and stimulate innovation to diversify the product and destination offer, to bolster and complement sun-sea-sand destinations with alternative offers. It also requires active measures to better spread the economic returns from tourism, and alleviate negative impacts on the environment.

According to the Sectoral Programme for Tourism 2013-18, Mexico is losing competitiveness due to a lack of supply-side innovation, including inadequate creation of new tourism products and services, consolidation of destination development, and harnessing of the country's competitive advantages. The sun-sea-sand product is showing signs of exhaustion and opportunities exist to generate greater value added, wealth and welfare and to stimulate regional development through the creation of attractive and sustainable tourism products (cultural, business, eco-and adventure, medical, sports, luxury). Tourism also has the potential to play an important role in promoting the sustainable use of natural resources and promoting biodiversity mainstreaming. Mexico has set out a plan to address these challenges, including taking steps to strengthen the competitive advantages of tourism, encourage market diversification, promote more sustainable destination development and distribute more widely the social and economic benefits of tourism.

Infrastructure development is a key part of this. The National Infrastructure Plan 2014-18 acknowledges the need to strengthen infrastructure in tourism destinations to boost competitiveness and meet domestic and international demand for transport and tourism services. Significantly, the plan includes a dedicated tourism investment portfolio for the first time and explicitly recognises the need for tourism to be taken into account in wider infrastructure planning (communications and transport, energy, water, health, urban development and housing).

This marks an enhanced recognition of tourism as a vibrant export-oriented sector within the wider Mexico economy, with potential to stimulate economic growth and regional development. Perhaps more importantly, it indicates an appreciation of the need to better align tourism and infrastructure policy. Tourism relies not just on tourism-specific infrastructure, but also on the existence of adequate network infrastructure to support tourism businesses and handle people flows to and around the country. However, the impact of such infrastructure on tourism, and tourism's role as a user of this infrastructure, are not always sufficiently taken into account in planning and feasibility assessment.

The tourism pillar of the National Infrastructure Plan 2014-18 aims to boost competitiveness and promote tourism as a key determinant of regional productivity and as a creator of social well-being, based on three strategies:

- improving existing structure and equipment in destinations with a highest influx of tourists,
- promoting the creation of new tourism infrastructure with a view to diversifying supply,
- promoting the development of infrastructure based on policies designed to increase competitiveness in matters of tourism.

Planned direct infrastructural investment in tourism is targeted to be MXN 181 billion for the creation of new and improvement of existing tourism infrastructure. This is equivalent to 2.3% of total investment foreseen under the plan, with 62% of this expected to come from private sources. Projects include the consolidation of Mesoamerican cultural heritage, reclamation of beaches and measures to counter beach erosion, revitalisation of the traditional coastal resort of Acapulco, construction of convention centres, and refurbishing the infrastructure and urban image in historic downtown areas.

Tourism also stands to benefit from wider infrastructural development investment foreseen under the plan. However, the extent to which this is realised will depend on how effectively senior policy makers across different institutions and agencies at national and sub-national level government co-ordinate their plans and work programmes. While tourism is not always a primary reason for allocating infrastructure development resources, it should where appropriate be recognised as a sector that provides strong supplementary reasons for investment decision-making. In this respect the Tourism Cabinet, as an instrument of public policy planning, has the potential to play a vital role in ensuring that the necessary co-ordination between government agencies - and their respective policy priorities – retains a consistent and clear focus on tourism development. The Ministry of Tourism will also need to be active in influencing those infrastructural developments which are the responsibility of state governments.

This strategic direction is ambitious, and the three areas of strategic focus align well with prevailing tourism priorities. The second focus area – creating new tourism infrastructure with a view to diversifying supply – particularly recognises the need to create new tourism infrastructure that will support a more diversified range of tourism product. While progress has been made on some projects, a number of high profile projects have been postponed or cancelled since the plan was launched, while recent budget cuts have also impacted on investment in tourism-supporting and tourism-specific infrastructure and development.

These plans are complemented by individual Regional Development Programmes 2014-18 for the North, Centre and South-southeast regions, which contain initiatives to attract tourism investment, develop eco- and other tourism opportunities to take advantage of regional assets, create region-wide tourism routes, design and offer new tourism products and professionalise human resources for tourism. The Programme for Sustainable Regional Tourism Development and Magic Towns (PRODERMAGICO) also provides subsidies to modernise the infrastructure and equipment in tourism destinations, contribute to the conservation and preservation of natural and cultural heritage sites, and promote supply-side innovation in the tourism sector. A Special Concurrent Programme (PEC) to support rural sustainable development projects focused on adventure and ecotourism was introduced in 2016.

Trends impacting tourism growth and development

Wider trends and developments are changing the global tourism environment and influencing the nature of tourism demand, with implications for consumer behaviour. Taking ample account of these trends is vital if Mexico is to develop a more competitive and sustainable tourism sector. Shifting trends on the demand-side invariably prompt a matching response on the supply-side. This supply side response moves beyond marketing and involves the development of basic infrastructure to enable visitors to access new tourism locations, and the development of new tourism products and services through which these experiences can be delivered. This requires active, innovative and integrated policy responses to ensure that tourism remains a competitive sector and continues to deliver economically and sustainably in the years to come.

Strong tourism growth in many emerging economies is reshaping tourism on a global scale, changing the nature of inbound and outbound tourism flows, shifting the balance of market share and relative size of tourism economies, and altering the competitive environment. Even with the recent economic slowdown in emerging markets, the pace of tourism growth in these economies is expected to continue outstripping growth in advanced economies. This long term trend is led primarily by the Asia Pacific region and China in particular. These developments create both opportunities and challenges for Mexico.

A key policy issue for Mexico is to understand how to strengthen Mexico's tourism economy and remain competitive with advanced and emerging destinations. This includes an assessment of the extent to which tourism in Mexico depends on the North American market, and the potential to grow new source markets. A particular area of focus here must be the readiness of Mexico to meet the demands of consumers from new and emerging markets, including Asia Pacific. Tourists from emerging markets demand different products from the existing tourism offer in Mexico, which largely caters to the traditional North American market.

Demographic and social trends are contributing to these changes. Rapid population growth in emerging economies is expanding the size of the potential outbound market, while the demographic profile in Mexico's most important source markets is also changing, with potentially important implications for Mexico's travel sector. The populations of countries in Europe and North America are aging, with a growing proportion of people aged over 50. Travellers from Mexico's main inbound markets are getting older, and multi-generational travel is also becoming more common, where three generations of a family holiday together. Mexico is already a well-established destination for retired people looking to travel to a warm climate and can take advantage of these trends.

Growing income disparities are also reducing levels of discretionary spending for some sections of the population, leading to increased price competition. At the other end of the spectrum, demand is increasing for customised, more exclusive and more luxurious travel experiences. One of the clearest indicators of this trend is the growth of the sharing or on demand economy, which is in part a creative response to increasing demand for more consumer choice and convenience, but for many is simply a strategy for attempting to do more with less – in the face of stagnating or declining discretionary income.

Consumer trends including changing travel interests and preferences are also changing the tourism landscape. While the origins are complex (globalisation, urbanisation, demographic change, technology), these trends are promoting different patterns of consumer behaviour and have immediate implications for tourism in Mexico. At the centre of this is a shift away from a large-scale commoditised tourism product based on relatively generic visitor services delivered to a high volume customer base, to a more authentic and differentiated tourism experience, with growing demand for more unique, personalised tourism experiences in alternative destinations.

Tourism is a major part of the experience economy, and consumers are motivated by expectations of what they can experience in a particular destination. This is the primary areas of focus for consumers, and the basis on which travel decisions are made. From a consumer's perspective, the hospitality component of tourism (where to stay, eat, drink) is a secondary demand and will only arise once the primary demand question has been satisfactorily addressed. For a destination like Mexico, the strong and natural comparative advantage enjoyed through the climate and coastline means that the sun-sea-sand resort product represents a ready-made solution. However, changes in consumer behaviour underscores the appropriateness of moving to a more diversified tourism offering in Mexico, which draws more heavily on the country's rich and diverse asset base.

While the baby boom generation continues to show high levels of interest in the sightseeing, golf and sun-sea-sand offer, younger demographic segments have a higher demonstrated level of interest in more active pursuits and more authentic cultural experiences. Interest in and demand for pre-packaged holidays is declining, while demand for customised vacations is growing, as is interest in booking locally (i.e. directly with destination tour operators and service providers). Another emerging trend is a shift toward short haul or regional travel, driven in part by reductions in paid vacation time and interest in shorter and more frequent trips. This potentially has important implications for Mexico, in terms of its continued reliance on the North American market to generate tourism growth, and its ability to increase arrivals from long haul markets and further diversify its market base.

The digitalisation of the economy is also transforming tourism. Travellers are increasingly connected to the internet and are using mobile applications, social media and online distribution platforms before and during their trip, to research, plan, book, rate, and share travel experiences. Mobile technology is now mainstreamed, enhancing connectivity and enabling real-time information provision. This is changing the relationship between consumers and producers, supporting co-creation and facilitating the more personalised travel experiences sought by consumers.

The heightened availability and accessibility of digital media has intensified competitive pressures in the tourism marketplace. The disintermediation caused by technology in supply and transaction chains means consumers have grown accustomed to the idea of designing tailored travel experiences based on their unique interests. These trends in consumer behaviour and expectations are necessitating a major shift towards digital marketing and promotion. Maximising the potential of these developments will require continued progress on reduced data-roaming charges, or alternative mechanisms to facilitate local internet access at modest cost, such as the steps taken by Mexico to provide free Wi-Fi to visitors in Magic Towns and elsewhere, to enhance the tourism experience. It has also been a powerful catalyst for innovation and the development of new business models, including the growth of the sharing economy in tourism. Peer-to-peer services for accommodation, transport and trips are active in Mexico, with local platforms operating in parallel with international platforms like Airbnb and Uber. While data is lacking on the full extent of these activities, the use of these platforms has grown in scale and is significant.

Internet access remains an issue for the operation of tourism businesses in regional and rural areas in Mexico, and is an important impediment to tourism SMEs looking to access global markets and value chains. Tourism businesses, and most particularly small and micro-enterprises, require high-speed broadband connectivity in order to open and maintain a virtual shop-window to their customers. Small tourism businesses that do not have access to broadband, and so do not have an online profile, are in effect closed out of the global market place where contemporary consumers plan and purchase travel. Investment in a new fibre optic cable network to provide more connectivity will improve this situation. Wider reforms in the telecoms sector intended to encourage real competition and support universal coverage will also play an important role in improving access and facilitating these developments, as will the Ministry of Communication and Transport's broadband access project.

Safety and security are important concerns for tourists around the world, with perception often as important as reality. These issues can affect the image of the destination, visitor arrivals and tourism growth, including where tourists have been the target of, or caught up in, security incidents or terrorist events, as has recently been the case in a number of OECD countries. The way governments respond to security issues is important, and the capacity to manage a crisis is a fundamental element of good governance.

Public safety and security are priority issues in Mexico. The security situation in the country has become more volatile over the last decade, linked with a rise in serious crime levels. Mexico's coastal tourism zones have largely been geographically removed from these developments. However, the situation is evolving and recent incidents have changed this. Security concerns may result in a reluctance among tourists from other countries to travel to Mexico, or even to include Mexico in their destination-consideration set, and can also mean that tourists regardless of origin are reluctant to travel to certain areas of the country. Continued attention to the security challenge is important for Mexicans in their day-to-day life, and also to realising the economic and regional development potential of tourism.

Mexico recognises safety and security as decisive elements of destination selection and critical issue for tourism development in the country. The Ministry of Tourism is working with the competent authorities to address these issues (Box 4.1). Mexico has introduced measures to provide a co-ordinated response in the event of an emergency or natural disaster, such as Hurricane Odile in 2014. Mexico has also sought to respond rapidly to the mosquito-borne Zika virus. The Mexico Tourism Board has created a map to help travellers understand where in Mexico cases of the Zika virus have been found, and this is updated with information from the Ministry for Health.

Box 4.1. Providing a safe and secure environment for visitors

The Ministry of Tourism has implemented a number of initiatives to provide a safe and secure environment for visitors to Mexico, working in conjunction with the responsible federal agencies and institutions, and the private sector. The Tourist Protection and Assistance Programme is multi-dimensional and takes into account public security, health protection, physical, psychological and economic integrity, crisis management and protection in the event of natural disasters, and response to unexpected events. It aims to provide assistance and protection for tourism, improve the security perception of tourism destinations in Mexico, increase trust in authorities, and create a collective sense of responsibility in destinations to protecting and assisting tourists. Initiatives include:

- **Holiday Safety Strategy** sees the deployment of additional Federal Police resources to ensure the safety of travellers during busy travel periods.
- **Centre for Attention and Protection of Tourists** provides information, support and guidance in the event of an emergency and helps victims and tourists who have broken the law.
- **Security Workshops** to enhance public and private sector co-operation in order to better plan for, prevent and effectively respond to tourism safety and security incidents.
- **Emergency and Disaster Response Manual for Tourism** to ensure tourism is considered in municipal civil protection plans, build strategic alliances and strengthen local capacity.
- **Tourism Victim or Transgressor Protocol** to provide a clear communication and decision-making system and support the establishment of services for tourists.
- **Green Angels** provide information, guidance and support to tourists, including road-side mechanical and accident assistance, and in response to emergencies and disasters.

Destination and product development

Over the past four decades, Mexico has adopted a model of tourism development largely built around the creation of integrated coastal resorts, designed to leverage the country's natural endowment of beautiful beaches, weather and Pacific and Caribbean coastline. This is reflected in the nature of the destination and product offer, and by extension, in patterns of tourism demand and the distribution of visitors across the territory. This has economic, environmental and social implications, concentrating the positive (and negative) impacts of tourism in defined geographic areas. It limits the potential to more efficiently use the full range of Mexico's tourism assets to diversify and grow the tourism offer, attract new markets and contribute to regional development across the territory. This core sun-sea-sand offer is also in need of investment to improve its competitiveness, due to wear and tear and the need to revitalise the product.

Profile of main destination and product offer

The core of Mexico's tourism offer remains the sun-sea-sand offer, in both traditional and planned coastal resorts. Six of Mexico's top 10 destinations are coastal areas, led by Cancún and the Riviera Maya in Quintana Roo and Acapulco in Guerrero (based on arrivals in hotels) (Table 4.1). Since 1974, FONATUR has operated a model of integrated planned resort development that has supported the creation of seven densely clustered resort developments on the Pacific Ocean, and two on the Caribbean Sea. All were developed based on Mexico's strong comparative advantage in the sun-sea-sand product. On the Pacific coast these resorts include Loreto, Los Cabos, Playa Espíritu, Costa Canuva (previously called Costa Capomo), Litibú, Ixtapa, Bahías de Huatulco. The two resorts on the Caribbean coast are Cancún, and Marina Cozumel.

Table 4.1. Mexico's top 10 destinations by market[1], 2014

	Total		Domestic		International	
	Arrivals	Nights	Arrivals	Nights	Arrivals	Nights
Mexico City	11 019 773	19 138 469	9 006 292	14 782 279	2 013 481	4 356 190
Cancún	6 020 823	21 269 570	2 018 363	6 218 383	4 002 460	15 051 187
Acapulco	4 590 910	6 416 828	4 481 115	6 181 665	109 795	235 163
Riviera Maya	3 712 818	22 079 503	105 643	310 003	3 607 175	21 769 500
Guadalajara	3 188 088	5 850 845	361 697	660 779	2 826 391	5 190 066
Veracruz-Boca del Rio	2 665 880	3 280 153	2 623 706	3 198 841	42 174	81 312
Puebla	2 093 835	3 890 466	279 168	473 608	1 814 667	3 416 858
Mazatlán	1 921 951	5 324 499	1 604 972	4 091 051	316 979	1 233 448
Monterrey	1 799 095	3 759 159	1 434 656	3 035 836	364 439	723 323
Puerto Vallarta	1 675 516	5 755 075	478 848	2 363 055	1 196 668	3 392 020

1. Based on arrivals in hotels.

Source: DATATUR, Compendium, extract May 2016.

Mexico has achieved considerable success with this model of tourism destination development, notably in Cancún, which was the first integrally planned resort in the country, and Los Cabos, where it has delivered in terms of attracting international tourism to the country. However, attempts to replicate this success in other destinations have met with more mixed results and raised concerns regarding the impacts of, and return on public investment from, these types of projects. Despite significant investment by the Federal government over an extended period, the planned destination of Loreto has not succeeded in stimulating the expected economic and social development in the region, for example. Insufficient transport connectivity and proximity to Los Cabos have been contributory factors.

Furthermore, many of these large-scale resort development projects are now reaching maturity and a significant number of both integrally planned resorts and more traditional resort areas are in decline. There is evidence that demand is weakening for central elements of the resort-based model (e.g. fewer Americans are now playing golf). There are also a number of significant environmental and sustainability challenges associated with this product, although recent developments in Huatulco in particular have sought to address some of these issues. Mexico's position in this market could be also undermined by competition from emerging destinations in the Caribbean region.

In considering tourism growth in the longer term, the resort-based model is vulnerable to challenge in a number of areas:

- Environmental considerations – the highly concentrated/highly localised resort product faces sustainability questions around water and energy consumption, sewerage capacity, waste management and impact on natural resources.
- Economic costs – associated with infrastructure maintenance and adaptation to new consumer preferences and market requirements, including new technologies for example.
- Changing consumer patterns – shifting lifestyle and leisure patterns are prompting some consumers to look beyond the purchase of a highly-concentred, single-location resort product. A significant consumer segment is increasingly interested in finding authentic tourism experiences rooted in an asset base that draws upon elements such as heritage, architecture, culture, gastronomy, nature and craft.
- Competitive advantage – the competitive advantage of the resort based sun-sea-sand product is vulnerable to competition. It can be competed away by new entrants to the regional industry possessing similar attributes that allow them present themselves as new and innovative resort destinations.
- Regional spread – the traditional resort model is highly concentred in a single geographic location. By extension, this tends to concentrate the economic gain associated with tourism in that single geographic location. In this model, tourism will not serve as an engine of economic distribution – it will have little impact in spreading the incomes and jobs associated with the industry across different regions of Mexico.

In terms of supporting a new phase of tourism development characterised by a more diversified product offering – in more geographically diverse regions – the tourism development model will need to evolve and adapt accordingly.

The Sectoral Programme for Tourism 2013-18 notes that public investment policies have resulted in the creation of accommodation, restaurant and second home services, but have not generated a more comprehensive range of tourism services to encourage spending and distribute the economic returns through the value chain, beyond these sun-sea-sand destinations. In the period 2008-12, the Ministry of Tourism allocated MXN 8.6 billion to tourism projects related to culture and the natural environment, sun-sea-sand, meetings and events, among others. During the same period, the National Fund for Tourism Development (FONATUR) channelled MXN 8.4 billion in real terms into sun-sea-sand destinations, in addition to MXN 761 million investment in the integrally planned resorts of Cancún, Ixtapa, Los Cabos, Loreto and Huatulco, as well as the construction of new resort developments in Playa Espíritu and Nayarit.

This focus on investment in sun-sea-sand destinations has resulted in limited investment in the diversification of the tourism infrastructure, deterioration of architecture and historic urban environment, and marginal investment in new tourism developments and attractions. Sustainably leveraging Mexico's natural and cultural tourism assets requires investment in new infrastructure, equipment and support facilities, as well as the development of new products and tourism services. Planning, and even more so, implementing and delivering this would also benefit from greater private sector participation.

Data on tourism services provides evidence on the nature of the tourism offer, and illustrates the degree to which tourism services, and demand, are highly concentrated in certain geographic pockets of the country (Table 4.2). In 2014, 692 351 registered rooms were available in 18 711 accommodation establishments across the country, the majority of which are located in sun-sea-sand destinations. Of these, 548 062 rooms were available in classified hotels which had an occupancy rate of 53.3% in 2014. Over half of these classified rooms are in four and five star hotels (25.6% and 33.4%), which attract a higher share of the inbound visitor market (international tourists account for 62.9% of arrivals and 74.7% of nights in the five-star category).

Table 4.2: Regional supply of tourism services, 2014

	Hotel establishments and similar	Rooms available	Bars and restaurants[1]	Travel agencies	Car rental	Convention centres
North	4 129	157 525	19 628	2 150	391	263
Centre	7 563	278 393	15 360	3 460	363	309
South-Southeast	7 019	256 433	15 256	1 342	316	232
Total	18 711	692 351	50 244	6 952	1 070	804

1. Including cafeterias and night clubs.

Source: DATATUR, Compendium, extract May 2016.

The majority of accommodation supply is located in the Centre and South-southeast regions (around 40% each), but within this, supply is highly concentrated in a number of destinations. The Ministry of Tourism has identified 70 main destinations in Mexico. Of these, five coastal destinations account for almost a third (30.9%) of hotel room supply in 2015 – Cancún, Riviera Maya, Acapulco, Los Cabos and Puerto Vallarta – with Mexico City, Guadalajara and Monterrey accounting for a further 22.4%.

Similarly, occupancy rates are highest in coastal resorts (64.8%) and major cities (63.8%), compared to 49.2% in destinations in the interior of the country. Cancún (77%) and the Riviera Maya (81.3%) have the highest occupancy levels, followed by Nuevo Vallarta (76.5%), Los Cabos (70.4%) and Puerto Vallarta (66.1%). However, in other coastal destinations occupancy rates are lower, falling to as low as 24.5% in the integrated planned resort Loreto, while occupancy is also declining in traditional resorts like Acapulco. As Mexico continues to develop coastal destinations based on the integrated resort model, this raises the question to what degree continued use of this model will generate incremental demand, or will redirect existing demand away from other resort destinations in the country.

Data on arrivals and overnights in hotels provides a demand side perspective to complete the picture. In 2014, over 99.7 million arrivals were recorded in accommodation establishments in Mexico, with an average stay of 2.14 nights, or 213.8 million overnights in total. Reflecting the concentration of the hotel room stock, the majority of arrivals are recorded in the South-southeast and Centre region. Five states account for just over two fifths of arrivals – Quintana Roo, Guerrero, Veracruz, Jalisco and Mexico City.

Table 4.3. Hotel capacity and occupancy in main destinations, 2005, 2014-15

	Available rooms			% occupancy		
	2005	2014	2015	2005	2014	2015
Mexico City	43 662	48 217	..	55.2	64.2	..
Cancún	10 525	32 129	31 711	78.7	75.3	77
Acapulco	16 518	18 544	18 603	40.8	38.9	40.1
Riviera Maya	..	36 115	36 541	..	79.5	81.3
Guadalajara	13 401	18 139	17 557	48.2	49.9	52
Veracruz-Boca del Rio	8 669	8 673	8 645	43	51.1	48
Puebla	4 751	7 049	7 947	51.9	65.7	66.4
Mazatlán	8 149	9 122	9 145	50.6	55.2	59
Monterrey	9 989	12 330	12 763	57.9	57.5	67.6
Puerto Vallarta	10 784	11 718	12 300	63.4	63.5	66

.. Not available.

Source: DATATUR, Compendium, extract May 2016.

The data particularly highlights the leading role of Cancún and the Riviera Maya. Tourism is the main economic activity in Quintana Roo, which accounts for 5% of accommodation establishments in Mexico, 12.8% of room stock and 24.3% of overnights, and enjoys the highest hotel occupancy rates in the country (75.3%). The Caribbean coast in Quintana Roo is the main destination for international visitors, while other areas cater more to domestic visitors. While Cancún has almost doubled the number of international tourists, other coastal resort destinations have seen a drop in the number of arrivals.

Towards a more inclusive model of tourism development

An immediate implication for tourism development in Mexico is the need to drive forward a strong, market-led destination and product diversification agenda, which in turn will support a regional development agenda. The need to diversify Mexico's product offering is now recognised as a central principle of policy and planning at government level. It also reflects a tourism industry which in the early phase of its development cycle leveraged the most compelling assets it possessed – its coastline and climate. This model is now maturing, its economic impacts are very localised in geographic terms, and its capacity to contribute to inclusivity and regional economic spread is limited. Notwithstanding this, Mexico's coastal resorts will remain a core element of the tourism asset base.

Product diversification allows Mexico to connect with new consumers and offer a new product base, without undermining its existing sun-sea-sand product and customer base. It also works well as a long term diversification strategy on the basis that if a contraction was experienced in the sun-sea-sand market, Mexico would be well positioned to pursue compensatory growth in the tourism experience market.

At the same time the industry has an important role to play in diversifying the tourism product portfolio to respond to changing trends among consumers and to meet the expectations of a public policy agenda which has prioritised inclusivity and regional economic spread. In parallel with pursuing this diversification strategy, Mexican tourism also needs to reconsider the well-established resort model to determine how it might be refreshed and reinvented so as to better deliver to the market and offer greater value-for-money to consumers, and insulate itself from aggressive marketing campaigns launched by emerging competitors in the region. Maintaining competitiveness in both mature and emerging tourism products will remain a key challenge and priority over the medium term.

The familiar infrastructure investment model will therefore need to evolve. In the resort development model of tourism growth, a central focus of tourism policy and planning has been on big infrastructure developments and the construction of hotels, restaurants, bars, and leisure parks. However, if Mexico is to achieve a long term tourism industry profile based on a more diversified portfolio of tourism products in order to pursue policy objectives related to continued industry growth, greater inclusivity, and a wider geographic spread of jobs and incomes, then other aspects of infrastructure development which focus more on enhancing the uniqueness of the destination and local development strategies will need to be prioritised.

This includes: preservation and conservation of natural and cultural assets, and supporting the physical carrying-capacity of these assets; information and communication technologies to facilitate the interpretation of these assets; access to and through natural heritage assets such as national parks; and facility development supporting adventure tourism, activity tourism, and eco/rural tourism. In parallel with this, interventions will be required to build capacity at firm level, to develop both operational and management skills as well as programmes to support small business entrepreneurs who are likely to become a more familiar feature of a diversified tourism landscape.

In addition, an emphasis on product diversification into non-coastal regions of Mexico will gain little if any traction in the absence of supporting infrastructure (transport access, water and air quality, sewerage facilities, waste and energy management, urban planning and public realm improvements). Developing this basic infrastructure is a pre-requisite for the development of accommodation, attractions and other tourism-specific infrastructure. The absence of these core infrastructure facilities at sites identified as having tourism potential can also prevent private sector development.

Investment programmes do not need to be fully tourism-centric in order to be tourism-relevant. They do, however, need to take adequate account of tourism's use of and requirements for infrastructure, to support effective infrastructure planning and enable the country realise its full tourism potential. Improvements in road and other transport infrastructure is particularly important, so that tourists can physically access new tourism products and activities in locations not currently considered to be primary tourism destinations. Projects focused on water and waste management, for example, will also help to reduce environmental impacts and support tourism-related development.

Paradoxically, it is in those areas with natural capital offering the greatest sustainable tourism potential where such infrastructure is lacking, especially in rural areas in the south and south-east of the country, and in indigenous communities in the north. FONATUR has played a key co-ordinating role in ensuring the provision of basic supporting infrastructure in the integrally planned resorts and tourism projects, but the situation is more complex away from these centrally planned and managed destinations. This implies a more central role for the Ministry of Tourism to ensure tourism is taken into account in infrastructure policy and planning in the future, alongside FONATUR.

Demand for activity and experience-based pursuits is growing rapidly and Mexico undoubtedly possesses the natural and cultural assets required to grow these markets. However, there are significant policy gaps that need to be overcome to fully exploit that development potential, linked with access and internet connectivity, visitor services, human capital and capacity building, training and technical assistance of SMEs, product development, and marketing support to effectively promote these destinations and more deeply penetrate these market segments.

This inevitably requires a change in mind-sets and behaviours. Diversifying the tourism product portfolio in effect means doing new things, in new ways, and in new places. It requires a new approach to policy making and to business development. It requires strong commitment and leadership from senior managers in both the federal and state government, and it requires careful co-ordination across a number of transversal agendas (infrastructure, physical planning, business development and skills development). Most importantly, the effective implementation of this diversification policy is likely to be realised only if there is a close working relationship between the private business sector and government policy makers.

Pursuing a destination development model on the basis of product diversification will particularly require an enhanced demand-side focus and understanding and will involve investment in marketing and market research. Whereas the sun-sea-sand product is typically targeted at a homogenous mass market, the market for tourism experience consumers – while sizeable – is more niche and fragmented, and marketing strategies in turn need to be more targeted. This will require more extensive market research and detailed intelligence on the motivating factors that prompt consumers to research and book a trip to Mexico. This extends to infrastructure development, which needs to be informed by demand side trend intelligence, and by a market-led understanding of product needs/gaps.

These developments are not entirely new, nor do they represent an entirely novel approach to tourism development. They are however a significant factor within the prevailing global tourism economy. Consequently they are important for Mexico, and should be positioned as a very important component of any tourism diversification programme.

The Ministry of Tourism, along with FONATUR and the Mexico Tourism Board, should thus review the destination development model and evaluate actions to move in this direction. This in turn may impact the work programmes of the Ministry, FONATUR and the Mexico Tourism board, and mark a (potentially challenging) reorientation from architect, master planner, and financier of large-scale tourism resorts, to an enabler of a new model of tourism development with a much more geographically dispersed portfolio of tourism experience clusters. While it is recognised the focus at the level of federal government is on policy and planning, consideration might also be given to the establishment of a delivery unit within the Ministry of Tourism to monitor progress on key aspects of policy implementation.

Sustainable tourism use of the environment

The geographic concentration of tourism in Mexico under the high density coastal resort development model generates high demand for natural resources in the main destinations and has consequences for natural habitats and species. An increased emphasis on product diversification will also have implications for the use and management of the natural and cultural environment. Mexico's rich and diverse tourism asset base is strongly linked with the country's natural and cultural resources and capitalising on these can create competitive advantages. However, some resources are more fragile than others and require management and protection. Infrastructure deficits and insufficient planning based on sustainability criteria are also contributing to environmental challenges (e.g. waste treatment). This damages the image of the destination and negatively impacts competitiveness and growth.

Like other countries, Mexico has to confront difficult trade-offs in pursuing its economic, social and environmental goals. While Mexico has strengthened its environmental policies and institutions and increased public investment in environment-related infrastructure, the OECD (2013) has called on Mexico to strengthen efforts to promote sustainable tourism. Mexico has been actively taking policy measures to address these issues for over a decade. Since first publishing a National Policy and Strategy for Sustainable Tourism in 2000, Mexico has sought to promote the sustainable development of tourism, with strategies to strengthen tourism destinations, promote well-being and support cultural and environmental preservation.

Mexico has a number of programmes to improve the balance between environmental protection and tourism development, as part of the Programme for Sustainable Regional Tourism Development and Magic Towns. Chief among these is the General Tourism Planning of the Territory Programme, which seeks to optimise the use of tourism resources and promote more suitable and sustainable land use. This programme involves the Ministry of Tourism, Ministry of Environment and Natural Resources (SEMARNAT), Ministry of Agrarian, Territorial and Urban Development (SEDATU) and FONATUR, in consultation with state-level governments. It is supported by joint work with SEDATU to map current and potential tourism areas throughout the country.

The Ministry of Tourism has also prepared guidelines to regulate tourism activities in specific destinations identified as sustainable development zones for tourism, with participation of the federal and state governments. Sustainable tourism development zones are clearly defined geographic areas with natural or cultural features which constitute a tourism attraction. Under the General Tourism Law 2009, these zones are established by Presidential Decree, at the request of the Ministry, and state and municipal governments and following an agreed evaluation process which also involves SEMARNAT, SEDATU and the ministries of the Interior (SEGOB), Communications and Transport (SCT). Such zones can be a useful instrument to co-ordinate public and private actions to develop tourism in these areas. However, they require effective and stable management over the long term.

Since 2014, the Ministry of Tourism has been developing a framework and guidelines to implement these initiatives. This has included organising workshops with public-private-community participation (with the World Wildlife Fund), identifying viable planning instruments and incentives and concept testing in planned destinations of Huatulco. High level co-ordination meetings involving the Ministry of Tourism, SEDATU, state and municipal authorities and the private sector have also sought to identify ways to promote a more comprehensive and sustainable approach to planning and development, and support more orderly growth in major tourism destinations to improve local living standards.

A further initiative has involved the development of an environmental certification programme for tourism businesses, *Distintivo S*, which has been developed and implemented in collaboration with the Rainforest Alliance and Earthcheck. This is one of a wider set of measures to improve the quality of Mexico's tourism offer (Box 4.2) and aims to promote sustainable development based on international norms and standards. However, participation can be challenging for small and micro tourism enterprises, as the costs can be high, and considerable investment may also be required to meet the standards and incorporate eco-techniques into their operations (e.g. using local materials, waste-water or solar or other renewable energies).

As part of Mexico's Special Climate Change Programme 2014-18, the Ministry of Tourism is undertaking six lines of action to support climate change mitigation and adaptation, including climate change diagnostics and vulnerability assessments in key destinations, a handbook on climate change adaptation and mitigation actions, energy efficient assessments in hotels in Boca del Río, Veracruz, ecotourism in protected natural areas, water management in destinations, and the development of a greenhouse gas emissions inventory to reduce emissions in tourism-related activities. The Ministry is also working to develop a new 5-year sustainable tourism model to ensure promote biodiversity and ecosystem conservation, better productive landscape management, energy efficiency and climate change resilience, with financial support from the Global Environmental Facility.

These measures represent the Ministry of Tourism's main activities to promote a system of sustainable development, in order to support the further growth and expansion of the Mexican tourism industry, and apply regardless of the scale of development.

Box 4.2. Improving the quality of the tourism offer in Mexico

To seek continuing improvement in product and service standards, the Ministry of Tourism's Under-Secretariat for Tourism and Quality Regulation is taking steps to: certify the quality of tourism products and services offered by companies, independent services providers and destinations; professionalise the service offered in different tourism sub-sectors; promote social, economic, and environmental sustainability and the continuous improvement of the sector; and operate for evaluation certification and re-certification mechanisms based on a scalable, incremental, and aspirational system. Within this context, a number of strategic projects have been set up and are currently being progressed. These include a National Tourism Registry, a System of Hotel Classification, a National Tourism Certification System, an Accreditation of Tour Guides, and a System for National Standards. In relation to the latter, the Ministry of Tourism will liaise with the Tourism and Related Services Technical Committee of the International Organisation for Standards (ISO). In progressing this work, it will remain important to ensure that quality standards and systems of regulation do not become so burdensome as to give rise to undue expense for the industry. Care should also be taken to ensure that the extent and requirements of such a system should not be such as to overwhelm both the industry and the regulatory authority required to oversee the system.

One of the advantages of the integrated planned resort approach is the potential to integrate sustainability principles into destination planning and development. This is evidenced by practices such as the use of greywater for golf course maintenance in FONATUR destinations, or the construction of waste water treatment facilities. However, planned development does not guarantee sustainable development and good environmental practices – this requires consideration of the appropriateness and scale of the development, a balanced assessment of the positive and negative impacts of tourism, and implementation of solutions. In common with all tourism destinations, the future performance of these integrated planned resorts will be required to follow increasingly demanding environmental and sustainability standards.

An indication of how progress can be made is evidenced in the case of Huatulco which adopted the Earthcheck environmental management system, and was also awarded the *Distintivo S* designation for its commitment to environmental sustainability. In 2013,

Huatulco received the EarthCheck Gold Certificate in recognition of its efforts to operate and maintain higher standards of environmental sustainability, and became the first destination in Latin America to receive the Earth Check Platinum Certification in 2014. Further innovation and improvement in the operating model of the coastal and integrated planned resorts will remain a priority concern into the future.

This is true also for the integrated planned resorts and tourism projects which are currently being planned and developed in both coastal and inland areas. FONATUR's plans to develop an ecotourism-based resort in Presa Necaxa in northern Puebla, and cultural tourism developments in Palenque, Teotihucán and Chichén Itzá, for example, need to take into consideration not only the appropriateness of this model of development for catering to the ecotourism and cultural tourism market from a demand-side perspective, but also the sustainability considerations and impact of such a development on the natural and cultural assets of the area. The submission of FONATUR projects for environmental impact assessment by the Ministry of Environment and Natural Resources, and development of projects in line with environmental standards and norms, is a positive development, although questions remain about the scale and impact of these developments.

It is important to take into account in this process not just the impact of the core of the project itself, but also the wider environmental and social impact. To minimise the undesirable environmental impacts of tourism, attention must be paid to the carrying capacity of destinations, enforcing environmental legislation, improving waste management and strengthening the capacity of communities. Tourism infrastructure also needs to be adapted, particularly in destinations most at risk from environmental pressures.

Beyond the Ministry of Tourism, the sustainability and other challenges associated with the continued development of the tourism resort model, along with the opportunities to realise wider policy priorities, have prompted policy-makers to focus on the tourism potential of the rich resource base.

The Ministry of Environment and Natural Resources has taken a proactive approach to tourism in Mexico which is largely unique among OECD countries, designing and developing environmental programmes, guidelines and standards to support more sustainable tourism development. A notable example of this is the working being done by SEMARNAT and the National Commission of Natural Protected Areas (CONANP) to support the development of nature based tourism in national parks and other areas of protected national beauty, including the development of ecotourism and certification of ecotourism centres and tourism-related businesses. Linked with this, CONANP has launched an ongoing process of good practice training in tourism-related projects in biosphere reserves and national parks. Projects can obtain certificates of compliance with environmental laws and regulations. This initiative recognises the green growth potential of ecotourism.

Other federal ministries and agencies, such as the Ministry of Social Development (SEDESOL) and the National Commission for the Development of Indigenous Peoples (CDI), are active in developing niche tourism activities which seek to harness the potential of culture and nature-based tourism in support of wider policy objectives. These projects recognise tourism's potential to create sustainable employment and income opportunities for marginalised rural communities located in areas with abundant natural resources. Environmental sustainability is a key component of these initiatives, which also target women and young girls. Greater co-operation can enhance these efforts, as the Ministry of Tourism can bring its knowledge, expertise and networks to help bring many of these initiatives to the market, while the other agencies bring knowledge of their respective policy domains to support more sustainable tourism development in regions beyond the coast.

Developing a new industrial policy for tourism

Stimulating regional and local development

The tourism and regional development potential of Mexico's natural and cultural asset base remains largely untapped. Mexico is arguably the richest country in the Americas and one of the richest in the world in this regard, from its biodiversity and ancient civilisations to living indigenous, Mestizo and Hispanic traditions. This asset base is unique to Mexico and offers a comparative advantage in an increasingly competitive global tourism market. It creates opportunities for Mexico to look beyond the sun-sea-sand market and develop high value segments linked with culture and the natural environment. This asset base is also distributed across the territory, and offers strong potential to support regional development. The creation of the Mexican Caribbean Biosphere Reserve, for example, will create the largest national protected areas in the region and will open up new tourism opportunities.

Moving towards a more geographically distributed model of tourism development requires some reimagining of the concept of a tourism destination as currently understood in Mexico. Conventional images of tourism destination development are usually associated with a single geographic point containing a variety of elements of interest to consumers (e.g. a coastal resort development with supporting infrastructure). An alternative understanding of a tourism destination could be developed around a collection of tourism experiences which are often thematically connected, and which can be explored at the visitor's own pace within a somewhat wider geography.

This is an approach which has been successfully used in other OECD countries to encourage visitors to disperse more widely, at local, national and transnational level (e.g. European Cultural Routes). Another favoured policy approach to help spread the benefits of tourism more widely is through active regional dispersal measures focused on identifying and promoting new tourism centres and niche products. These are approaches that Mexico can also benefit from to take advantage of and better utilise the country's rich and diverse range of tourism assets.

The Sierra Mágica Routes Programme in the state of Puebla provides one example of where different levels of government have come together to capitalise on this potential by developing routes around different themes, as part of a wider brand (Box 4.4). Plans to develop an ecotourism route in Tuxtlas, Veracruz (led by the Ministry of Communications and Transport) and wine route in Valle de Guadalupe in Baja California, along with plans for natural and archaeological routes in the Cancún Riviera Maya Tourism Corridor (led by FONATUR) are further examples of where this type of initiative can better leverage Mexico's tourism assets and spread visitors more widely.

This type of tourism development relies on co-operation between different levels of government and different actors along the route, as well as the provision of supporting infrastructure and facilities including transport, signage, information provision and tourism services for visitors.

One example of co-operation and collaboration between a large group of tourism stakeholders that share a common resource or a common business interest is provided by the Brothers Grimm Fairy Tale route in Germany. This example is particularly interesting as it is based on intangible cultural heritage and demonstrates the potential to create an engaging and attractive product which can draw visitors to areas they would not otherwise have known about. The outcome of this collaboration is the creation of a new business entity that trades on a more integrated and potentially more compelling basis. This allows for a new model of destination development through the creation of a tourism corridor. The particular relevance of this example in the context of tourism destination development in Mexico is the opportunity to reimagine tourism destinations as other than a fixed-point geographic location, and the connections with Mexican folklore, myth, and legend as a platform to meet the interests of those tourists seeking an authentic Mexican experience.

Box 4.4. Developing Sierra Mágica thematic routes in Puebla

The Sierra Mágica programme is the result of a joint effort across three levels of government – federal, state and 17 municipalities - to boost tourist activity in the Sierra Norte de Puebla region. The core idea was to develop tourism routes that would support the Sierra Mágica brand created to profile and integrate the human, tourist and cultural resources of the area. Four routes allow tourists to experience and participate in regional heritage and customs. The economic benefit is captured directly in local communities, increasing the number of active tourism firms and people employed in the sector, and enhancing the quality of the visitor experience. The routes were developed with a focus on particular themes indigenous crafts, well-being and health, gastronomy, and nature and include:

Route of the monastries: Includes three Poblanos monasteries considered UNESCO cultural heritage of humanity, clustered into a promotable tour which includes complementary activities of cultural and traditional interest that enables tourists to understand and appreciate the region.

Route of the historical footprints: Links two municipalities which are part of the biosphere reserve of Tehuacán-Cuicatlán shared with the state of Oaxaca. It aims to cluster nature tourism and cultural attractions with a choice of routes offering a flexible, clustered package to visitors. A guide brochure contains information on the attractions on the route, distances and times, and recommended places to eat and stay.

Route of the high and middle mountain: Developed jointly by the state and Malinche National Park, it draws on the natural heritage assets of the park to generate sustainable economic activity for the local population. It has been undertaken with a deliberate emphasis on environmental sustainability and the conservation of the cultural and natural heritage, so as to improve the quality of life of local communities and enable visitors to access and fully understand the attractions of the national park.

Gastronomic City of Puebla: This is a fusion of cuisine rooted in centuries of Arab rule in Spain and the inspiration of ingredients in Mesoamerica, with recipes including Mole Poblano and Chiles en Nogada. This initiative is promoted under a Gourmet Calendar brand which aims to stretch the tourism season in Puebla.

Source: http://eleconomista.com.mx/industrias/2013/12/16/presentan-ruta-sierra-magica

The Tequila region of Jalisco provides an example of a region taking steps to leverage its natural and cultural assets to stimulate tourism-led development, notably its status as a UNESCO World Heritage Site and associations with the drink tequila. This has included the creation of new tourism services, products and routes, which help to link the city with the wider region. It has also included the creation of a web site and interactive guide to promote the variety of experiences on offer in the region and help visitors plan their visit. Tequila seeks to add value for visitors to the town and encourages them to travel more widely around the region, for example by targeting niche markets with tourism products including the Haciendas and Aromas del Arenal bike tourism through the Tequila Agave Landscape. The private sector and local community has played an important role in this, through the leadership of the Jose Cuervo Foundation and with the support of the municipal, state and federal government. National and international programmes have provided a framework for developing the destination, supported by a local committee (Box 4.5).

Box 4.5. Culture and nature-based tourism development in the Tequila region

Tequila is a rich, biologically diverse destination surrounded by the Cerro Azul (Blue Hill) and the agave landscape which has UNESCO World Heritage status and includes archaeological ruins of the Teuchitlan cultures that date back to the sixteenth century. The town is home to traditional artisan distilleries and historic churches, while near municipalities produce opal crystals. Tequila was designated a Magic Town in 2003 in recognition of the town's customs, traditions, urban environment and surround natural landscapes, and the Council for Integral Development of Tequila was established to bring together local actors and develop a long term vision for the town. Between 2007 and 2015, public investment in infrastructure the Magic Town of Tequila totalled MXN 101.3 million, from a combination of federal, state and municipal sources. Visitor numbers to the town doubled over this period, with' the majority of visitors coming from the state of Jalisco, and elsewhere in Mexico.

Tequila has also benefited from private sector investment by Jose Cuervo to create Tequila Espíritu Cuervo and investment by the Inter-American Development Bank in the Ruta de Tequila. It has also benefited from participation in the National Geographic Tequila Geotourism Programme. This project is private sector-led and municipal, state and federal government supported. It is centred on the concept of place-based authenticity and through a geo-located mapping process and engages the entire community to identify and promote authentic travel experiences. Visitors are encouraged to buy locally made products and services, eat in local restaurants and visit the historic sites. A website and interactive guide provides tourists with the information needed to plan a trip with Tequila's major attractions and activities, including festivals and events. The Tequila project was initiated by the Jose Cuervo Foundation, as a component of the region-wide sustainable tourism development project, Mundo Cuervo, and is supported by the Council for Integral Development Tequila, City of Tequila, Magic Towns, Ministry of Tourism of the State of Tequila and the Federal Ministry of Tourism. It has also benefited from support from the Inter-American Development Bank, US Agency for International Development and the World Bank.

Source: SECTUR, http://www.tequilatourism.com/guide

Making the most of Mexico's under-utilised tourism assets to support regional and local development extends to more efficiently using the existing tourism infrastructure in the country and promoting new markets. The Let's All Travel for Mexico (*Viajemos todos por México*) initiative focuses on encouraging and facilitating travel for Mexicans in the low season, taking advantage of under-utilised infrastructure and capacity. It aims to enhance the accessibility of tourism to the local population, including people from a low income background, indigenous people and other marginalised sectors of the population, as well as strengthen local economies, generate new tourism products and create new opportunities for local businesses.

As part of this initiative, tourism service providers have begun to propose special offers and create packages, routes and circuits, while businesses have been invited to introduce incentive programmes for employees. State and municipal governments are being encouraged to actively support this initiative, and work with local industry and the Mexico Tourism Board to develop and promote the offer. The Ministry of Tourism plays a co-ordinating role between these actors.

An initiative to leverage the good quality hotel infrastructure developed to cater to business travellers linked with the oil industry in Campeche and Tabasco is similarly looking to make better use of existing tourism infrastructure in the region. Work is underway to develop nature-based travel services to attract tourists to the area and take advantage of the excess accommodation capacity, following the decline in oil prices.

Promoting new tourism clusters

A key feature of successful tourism destinations is their capacity to cluster a number of different tourism experiences into a single destination offering. This provides a richer visitor experience than a single-attraction product such as a beach with a fixed and pre-determined accommodation and food offering. This layering of the tourism offer may involve developing new products and attractions which can complement and be combined with the existing sun-sea-sand offer in Mexico, as well as developing tourism services clustered around new destinations catering to new markets. Cross-sectoral clusters may also establish linkages between tourism and other sectors.

This is something the Ministry of Tourism has sought to do with the Magic Towns Programme (*Programa Pueblos Mágicos*), which brings together federal, state and municipal resources to develop the tourism potential of towns with historical significance or cultural heritage assets (Box 4.6). The initiative is in effect an example of clustered tourism destination development for accredited towns in Mexico. The programme seeks to support the development of the tourism offer in the individual towns, while the designation links these towns under a common umbrella brand.

The Magic Towns programme takes some of the elements of the integrated planned resort approach (identification and mapping of tourism site, destination plan, focus on infrastructure development) but attempts to support a more inclusive, bottom-up approach to tourism development within the designated towns. Local communities can request Magic Town's status and the programme is co-ordinated and managed by a local committee which also acts as a medium through which public funding is channelled for the upgrade and maintenance of the urban public realm. These factors help build social capital, in addition to the physical refurbishment of the town.

The adoption of a more strategic approach to the Magic Towns programme and implementation of recent changes to the rules and operating procedures should help to strengthen this initiative and better realise the tourism potential. The new rules set out the process and application of a clear set of qualifying criteria which aspiring towns are required to meet to obtain and, equally important, retain the designation. Integration of the programme into what is now the Programme for Sustainable Regional Tourism Development and Magic Towns also provides a framework for a more co-ordinated and integrated approach to this initiative, within a wider tourism development framework. Access to many Magic Towns is a key impediment to developing their tourism potential, for example, while proximity to existing tourism centres may provide an opportunity to encourage visitors to coastal resorts to visit one of the Magic Towns (e.g. near Puerto Vallarta). The potential to attract international visitors to these towns also remains untapped.

Box 4.6. Promoting cultural tourism in Magic Towns

The *Pueblos Mágicos* or Magic Towns Programme was created by the Ministry of Tourism in 2001 to promote tourism to towns with historical significance or cultural heritage assets. The programme aims to develop local infrastructure, promote local development and preserve culture and identity, foster domestic tourism and complement the sun-sea-sand offer. The designated towns receive a combination of federal, state and municipal funding and supporting, involving a range of actors. A local committee with community stakeholder's co-ordinates and manages the programme, which starts with a diagnosis of local needs. By 2012, 83 towns had been designated and supported through the programme, with each required to have a feature that makes them culturally special, a destination plan, and an annual programme to evaluate economic impact (including regional impact). Work focused on reconstruction of historic sites, enhancement of infrastructure and signage, undergrounding of electrical wiring, development of tourism attractions and facilities, reorganisation of the tourism trade, and provision of training. Specific challenges have included the regular change in local government, lack of support for marketing and packaging the product, and limited capacity for delivery.

In 2013, an analysis of the programme concluded that changes were required to maintain its value. A more strategic approach has since been adopted. The programme was re-launched in 2014, with the intention of establishing clear rules to promote more effective co-ordination between the three levels of government, strengthen participation by civil society, enhance competitiveness and productive inclusion, and promote sustainable and community development. Dedicated resources were allocated to the programme for the first time. The process of incorporation involves 4 steps: a technical visit to verify town's tourism potential, review of tourism-related indicators compiled from online data (prices, reviews etc.), documentary evidence of unique attributes and local support for designation, and assessment of existing tourism offer. From the 180 towns that applied for registration in 2015, 28 highest scoring municipalities were successful, making a total of 111 unique Magic Towns. Implementation of the rules of permanence remains pending.

Promoting new tourism centres and niche products opens up the potential to link these across a wider geography to create a new distributed tourism destination. The five Magic Towns in the state of Jalisco (Tequila, Tapalpa, San Sebastián del Oeste, Lagos de Moreno, and Mazamitla) are promoted as an integrated tourism experience, for example. The visitor proposition is rooted in local heritage, culture, gastronomy, and an opportunity to explore an attractive and accessible natural environment. Although the five towns are spread across the state, they represent an integrated tourism itinerary and provide a shape and structure which gives the destination definition. This is not a destination in the conventional sense of a narrow geographic point. It is a multi-location destination, and it is one which has a coherence and integrity because it offers the visitor the opportunity to experience authentic aspects of these towns, on the basis of moving around within a well-defined but still wider geographic area.

This type of offering aligns well with the interests of those seeking tourism experiences. The important point for these visitors is that this thematically coherent travel itinerary provides a focus and structure for their visit, but leaves it entirely to the consumer as to how, in what manner, and over what time-span they wish to experience what the area has to offer. It allows for a greater flexibility in what is in effect a reimagined tourism destination. A strong narrative with compelling information about the towns and how to navigate the destination is essential to bring the elements of the experience together for the consumer. Where it is well structured and resourced, such a model is equally applicable across other parts of Mexico.

The destination innovation potential of this kind of cluster development is that the experience offered to consumers is not limited to a single location. A great deal more is clustered into the experience. While any one individual attraction might struggle to draw attention to itself and secure a customer base, when it is included within a wider set of attractions and presented within a themed tourism itinerary, a more intense level of scale is achieved and a stronger profile is secured in the noisy world of tourism marketing.

However the real potential of emerging clustered destinations is their capacity to deliver on the policy agenda of government, particularly when they involve community and private sector participation. Tourism clusters can help deliver on the ambition to spread the economic gains associated with tourism activity beyond the conventional tourism hubs. They represent real locations where the policy-led ambition for product diversification can be realised in practice.

By leveraging the asset base in a more innovative way, tourism clusters give consumers a reason to visit the area and extend dwell time, and so facilitate higher visitor spend and greater economic gain in the local economy. This in turn generates local employment opportunities for workers, and improved access to supply chains for local small businesses. This also supports a more vibrant local economy thereby improving the employment prospects, including for women, young people and people with disabilities.

The development of tourism clusters has gained considerable attention as a tool for product diversification and competitive advantage. A tourism destination by its very nature creates a geographical concentration of service providers, creating in turn the conditions for cluster development. However, clusters are not necessarily a tourism phenomenon that naturally or organically falls into place. More typically they need to be nurtured, supported, and co-ordinated.

Some significant challenges persist in relation to tourism product clustering which are relevant in the Mexico context. The highly fragmented nature of tourism and large number of SMEs in the sector can frustrate the establishment and operation of tourism clusters, while lack of awareness of clustering opportunities is also a challenge when developing effective tourism clusters (Box 4.7). Intervening to address these challenges could emerge as a key role for local government agencies as they support a programme of tourism product diversification at local level.

Successful clusters usually require some form of central co-ordination. It may be something as simple as a part-time co-ordinator in a group of rural ecotourism enterprises, or it could be a structured and sophisticated arrangement as in the Mexican medical tourism cluster (Box 4.8).

Medical tourism in Mexico provides a good example of where strong policy-making and government support, allied with local actors willing to collaborate, and based on an intrinsic source of competitive advantage, can combine to form a tourism sub-sector which is built on an asset base other than sun-sea-sand. The development of medical tourism clusters in Mexico is an example of cross-sectoral clustering, which seeks to leverage the linkages between tourism and another sector to generate value. Building on progress to date in developing medical tourism clusters in Baja California and elsewhere, co-ordination efforts have been brought under the Tourism Cabinet working group on Innovation, Competitiveness and Tourism Product Development in a bid to further strengthen the value proposition.

Box 4.7. Tourism cluster development challenges

A destination is an amalgam of tourism services and experiences (accommodation and food services, attractions, activities etc.), which are at the same time competing and complementary. Effectively clustering these services and experiences allows destinations to provide a seamless and high quality visitor experience. It also helps to build a critical mass to enable tourism providers to take advantage of operational synergies, generate economies of scale, increase productivity and innovation and be more competitive. A cluster thus represents a group of tourism providers that serve broadly the same market and thereby creates a physically close group of companies that may either compete and/or co-operate with each other (OECD, 2008).

Challenges include:

- Large tourism businesses usually possess the resources to be autonomous and self-sufficient. They seldom have much incentive to cluster with other businesses.
- By definition therefore tourism clusters tend to be more appropriate to SMEs and micro-enterprises. They benefit most from bulking up to build some economic scale. Alternatively, a tourism cluster could be formed to serve as a stronger integrated service provider into the supply chain of a larger tourism firm.
- However smaller businesses tend to be wary of sharing or pooling resources with other firms. Typically they fear a zero sum game where some other member firm within the cluster will prosper at the direct expense of another member.
- Smaller businesses also tend to be reluctant to pool business performance data or financial information - typically they might be fearful of drawing the attention of official agencies, tax authorities, or other government regulatory bodies.
- Equally smaller businesses are usually preoccupied with simple day-to-day operational (trading) matters – simply keeping the shop open for business. They have little time to explore clustering opportunities with other related businesses in the area.

The lessons emerging from the experience in Baja California are that even in a sophisticated and mature business environment such as the medical sector in Baja California, capturing the potential gains associated with medical tourism required a willingness to pool resources, and a strong central co-ordination mechanism to ensure that the cluster remained active, engaged, and aligned with its business objectives. Developing an offer around providing medical services to international visitors involves a range of public agencies and institutions and medical and tourism service providers, and also raises practical challenges, including insurance, accessibility and integration of the service chain.

A mapping exercise has clearly identified the components and actors of a medical tourism cluster, and how they relate to each other. In total, ten regional medical tourism clusters have been identified, including in areas where tourism is less developed, and with limited natural tourism assets (e.g. Chihuahua). The Ministry of Tourism is also considering establishing an advisory council on medical tourism bringing together public and private stakeholders, to promote further cluster development.

The experience in co-ordinating across a diverse range of actors and interests may serve as a useful template developing other cross-sectoral clusters, such as the food industry-tourism cluster in the Yucatán Peninsula. Food connects tourists to culture and heritage and is becoming one of the most noticeable examples of the tourism experience.

Food also plays an important role in local development. As part of the National Gastronomy Promotion Policy, Mexico is seeking to leverage the supply-chain linkages between agriculture, food and tourism. Traditional Mexican cuisine is a comprehensive cultural model comprising farming, ritual practices, age-old skills, culinary techniques and ancestral community customs and manners. It is made possible by collective participation in the entire traditional food chain: from planting and harvesting to cooking and eating (UNESCO, 2010).

Box 4.8. Developing the medical tourism cluster and offer in Baja California

The Medical, Dental and Hospital Cluster of Baja California was established in 2011. Prior to the global economic crisis, Baja California welcomed around one million patients each year, but this had dropped to 350 000 by 2010. Two factors had supported the development of medical tourism in Baja California up to this point: the proximity of a large market of consumers in the United States and Canada attracted by the availability of high-quality and cost-competitive health care; and the region's reputation from manufacturing high-quality medical devices and medical technologies. This facilitated the emergence of a medical services industry for visitors, which in turn facilitated the emergence of an allied cluster of services in the hospitality and tourism sectors. However, to get ahead in the medical tourism sector, providers have had to pool efforts, consolidate their operations, get certified, promote themselves as a group, and earn the trust of their prospective customers. The Baja California Cluster cluster enables the hospital services in the region to provide a comprehensive and diversified offer to meet the needs of medical tourists. It also optimises the eco-system of complementary services such as lodging, food, and entertainment among others. By 2015, the number of medical tourists travelling to Baja California to receive medical treatment had risen to an estimated 800 000. Most medical tourists attend for minor procedures, so there is a greater chance they will extend their stay as a mini-vacation and visit local tourist attractions.

Mexico is seeking to position itself as a leading provider of quality, safe and competitively priced medical services to visitors. Ten medical tourism clusters have now been identified for development in Mexico: Baja California, Sonora, Chihuahua, Nuevo León, Tamualipas, Jalisco, Guanajuato, Puebla, Quintana Roo and Mexico City. Actions include strengthening the medical tourism service chain, holding regional meetings to raise awareness of the importance and potential, encouraging certification and accreditation of services and products, and implementation of *Distintivo H* and *Punto Limpo* hygiene certifications, and attracting investment and encouraging financing through the development banks, as well as actively promoting Mexico as a medical tourism destination. Medical tourism revenues in Mexico were estimated to exceed USD 3.1 billion in 2014.

Source: ProMéxico.

Integrating SMEs in tourism supply chains

Facilitating the participation of small and micro-enterprises in tourism supply chains is one way to make progress towards government policy of securing greater inclusivity in tourism. This can remain an area of particular challenge in rural areas, and in areas which are not traditional tourism hot-spots where business models may not be well defined and understood. It can also be a challenge in integrated resort developments, as larger tourism businesses may have well-established supply chains and it can be difficult for local businesses to access these supply chains. Where this is the case, certain barriers – whether intentional or otherwise – can frustrate small and micro-enterprises in accessing tourism supply chains.

Tourism supply chains comprise the suppliers of all the goods and services that go into the delivery of tourism products to consumers. It includes all suppliers of goods and services whether or not they are directly contracted by tour operators or by their agents or suppliers. Tourism supply chains involve many components - not just accommodation, transport and excursions, but also bars and restaurants, handicrafts, food production, waste disposal, and the infrastructure that supports tourism in destinations (Tapper and Font, 2004, Travel Foundation).

The OECD has identified closer collaboration across tourism value chains as a key component of increasing the economic value of tourism activity, facilitating more ready access for small and micro-enterprises in particular. It can help overcome the high level of fragmentation in the sector, deliver a total tourism experience and support a better use of existing infrastructure, staff and resources. Increasing the economic value of tourism is an important concern for advanced tourism economies looking to remain competitive in the global tourism market place and vis-à-vis other industries.

In Mexico, small tourism firms in sub-sectors such as gastronomy, indigenous craft, ecotourism, adventure sport, and heritage tours, can find it difficult to access tourism hot-spots with high visitor volume, or to access larger firms in the accommodation sector that may have visitor volume, but for whom these smaller firms are simply not visible. Currently, only 5% of the tourist market inputs come from local companies, according to the Regional Development Programme of the South-Southeast Region 2014-18 which, among other things, seek to develop local suppliers in the tourism market to generate greater local benefit.

The example of medical tourism shows that increased collaboration in the value chain was essentially prompted by the medical sector which quickly recognised that it need the collaboration of the hospitality sector to maximise the business opportunity it had identified. The medical economy was therefore the catalyst that identified an opportunity which in turn led to a related expansion in the tourism economy. This was accomplished by the introduction of the hospitality sector as a component within the wider medical tourism supply chain.

This carries an implication for the tourism clustering initiatives previously referenced. Whereas the medical sector prompted the tourism sector to join its value chain, tourism clusters – when they can be created and supported – essentially represent a coming together of a diverse set of fragmented small tourism service providers into one single coherent value chain. Tourism clusters not only represent improved outcomes for tourists and the experiences they encounter (demand side effects), they also have the potential to pull small businesses into the tourism value chain and so capture the increased collaboration noted by the OECD (supply side effects).

Building capacity

The capacity of organisations and individuals to develop and implement tourism policy is an important and ongoing challenge in Mexico. This includes capacity of policy makers at each level of government to design and implement effective, joined-up tourism policies to re-invigorate the coastal tourism offer and support a more diversified model of tourism in Mexico. Developing a more diversified model of tourism in Mexico also raises different policy issues and requires tailored policy responses, compared with large-scale tourism development. A particular challenge in Mexico is to bridge the gap between central level, which is responsible for programme design, and local level, which plays a lead role in programme implementation, and in developing the product offering.

An emerging tourism development paradigm based on a growing level of product diversification, will require new skills in the areas of strategic planning, policy implementation, and both horizontal and vertical integration of action plans. At local government level it will also require a strengthened model of collaboration between local government, business groups, and civil society. The participation of the latter is important in order to ensure that the full potential for employment in an expanded local tourism sector is realised. It is important to note also that while planning for tourism and destination development will continue to require leadership and support at the central level, the tourism experience which the consumer encounters will always be delivered by people and firms at the local level.

The capacity of tourism businesses to capitalise on the country's tourism assets and develop a competitive tourism offering is a further challenge. The conventional resort development model is frequently led and operated by large and sophisticated business corporations, which usually possess a full suite of business competencies across functions such as financial management, information technology, marketing, business strategy, and forward planning.

A more diversified model of tourism and product development operates on a different basis and requires different policy supports. It opens up new entrepreneurship opportunities, including for women and indigenous populations. A more diversified industry will be characterised by a greater number of small businesses, operating in a loosely affiliated coalition. This small and loose affiliation is the mechanism that allows for greater inclusivity and employment, and so is to be valued. It offers an alternative to tourism delivered on a concentrated localised scale in one location only, and instead offers an opportunity for small businesses to prosper within a wider cluster. However, it could perpetuate a system of many small fragmented service providers persisting with less than efficient business practices.

Unlike larger firms, these small businesses may lack the means, experience and know-how required to start and run a tourism business. They may also need assistance to connect with other tourism businesses in their areas, and to access tourism value chains. Policy supports to promote entrepreneurship and assist owners of small and micro-enterprises to manage and grow their business will therefore be important, and will need to be easily accessible at local level. This is particularly the case in rural tourism initiatives based on the natural environment, local food and artisan products, for example. These are largely composed of families or entire communities and *ejidos*, which need to be accompanied in the early stages of the initiative with training and support to put in place effective planning and management systems (including creating a collective tourism fund and developing conflict resolution strategies), learn new cultural habits, communicate local customs and deliver quality tourism services to visitors.

A locally delivered programme of training and mentoring could assist in helping small businesses to develop the management skills they need, and also to identify opportunities to formalise business networks and perhaps consider opportunities for local mergers. This training would be best delivered across clusters of firms (rather than to individual firms) and is more likely to be effective if delivered on the basis of action-learning and peer learning principles drawing on the existing knowledge and insights of the participants, rather than on more formal education modules. Adult learners, particularly those running their own small business, very often learn best from peer knowledge exchange (most usefully facilitated by a skilled trainer or mentor) rather than by traditional academic models of learning.

One example of local training in action in Mexico is the FONATUR-sponsored Enterprising Women Programme (*Programa Mujeres Emprendedoras).* The programme is designed to support women entrepreneurs in tourism and addresses issues relating to entrepreneurship, creativity, strategic planning, competitive positioning, business planning, communications, and leader's attributes. Training such as this represents an early intervention in capacity building for small businesses in tourism. It always needs to be followed up, and reinforced. Following a successful pilot of this two-day training programme in in Huatulco, Oaxaca, Ixtapa-Zihuatanejo, Guerrero and Los Cabos Baja California Sur in 2015, the goal is that this programme will operate in all integrated planned resorts and tourism projects by 2018. This may also serve as a model in other destinations also. It can also support the work of the Gender Equality Unit in the Ministry of Tourism which was established in 2014 and looks to strengthen the employability of women, promote job training and empower women working in low-skilled jobs through mentoring and technical advice.

An initiative to strengthen rural tourism in the Andean region may also serve as a model to support community tourism and female empowerment in Mexico. The RUTAS initiative is based on three dimensions: tourism competitiveness, including ensuring that the quality of the supply meets demand expectations; sustainable marketing, managed by the rural communities; and strategic public-private-community partnerships, generating mutual benefits and business opportunities. It has been implemented in Ecuador, Peru, and Bolivia, and apart for its poverty-alleviation role, has the specific objective of empowering women in those communities. To be successfully applied in other contexts, there needs to be a strong commitment from the rural communities, potential for tourism inflows, and adequate access and basic infrastructure are in place prior to the programme development.

More generally, the programme of technical assistance for states and municipalities operated by FONATUR may be an effective instrument to support SMEs and build capacity in the tourism sector. FONATUR has conducted more than 183 assessments and identified more than 500 potential tourism projects through this programme. However, the application and implementation of these projects falls under the responsibility of the states and municipalities, beyond FONATUR scope. Consideration should be given as to whether, in addition to existing support programmes in project identification, project evaluation, and project financing, FONATUR could expand its capacity building operations so as to support emerging projects in tourism product diversification.

Evolving public supports and policy interventions

In the context of a new model of tourism development, the role and expertise accumulated by FONATUR over the past four decades continues to be relevant and significant in terms of Mexico's tourism development agenda. Since its creation, FONATUR's primary role has been to identify potential large-scale tourism development projects, assist and support state government in the planning of local projects, participate in the construction of basic infrastructure in tourism destinations, and attract private investment.

FONATUR's core business model has been based on long-term destination planning and development of Integrally Planned Resorts (CIPs), in addition to Integral Tourism Projects (PTIs) which have a shorter planning horizon. This has involved identifying areas with tourism potential, conducts feasibility studies (environmental, technical and financial), developing destination master plans, building and developing the required basic and tourism supply infrastructure, managing projects, planning and off-loading land supply, attracting private equity investment, and managing financing. It also provides maintenance for public spaces and operates business units.

Implementing a model of tourism development based on the creation of a more diversified product and destination offer will require an adaption of this role, with FONATUR moving to a less interventionist but no less central role. Rather, this would evolve into a supporting role guiding and informing the development of the destination and product offer, led by private sector investment, including in small scale or niche segments. Wider tourism trends also call for a more detailed examination of FONATUR integrated master plans for the development of traditional visitor services, such as large resort hotels or golf courses, particularly those slated for development near some of the country's most significant archaeological sites, not only in terms of whether this type of development is responsive to new market demand, but also whether it is financially and environmentally sustainable.

In recent years FONATUR has undergone an organisational restructure and a redefinition of its mission to support the development of tourism which is close to the market, in co-ordination with the private sector and three levels of government, under its institutional plan for 2013-18. Under this new business model, FONATUR has set out an agenda to implement strategies aligned with market needs and support large and small tourism businesses, to strengthen and diversify the tourism offer, stimulate job creation and promote the economic and social benefits from tourism. This includes strategies to update the integrated planned developments through: the creation of a portfolio of tourism projects; identification of infrastructure and tourism equipment requirements; definition of a programme to increase awareness of tourism destinations; encouragement and support for SME investments, facilitating in particular access to finance; encouragement of urban development to increase value added for tourism; advice on development or realignment of tourism projects; and measures to ensure the environmental sustainability of projects.

Recent FONATUR initiatives also point to a move in this direction and this needs to be supported and strengthened, to ensure the success of the new institutional mission and the inclusion of a multiplicity of local SME partners. This includes an increase in technical support in tourism related activities provided to SMEs and vulnerable groups, as well as technical assistance to states and municipalities, evaluation and assessment of projects for small and micro-enterprises and the entrepreneurship training for women, discussed above.

Moving to a new model of tourism development based on product and market diversification will also have implications for the Mexico Tourism Board, and will require a reorientation of its activities. The aim of the Mexico Tourism Board is to strengthen Mexico's image as a tourism destination by promoting the quality, diversity and authenticity of the offering; promote products, segments and market niches with greatest potential to encourage economic benefit; stimulate the domestic market; increase the promotion of Mexico in traditional markets; encourage source market diversification; and promote better air connectivity to open up destinations and markets.

As a consumer-facing organisation, the Mexico Tourism Board has an important role to play in promoting demand-led tourism development and informing the development of supply-side policies which are close to the market. This role will require strengthening, while the move to a more diversified, experience-based model of tourism will also require new marketing strategies. While this was not the focus of this review, Mexico's tourism marketing messages and resources will need to be reviewed and where appropriate repositioned to reflect this change in focus. The Mexico Tourism Board may also have to adjust the types of supports and resources that are made available to tourism businesses to assist them in responding to demand-side trends, particularly small and micro-enterprises.

References

Dupeyras, A. and N. MacCallum (2013), *Indicators for Measuring Competitiveness in Tourism: A Guidance Document,* OECD Tourism Papers, 2013/02, OECD Publishing. http://dx.doi.org/10.1787/5k47t9q2t923-en

OECD. (2015a). *OECD Economic Surveys: Mexico*, OECD Publishing. http://dx.doi.org/10.1787/eco_surveys-mex-2015-en

OECD. (2015b). *Economic Policy Reforms 2015: Going for Growth,* OECD Publishing, Paris.
DOI: http://dx.doi.org/10.1787/growth-2015-en

OECD (2015c). *Fostering Investment in Infrastructure*, https://www.oecd.org/daf/inv/investment-policy/Fostering-Investment-in-Infrastructure.pdf

OECD. (2013). *OECD Environmental Performance Reviews: Mexico 2013*, OECD Publishing, Paris.
DOI : http://dx.doi.org/10.1787/9789264180109-en

OECD. (2012). *Food and the Tourism Experience: The OECD-Korea Workshop*, OECD Studies on Tourism, OECD Publishing, Paris.
DOI: http://dx.doi.org/10.1787/9789264171923-en

PWC. (2014). *Analysis and Summary of the National Infrastructure Programme 2014-2018,* https://www.pwc.com/mx/es/industrias/archivo/2014-05-analysis-pni.pdf

Tapper and Font. *(2004) Tourism Supply Chains* – A report from Leeds Metropolitan University for the Travel Foundation. http://icrtourism.com.au/wp-content/uploads/2012/09/TourismSupplyChains.pdf

UNESCO. (2014) *Sustainable Tourism and location communities in the Agave Landscape of Tequila*, World Heritage No.71, http://whc.unesco.org/en/review/71/

Warwick, K. (2013). *Beyond Industrial Policy: Emerging Issues and New Trends*, OECD Science, Technology and Industry Policy Papers, No. 2, OECD Publishing. http://dx.doi.org/10.1787/5k4869clw0xp-en

Chapter 5
Financing tourism development in Mexico

Access to finance is one of the key underlying conditions required if tourism in Mexico is to deliver on its economic potential and provide skilled jobs, increase productivity and contribute to inclusive growth. Opportunities exist to better target financing to viable tourism projects of all scales and mobilise private sector funds to support more diversified model of tourism development. This chapter provides a systematic analysis of tourism-related investment and financing policies, and outlines the current framework conditions and main public actors influencing financing in the sector. It examines the effectiveness of existing mechanisms in mobilising private investment for large scale infrastructure projects, and in improving access to financing for small and micro-enterprises in particular.

Introduction

Access to finance is one of the key underlying conditions required if tourism is to deliver on its economic potential and provide skilled jobs, increase productivity and contribute to inclusive growth. Mexico has in place a comprehensive public framework to provide finance for tourism-related projects under the existing model of tourism development. However, this framework has been less successful in promoting supply-side innovation and the finance instruments will need to evolve to mobilise private sector funds to support greater product and destination diversification under a new model of tourism development. Financing tourism development and infrastructure in this context will involve the investment and maintenance of large-scale resorts as well as the development of local firms, particularly small and micro-enterprises, with different finance needs requiring different approaches.

The activity of providing finance implies matching borrowers and lenders, who usually have different desired maturities for their finance products, and entails non-linear transaction costs. This is particularly important in the tourism sector. Large investment projects usually need a long period of maturity of about five years in Mexico, while small tourism firms looking for finance usually demand lower funding amounts than which would make the project profitable for the private sector. Finding finance for tourism activities involves therefore solving supply and demand issues.

From the supply side, the banking system can provide direct and indirect instruments, the most common instruments being loans and guarantees, respectively. Non-bank finance options include capital markets, venture capital, crowdfunding and other instruments with different degrees of risk-return (e.g. asset-based finance, subordinated debt, or equity instruments). All of these finance instruments are available for tourism SMEs in Mexico, where due to the underdevelopment of the banking system and other structural reasons, large and small investment projects have a strong component of public funding. Tourism is also heavily reliant on public goods and infrastructure involving public support. From the demand side, the financial education and capacity of borrowers, along with managerial skills need to be assessed, for financing to be used in a profitable and efficient way.

This chapter provides a systematic analysis of investment and financing policies and strategies to support tourism development in Mexico. The current framework conditions influencing investment and financing decisions are outlined and the main public actors identified. The chapter examines the effectiveness of existing mechanisms in mobilising private investment to support large scale infrastructure projects and improving access to financing for SMEs, and small and micro-enterprises in particular.

Aligning investment, SME financing and tourism policy

The need to make financing available to boost economic development is recognised in the National Development Plan 2013-18, including for tourism which is identified as an important and strategic sector. The plan aims to develop the capital market and target lending to viable SMEs and infrastructure projects through Mexico's development bank system, which is also charged with developing products that promote gender equality and foster inclusive growth. It also aims to reduce informality, which is a barrier for many businesses when seeking to access external finance. The Sectoral Programme for Tourism 2013-18 in turn recognises the need to attract public and private funding to boost investment to support tourism development, while the National Infrastructure Plan 2014-18 specifies a number of projects linked to the tourism sector. The actions foreseen under these plans will benefit tourism, directly and indirectly.

Mexico has an underdeveloped banking system with high bank concentration for those who have an account and with a large proportion of people outside the financial system, particularly women. The proportion of domestic credit as a percentage of GDP in Mexico was less than 30% in 2013, compared to 70% in Colombia, 110% in Chile, and 115% in Brazil, and 246% in the United States (OECD, 2015a). Preliminary figures for 2015 show that the indicator is in the 35-36% range, on target to reach the 40% objective by 2018. Around two thirds of this entire lending portfolio is concentrated in five banks. Only 30% of women in Mexico owned a bank account in 2012, compared to 42% of men. In this context, public development banks play a strong role, as measured by both the size of assets and by geographic coverage.

Since 2014, a structural financial reform has been underway to increase the credit available for productive activities and promote financial inclusion, in addition to temporary measures to increase the flow of credit to SMEs through the development banks. The tourism sector stands to benefit from the anticipated decrease in the cost of borrowing as an outcome of the financial reform, and the proposals to increase credit to SMEs and develop of gender-specific products will benefit the whole population (Box 5.1).

Box 5.1: Four main pillars of Mexico's financial reform

Mexico's structural reform agenda aims to generate better conditions and development opportunities in the country to boost investment and sustainable economic growth. These reforms can also help to exploit Mexico's tourism potential by generating greater economic benefits through foreign currency flows, employment opportunities, regional development and supply-chain consolidation. A financial reform that strengthens regulation, increases financial competition and decreases the cost of borrowing is operating since 9 January 2014. Impacting more than 30 laws and regulations, the Financial Reform aims to increase competition in the financial sector and expand the supply of credit, facilitate the mobility of guarantees and operations, promote transparent economic conditions to benefit the users of financial services, and boost investor confidence. The domestic economy requires greater penetration of the financial sector, especially the tourism sector. According to the Mexican Foreign Trade Bank Bancomext, the Financial Reform has enhanced the role of development banks to boost growth engines in strategic sectors, including tourism. Bancomext supports the tourism sector through financing for infrastructure development and is a strategic player in financing hotel infrastructure, and adopted a counter cyclical strategy to inject liquidity into the sector in response to contracting international flows in recent years.

The four main pillars of the financial reform are to:

- **Increase bank competition**: forbids forced uptakes of other banking products when borrowing.
- **Increase credit to development banks (MXN 1 billion):** to develop infrastructure and SMEs, fender-specific products, innovation and patents.
- **Increase credit to the private sector:** to promote productive activities.
- **Increase solvency and incorporate prudential (Basel III) regulations.**

Source: National Development Plan 2013-18

These reforms and measures targeted at the whole population will benefit tourism firms and support destination and product diversification by improving credit provision to tourism entrepreneurs, including in rural areas and communities away from the sun-sand-sea destinations. However, it is important that an ex-ante assessment is conducted to verify the viability of projects and their implied fiscal cost. These measures are not cost-free and an evaluation of alternative uses of public funds to assess the optimality of decisions is usual good practice in OECD countries.

Tourism in Mexico has benefited from considerable public investment. At federal level, for example, the Ministry of Tourism channels federal subsidies for infrastructure developments at the local level through the Programme for Sustainable Regional Tourism Development and Magic Towns (PRODERMAGICO). The amount of subsidies under this programme has increased from USD 12.9 million in 2002 to USD 91.5 million in 2015, and account for around a third of the Ministry of Tourism's total annual budget (Box 5.2).

Box 5.2. Using subsidies to finance tourism infrastructure

Tourism in Mexico benefits from considerable public investment. The Programme for Sustainable Regional Tourism Development and Magic Towns (PRODERMAGICO) provides subsidies to modernise the infrastructure and equipment in tourism destinations, contribute to the conservation and preservation of natural and cultural heritage sites, and promote supply-side innovation in the tourism sector. Through this initiative the Federal Ministry of Tourism works directly with the state governments by providing economic resources to improve destinations. One characteristic of this programme is the private sector does not participate – only public funds are involved in the form of subsidies. The funding can only be used for investment in infrastructure and equipment and is allocated on a project-by-project basis. State governments submit a project proposal and funding request which is then evaluated by the Federal Ministry of Tourism in accordance with new operating rules established in 2014 to support more transparent and efficient work. Once funding has been approved, the state governments are responsible for transferring the economic resources and implementing the projects.

In 2014, the Federal Ministry provided MXN 1 494 million in funding for this programme, with the state governments providing a further MXN 1 164 million. One of the main concerns with this programme is the limited budget available to carry out and implemented the projects, although there is potential to fill this gap with alternative finance. However, inefficiencies have also resulted in budgetary amounts being left unspent in some cases. Implementation of the funding is the responsibility of local governments, with implications for the impact and return on investment from these public funds. The technical capacity of local governments is variable, while the lack of a long-term vision and political issues also has an impact. A significant share of the funding available remains focused on the maintenance and upkeep of integrated planned resort developments and tourism projects. Also, a diagnostic of infrastructure modernisation needs is not systematically available at destination level, and greater co-ordination is needed with the Ministry of Tourism.

Mexico has also had considerable success in attracting private investment and financing to support the existing model of tourism development over the last four decades, notably through the activities of the National Fund for Tourism Investment (FONATUR), which is the lead agency responsible for attracting investment for tourism development in Mexico, including the integrally planned resorts and projects. It co-ordinates the Tourism Cabinet working group on Investment Planning and Facilitation and works with other public agencies to match tourism projects with financing.

The Ministry of Economy is also involved in investment and finance decisions and has two institutions which identify and in some cases fund tourism-related activities: ProMéxico, the National Trade and Investment Promotion Agency, and INADEM, the National Institute for Entrepreneurship. The main funding actor, however, is the Ministry of Finance (SHCP), through four of its eight public development banks – the Mexican Foreign Trade Bank (Bancomext), which is the largest bank in Mexico by asset size; the National Bank of Public Works and Services (Banobras), which finances major public infrastructure projects; National Financial Institute (NAFIN), which targets new entrepreneurs and SMEs; and National Financial Institute for Agriculture, Rural, Forestry and Fisheries Development (FND), which provides for small working-capital needs in rural areas.

Public development banks play a central role in Mexico's banking system, alongside the central bank, commercial banks and public trusts. They are a key tool to promote development, solving the problem of access to finance and improving conditions for those sectors that stand out for their contribution to economic growth and employment. Public funding through development banks to tourism increased from MXN 3.2 billion in 2004 to MXN 7.5 billion in 2014. As part of the financial reform, development banks have been given more scope and funds to lend to SMEs and entrepreneurs and were required to align their mandates to promote credit to priority sectors, including tourism. This is already reflected in an increase in credit, as by 2015, development bank financing to SMEs had increased by 19% and private bank financing by 13% in real terms (Figure 5.1). Specifically for tourism-related activities, Bancomext increased credit to tourism enterprises by around 30% between 2013 and 2015.

Figure 5.1. Development bank financing, 1995-2014

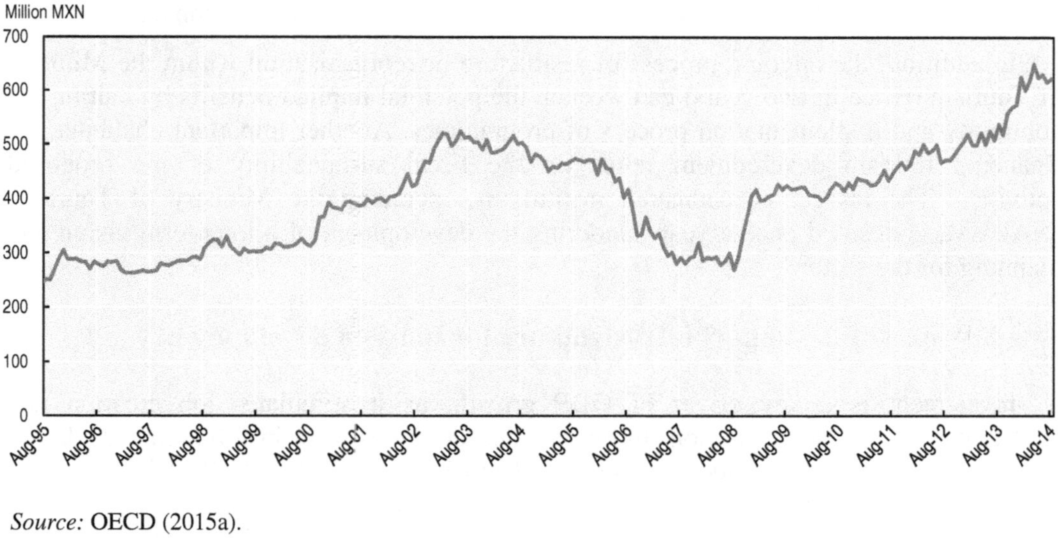

Source: OECD (2015a).

FONATUR, INADEM and ProMéxico are not financial institutions but rather identify viable projects and link them with the appropriate public development bank to access funding. Depending on the size of the private counterpart and tourism related project, FONATUR (for large-scale projects) or INADEM (for SME-led projects) channel funds through the development bank system, which in turn either lends directly (for projects larger than USD 3 million) or issue credit guarantees to promote private sector lending (for projects smaller than USD 3 million). FONATUR and INADEM have ample autonomy to co-ordinate project financing through the development bank system and also provide technical assistance.

This model of tourism financing has been functional in supporting the existing model of tourism development, notably basic infrastructure and hotel developments in coastal resort areas. However, it does not sufficiently incorporate the financing of the type of innovative and diversified tourism development projects which could support further regional development and inclusive growth. This model has also suffered from the external and internal setbacks including budget cuts and organisational restructures which have led to the suspension or delay in the implementation and delivery of results.

Moving to a new model of tourism development also raises questions about how government agencies signal tourism development opportunities to the private sector. In the well-developed model of clustered high-density resort development, this signalling issue is less challenging. In this case the model is familiar, and both government and private sector have had a lot of opportunity to develop expertise in its successful execution. Within the less familiar strategy of attempting to diversify the tourism product, and disperse it to multiple locations around the country, the signalling impact of tourism-related infrastructural development will serve as an important instrument to alert the private sector to emerging tourism opportunities.

Another challenge in aligning investment, SME financing and tourism policy is the vertical co-ordination of activities which is not always ensured, given that infrastructure activities such as road construction are decided and financed at the sub-national level. There are also well-recognised issues with the implementation of the set of reforms proposed in the National Development Plan 2013-18, including the capacity at the states and municipality level, and also in the collaboration with the private sector. SMEs that have been successful in securing financing through the various instruments do not always have the capacity to bring the project to success, lessening the potential impact.

In addition, the ongoing process of restructure or reorganisation within the Ministry of Tourism (twice in two years) can weaken the potential implied benefits by halting the continuity and implementation process of programmes. Another important challenge for financing tourism development relies on the fiscal sustainability of the proposed activities. The budget of dedicated institutions, including the Ministry of Tourism, INADEM, is decided once a year, hindering the development of a long-term vision and planning for the sector.

Mobilising investment to support infrastructure for tourism development

Investment is a key driver of GDP growth, as it stimulates job creation and contributes to income generation. In the last decade, investment in infrastructure driven by the public sector in Mexico has increased from 3.1% to 4.5% of GDP. While this has satisfied some of the infrastructure requirements for tourism, opportunities remain to better reach and take greater account of small and micro-firms in infrastructure design and planning, which are a key component of tourism-related activities.

Public investment depends on strategic government decisions and availability of resources, including fiscal capacity and access to internal markets for finance. Private investment decisions depend on expected sales, interest rates, and general macroeconomic environment. Ensuring a stable macroeconomic environment is therefore a precondition to attract investment inflows, including for tourism. Since 2013, the Bank of Mexico has consistently ensured a low annual inflation rate (below 3% since 2015).

This has boosted confidence among investors and consumers, who are now able to borrow at long-term rates below 10%, unthinkable a couple of decades earlier.

Tourism investment is an issue for countries around the world in order to stay competitive. Destinations compete not just to attract visitors, but also investors. In Mexico, the majority of investment in tourism is of domestic origin, which represented 74% on average in the period 2004-14 (CNET, 2014). However, attracting international investment can provide an additional indirect benefit, as it can enhance the image of a country as a tourism destination. Investment in tourism-related activities has been found to bring in welfare gains for Mexico at the local and aggregate level (Faber and Gaubert, 2016). Investments in infrastructure also help diversify and open up new destinations. However, they are very intensive in capital and often involve a strong component of public funding.

The National Infrastructure Plan 2014-18 proposes a total investment in tourism-related infrastructure investment portfolio of MXN 181.2 billion for the period 2014-18 from public and private sources. About 80% of this investment corresponds to new infrastructure investments related to tourism, with the purpose of diversifying the offer. This includes the revitalisation of sun-sea-sand destinations (MXN 6 billion), diversification of historical centres and colonial cities (MXN 780 million) and infrastructure support in Magic Towns (MXN 4 billion). It is planned that about MXN 112.2 billion are private sector investments. The remaining 20% of the planned budget is aimed at improving the existing tourism infrastructure in the main destinations. Financing options include federal budget (MXN 17.5 billion); subsidies (MXN 12 billion); and PRODERMAGICO state budget (MXN 4.1 billion). By 2015, total investment in tourism amounted to MXN 16.6 billion, representing 3.5 % of total investments in the economy.

Mexico has a broad set of finance options to attract private sector investments and support tourism-related investment projects at large scale. These include special long-term credits, mainly managed by FONATUR but also through independent tourism-related programmes managed by Bancomext and Banobras and specific investment vehicles for real-estate development in the capital market. Mexico also has a long-track record of using public-private partnerships for network infrastructure-related activities (transport, energy, urban development) at the sub-national level to benefit from private sector expertise in infrastructure investments that can be catalysed to tourism-related investments (Figure 5.2). These finance instruments support the existing model of tourism development, focusing on hotel and other real-estate developments, but are less supportive of a more diversified range of tourism activities.

Evolving the model for attracting private investment

The FONATUR model has been successful in attracting private investment to the integrated resort development and tourism projects in coastal areas, notably in Cancún where land value has gone up by 6 363% since 1974. However, more recent developments such as the integrated planned resort in Loreto have fallen short on expectations and struggled to attract the attention of investors and tourists, demonstrated by the observed occupancy rates. This model also blurs the line between public and private components of tourism investment, as it entails a strong public role in planning and financing tourism development.

Figure 5.2. Financing tourism-related investments

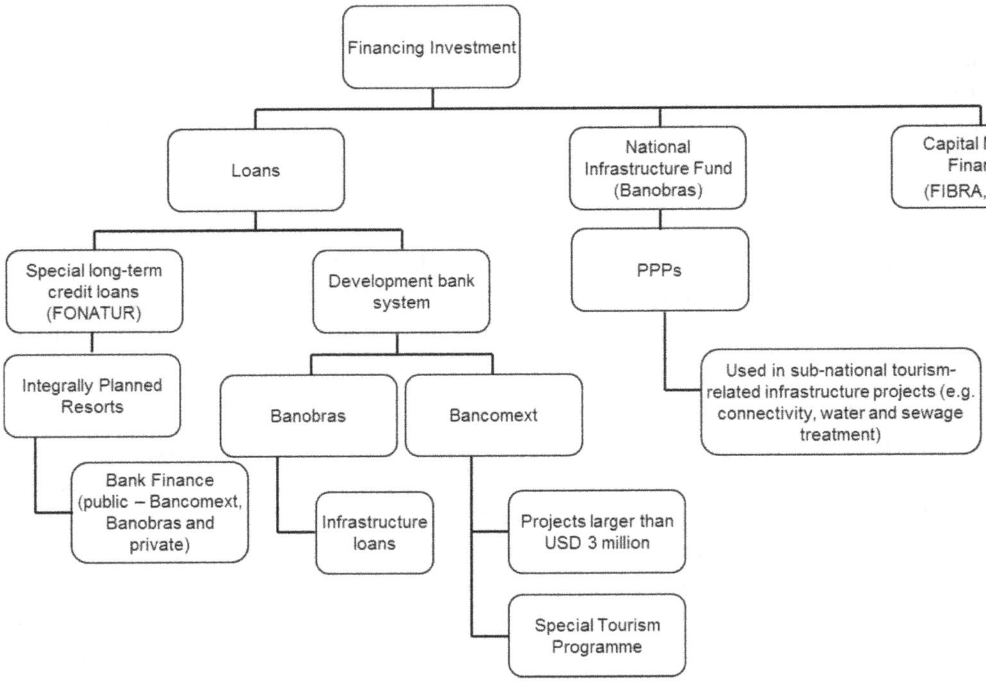

The FONATUR approach to mobilising private investment is based on a supply-side concept, with two different models. The original model involves FONATUR planning and developing a centrally planned destination in a coastal area, including constructing the necessary infrastructure using public finance, before selling it to the private sector. An alternative model, which is being used in Costa Canuva/Capomo in Nayarit for example, involves FONATUR providing the overall planning and acquiring and selling land (government or privately owned) to the private sector, which is then responsible for developing the infrastructure in accordance with a previously approved FONATUR master plan. Both approaches involve a significant public financing component (Table 5.1).

In recent years, FONATUR has had to deal with inventories unattractive to investors as a consequence of having exhausted its strategic land reserve, with rigid marketing schemes, ineffective sales strategies and inadequate investment models (PIT, 2013). There are demand-side conditions that also explain the decline in the uptake by private investors in integrated planned resorts, such as the rise in demand for more individualised visitor services and experiences, and the decline in golf. In addition, the 2008-09 financial crisis hit FONATUR finances, which added to the drop in land sales and in income generation from tourism investments. FONATUR had an outstanding debt of MXN 4 464.6 million as of November 2012.

In 2014, FONATUR underwent a financial and organisational restructure that reduced the interest rate conditions for the outstanding FONATUR debt from 276 to 151 basis points and extended repayment terms to 20 years, with a two year grace period. FONATUR has been successful in reducing the outstanding debt by 30% in 2016, from MXN 4 465 million in 2013 to MXN 3 156 million. The financial restructure gave room to FONATUR to diversify the offer including urban rehabilitation projects.

Table 5.1. FONATUR historical investment in integrated planned development, 1974-2015

	Period	MXN, constant price
CIP Cancún	1974-2015	13 929 436 417
CIP Ixtapa	1974-2015	5 622 016 352
CIP Los Cabos	1976-2015	3 666 730 369
CIP Loreto	1976-2015	5 488 646 824
CIP Huatulco	1984-2015	9 993 082 764
CIP Nayarit	2004-2013	1 993 629 479
PTI Litibú		
PTI Costacapomo		
PTI Marina Cozumel	2005-2015	629 685 650
CIP Playa Espíritu	2008-2015	6 823 113 533
Total		48 146 341 388

Base year 2016.

CIP: Integrated Planned Resort

PTI: Integrated Tourism Project.

Source: FONATUR.

The organisational reform has enabled FONATUR to ease procedures for promotion, facilitation, and environmental processes, and increase technical support in tourism-related activities for SMEs and vulnerable groups, including indigenous communities and women. FONATUR has also taken steps to enhance synergies with development banks and the private sector to strengthen and diversify the tourism offer. In 2015 FONATUR provided technical advice to 105 SME-led tourism development projects, representing about MXN 728.9 million of potential SME investments. As of July 2016, the annual target of 52 projects is on track for evaluation, of which 30 assessments were already conducted by June 2016, representing MXN 323.7 million.

Nevertheless, FONATUR has still to show how to leverage the existing model to revitalise current projects and develop new destination products that are capable of supporting regional development and are in accordance with new market trends. The finance options might be suitable to leverage the existing model of tourism development, but have not evolved to support tourism development beyond hotel and resort construction. An additional complexity is that the tourism firms and state authorities that are responsible for implementing approved projects may lack the capacity to bring the project to success, underscoring the need for financial supports to be complemented by non-financial supports.

As of 2016, FONATUR has taken steps to improve co-ordination with other agencies to follow up and support the implementation of viable SME projects, signing several agreements for technical advice on tourism-related SME projects with other government institutions, including INADEM, NAFIN and the National Commission for the Development of Indigenous Peoples (CDI), and the private sector (Confederation of National Chambers of Commerce – Services and Tourism, CONCANACO-SERVYTUR, Mexican Association of Tourism Developers, AMDETUR) in order to increase awareness and uptake of the FONATUR supports. Both financial and non-financial supports are needed to deliver on these new initiatives.

If FONATUR is to play a role in broadening the options to design and finance tourism developments beyond sun-sand-sea destinations and implementing a new model of tourism development, this re-orientation of its business model and activities needs to be given more support. While FONATUR has undertaken to be the facilitator of demand-led private investments, it has not yet shown a clear evolution of its role and activities in boosting new products or new types of developments. To solidify and ensure a long-term vision for FONATUR, more institutional support can be given, reinforced on the side of FONATUR by enhanced evidence-based assessments of its project developments.

Expanding credit for tourism investment projects through the development banks

Credit loans are the standard instrument to finance tourism, and the main finance option available to FONATUR to leverage private investments for integrated resort developments. Both the development bank system and private banks participate in these funding activities. In addition, Bancomext and Banobras have special programmes for the development of tourism related projects. These include basic infrastructure development, through Banobras, and a special tourism development programme offering hybrid instruments, through Bancomext.

FONATUR offers long-term credit loans with a maturity up to eight years at market interest rates. About a quarter of the FONATUR tourism loan portfolio is covered by Bancomext, with the remainder shared among the commercial banks, including BBVA Bancomer (20%), Banorte (14%) and Santander (11%), and the capital market, which accounts for less than 10%.

Bancomext is the largest public development bank in Mexico and has a portfolio of loans larger than all of Mexico's commercial banks combined. It is a strategic player in financing hotel infrastructure in particular. Bancomext adopted a counter cyclical strategy to inject liquidity into the sector, in response to contracting international flows and falling commercial bank finance for tourism projects following a downturn in Mexico's lodging industry between 2006-09. It increased its share in the credit market for tourism real-estate projects, and provided financing relief to meet the needs of investors.

Bancomext is a key partner and catalyst for the promotion of investment in FONATUR-sponsored integrated resort developments. Bancomext facilitates access to credit through a variety of instruments, including direct loans, loan syndication, guarantees and letters of credit. During the period 2010-14, Bancomext increased both the credit provided to, and the number of companies financed in, the tourism sector. This has supported the existing model of large-scale tourism development.

Beyond its role as a FONATUR partner, Bancomext also offers two other funding modalities for tourism-related projects: direct finance for investment projects larger than USD 3 million, and indirect finance including credit guarantees and second-tier loans for projects up to USD 3 million. Under the National Development Plan 2013-18, Bancomext has a specific programme for tourism, which covers loans with long-term maturity of up to 17 years and alternative finance instruments, including syndicated debt and club deals. The targeted sectors within tourism are: sun-sand-sea, business, luxury, megaprojects, sport and medical tourism.

Between 2007 and 2014, Bancomext increased its tourism portfolio balance by more than 400%, injecting MXN 32.8 billion in loans. In 2014, Bancomext reached out to over 1 000 tourism firms by providing MXN 17.7 billion through direct lending and MXN 1.9 billion through guarantees via commercial banks. The 2015 balance of Bancomext portfolio to the tourism sector was MXN 22.5 billion. Measured in hotel rooms, Bancomext's financing activities have resulted in an estimated additional 12 000 new hotel rooms per year since 2013. In addition, Bancomext put in place a contingent line of credit and lent MXN 3.5 billion in the six months following the passage of Hurricane Odile in September 2014. This was part of a wider response strategy from the development bank system to help reactivate the area and to support tourism businesses in Baja California South.

Banobras is the public bank in charge of leveraging private investments in basic infrastructure through public-private partnerships, most of them conducted at sub-national level. It is an important FONATUR partner in providing the financing for development of the basic infrastructure required for large-scale integrated resort development, including roads, airports and waste treatment facilities. Banobras provides access to credit for both public and private tourism projects through a variety of finance and non-finance services, including project financing, financial restructuring, guarantees, trust management, and specialised technical services. It particularly supports sub-national governments.

Between December 2012 and May 2015, Banobras extended credit for tourism development projects for over USD 9 billion, under three modalities: public-private partnerships for the development of connectivity projects to promote tourism (USD 2.9 billion); credits to the private sector to develop tourism projects (USD 240 million); and national and sub-national government financing to develop basic infrastructure and public works for USD 5.8 billion.

Bancomext and Banobras also finance tourism development projects at the sub-national level with own funds as well as channelling federal funds to ear-marked projects, with the objective of transversally impacting economic growth. Direct credit loans to firms irrespective of size are offered to states and municipalities. The uptake varies by state, depending on inter-related dimensions. Bancomext has channelled federal funds targeting the economic recovery of southeast Mexico, for example. This programme supports the operational and financial sustainability of the tourism infrastructure in Chiapas, Guerrero and Oaxaca by providing finance to tourism companies and related activities. The programme offers long-term loans ranging from MXN 5 million to MXN 60 million for up to five years at preferential rates for working capital, machinery and equipment, and up to ten years for building acquisition, reconstruction, or renovation. Up to 80% of the loans are guaranteed by the Federal Government.

Bancomext second-tier lending to tourism-related projects at the sub-national level targets: working capital and acquisition of fixed assets for enterprises linked to tourism; hotel acquisition, expansion, remodelling, and furnishing; restructuring and sustainable hotel improvements (technological, environmental, energy saving, fuel and water); brand-up grades; and medical tourism, including construction and equipment of hospitals and clinics. Quintana Roo (22%) receives the highest proportion of credit allocated to states, followed by Sonora (14%), Hidalgo (7%), Querétaro and Michoacán (6% respectively). From the private counterparts, the most active lending bank is Banorte (48%), followed by Santander (31%) and Banamex (10%). Note, however, that a room hotel key in Cancún is more costly than in other areas, such as Guanajuato in the automotive corridor in central Mexico. Hotels in Cancún also tend to be larger in size than hotels in other regions, due to demand-side reasons.

Apart from financing traditional working capital needs, Bancomext is the implementing partner for an innovative pilot programme to finance sustainable solar water heating in tourism hotels, for example. This pilot is being implemented in Yucatán, Quintana Roo and Campeche since 2015, with Bancomext providing MXN 16 billion through a guarantee fund. The programme provides finance and technical advice for the acquisition and installation of solar panels and is an initiative of the Federal Government, the Secretariat of Energy (SENER), the National Commission for the Efficient Use of Energy (CONUEE) and the United Nations Development Programme (UNDP). This is an example of how Bancomext can expand and diversify its credit offer to attend new finance needs, beyond hotel construction.

One potential good practice example of public support for tourism development in Mexico is that of another federal OECD country. Canada offers public financial support in co-ordination with sub-national governments and the private sector to promote regional tourism development, including the integration of SMEs in the tourism value chain. The main uptakes from this experience are in the framework conditions for public participation and the interaction with other key players, as well as in the role of public intervention in supporting demand-led developments. Canada has set up a strategy that incorporates all levels of government and the private sector to boost productivity in tourism, offering support from public banks for direct and indirect tourism-related activities, in particular SMEs that could serve a good example of horizontal and vertical co-ordination (Box 5.3).

Box 5.3. Financing tourism to support regional development in Canada

In Canada, financial support for the tourism sector is provided in partnership with other levels of government, with Aboriginal communities, and other private actors. In 2008-09, federal direct support for the tourism sector amounted to CAD 530 million for product development and tourism infrastructure such as convention centres, and CAD 113 million for tourism marketing. Furthermore, CAD 782 million was spent on artistic, cultural and sports-related activities that have an indirect impact on tourism. The Business Development Bank of Canada has invested CAD 1.97 billion in the tourism sector. Further support is provided from the direct control and operation of iconic tourism attractions and programmes to market Canada as a destination (Industry Canada, 2011). In particular for SMEs, which amount to 98% of tourism firms, Canada offers strategic promotion activities, training, market readiness, quality assurance and mentoring programmes in a co-ordinated fashion across the three levels of government.

Source: Canada (2013), Industry Canada (2011).

Leveraging public-private partnerships to finance tourism-support infrastructure

Public-private partnerships (PPPs) can be leveraged to finance public infrastructure projects required to support tourism. PPPs are long term contractual arrangements between the government and a private partner whereby the private sector delivers and funds public services using a capital asset, sharing the associated risks. The OECD supports the use of PPPs whenever they bring in value for money and has developed a set of principles for their governance (OECD, 2012). The main reasons to foster the use of PPPs are to harness the expertise of the private sector in the specific area for development and to reduce public spending (OECD/IDB, 2014). PPPs may also help ensure that tourism developments are aligned with market demands.

PPPs are generally used to finance basic public infrastructure (e.g. road construction, water treatment facilities). They may be less suitable for other types of infrastructure development which are more commercial in nature (such as hotel developments), and where the rationale for public intervention might be blurred. One exception here may be the construction and operation conference centres and convention facilities, which require significant upfront investment, or where the development of leisure facilities can also cater to the local population. Given the supply-side focus on tourism development in Mexico, greater private sector involvement may help increase awareness of the demand-side objectives and interests and contribute to ensure the sustainability and efficiency of projects.

Box 5.4. PPPs for infrastructure development at the sub-national level

The Programme for the Promotion of Public-Private Partnerships in Mexican States (PIAPPEM) is an initiative from the Multilateral Investment Fund of the Inter-American Development Bank. It aims to provide technical and financial support to create the technical, legal, and institutional framework for the development of public-private partnership projects at state level through alternative mechanisms to traditional public investment to infrastructure and services. PPPs can help governments to reduce the budget required for the development of large-scale projects, while benefitting from the experience of the private sector on the specific sector (e.g. transport infrastructure, construction). In recent years in Mexico, the Federal Government has developed PPP projects under different modalities (e.g. concessions, service provision projects, projects for long-term productive infrastructure). Also, at the state level, Oaxaca, Mexico City, Zacatecas, and Mexico City have developed public investment projects with the participation of the private sector under concession schemes, service contracts and public works and, more recently, under the model of Projects for provision of Services. The PIAPPEM programme has worked with 13 of 32 Mexican States. The 2014 Infrascope report from the Economist Intelligence Unit (EIU) evaluates the performance of PPP in Mexico at the sub-national level. It situates Mexico in the upper group of Latin American countries and ranks it as "developed" for implementing PPPs. However, the EIU finds that Mexican institutions are highly fragmented, and each sector of government is responsible for the planning, implementation and supervision of PPP projects. Other challenges identified relate to institutional capacity, the legal and regulatory framework, contract design, and financing issues.

Source: http://www.piappem.org/index.html and EIU (2014).

In Mexico, the Public-Private Partnerships Law 2012 regulates PPP projects at the federal level, and at the state level when the federal state finances more than half of the project. The law simplifies the regulatory framework, facilitates contract adjustment, reinforces creditor rights, and ensures that projects are structured according to the principle of reasonable project-risk allocation. Efficiently using PPPs requires strong governance and solid regulations.

Financing infrastructure development through PPPs is a key approach adopted in the National Development Plan 2013-18 and the National Infrastructure Programme 2014-18, especially for tourism-related projects. Mexico has experience using PPPs to promote long-term private participation in infrastructure investment at both at the federal and sub-national level, including the development of basic infrastructure supporting tourism in Yucatán. The public bank channelling PPP investments is Banobras (Box 5.4).

France's experience mobilising public-private investment for tourism development highlights the importance of a long-term investment strategy and different approaches. Three distinct types of projects are supported, each with its own funding modality. To finance commercial tourism developments, a real-estate fund will initially invest in quality accommodation in areas with potential for development, seeking institutional investors to develop the project. To finance basic tourism infrastructure, public investments will be matched with private co-investors. Finally, to finance the development and diversification of tourism related activities by SMEs, public participation from Bpifrance will seek to leverage private participation (Box 5.5).

Box 5.5. Mobilising investment for tourism development in France

In October 2015, France has implemented a new integrated initiative led by the group Caisse des Dépôts (the national long-term investment agency) whose ambition is to mobilise nearly EUR 1 billion over the next five years to support the tourism economy, with three main targets: 1) accommodation; 2) equipment and infrastructure; and 3) businesses. This new platform for investment dedicated to the development of the tourism sector in France is composed of three main actions, with distinct investment aims and targets:

1. Investment for accommodation – The creation of this real estate fund (Foncière de Paris), open to investors, aims to support capacity improvement and quality accommodation in tourism destinations. The fund will primarily invest in physical infrastructure for the construction or the renovation of hotels and tourist residences in destinations with a strong potential for development. A fundraising strategy will be launched targeting institutional investors with a target of EUR 500 million, with the Caisse des Dépôts participating in the initial investment.
2. Investment for equipment and infrastructure – Caisse des Dépôts capital will be mobilised for investment in tourism infrastructure facilities (marinas, exhibition centres, spas, cultural tourism attractions etc.) in all types of territories/destinations, including for accommodation that would not be targeted by the specific fund (see above). The funding will be close to EUR 400 million and investment will involve private co-investors in each case.
3. Investment for tourism SMEs – A capital development fund (France Tourism Investment) has been created by the public investment bank (Bpifrance) for tourism SMEs, with a proportion of investments earmarked to financing innovation and e-tourism. This fund will be open to third party contributors and fundraising of between EUR 80 million and EUR 100 million is expected with a commitment of Bpifrance for EUR 50 million.

Source: OECD (2016c) based on Ministry of Foreign Affairs and International Development, Bpifrance, Caisse des Dépôts.

Financing infrastructure investments with PPPs poses significant challenges and many countries have opted out of this option, including several states in Germany, because once the PPP has been signed off, the government loses bargaining power in the renegotiation of the contract terms. However, to afford not to use such instrument, a government needs to have an alternative funding source to enable the construction of the required infrastructure project.

Facilitating tourism development with Foreign Direct Investment

Foreign direct investment (FDI) is a facilitator of economic development and is sought after for the anticipated benefits. This not only includes the direct contribution to GDP growth, but also the diffusion of technology and expertise, and the creation of linkages with domestic firms, in particular SMEs. Thus, while FDI is a financing approach suitable for the development of new commercial large-scale tourism projects, it also has the potential to indirectly benefit tourism SMEs. ProMéxico works with the Ministry of Tourism and FONATUR to identify and promote tourism foreign investment in tourism-related projects. ProMéxico has significant in-house tourism expertise and is mandated to promote investment in large-scale projects, including large commercial hotel and resort developments.

Since 1999, total FDI inflows to Mexico have represented on average 2.7% of GDP, amounting to USD 28 billion in 2015. However, FDI inflows are subject to the macroeconomic conditions of the source and the host country, as evidenced by the decrease in FDI inflows from the two most important source countries, United States and Spain, in the aftermath of the global financial crisis. According to the Sectoral Programme for Tourism 2013-18, FDI investments in tourism-related projects decreased from USD 435 million in 2004 to USD 106 million in 2012.

FDI in tourism-related activities can have an impact on a number of dimensions: on demand patterns, as tourism-related multi-national enterprises are said to have enhanced country images as tourism destinations; on capital, technology and skills, such as the diffusion of technology through staff movement to local firms; on human resources, as tourism-related multi-national enterprises are said to generate more employment than local firms; on local firms, by establishing local linkages with suppliers and distributors; and on balance of payment impacts through the revenues spent by tourists (UNCTAD, 2007).

Nevertheless, the opportunities for productive business linkages are contingent on the type of FDI attracted. There are some policy options that can enhance value creation of FDI investments: for example, increasing linkage prospects with local firms by stipulating the use of local inputs, transferring managerial skills and techniques, and supporting local firms with finance and non-finance products in order to be able to reach international standards (UNCTAD, 2007).

The OECD Policy Framework for Investment (PFI) (2015b) notes that investment promotion and facilitation policies need to put the focus on the activities undertaken in the value chain, rather than on individual industries. Tourism development implies a cluster of different activities and industries, and can especially be beneficial for knowledge transfers, including for SMEs. The PFI discourages the use of tax policies for infrastructure investment in tourism, given that the location-specific characteristic of the investment can make it profitable even with a higher-than average tax rate.

For most countries, the share of FDI in tourism is low compared to FDI penetration in other sectors, or to domestic investment in tourism (UNCTAD, 2007). This is also the case in Mexico. There are opportunities to develop (mainly backward) linkages with FDI investments in tourism-related activities, for example, through developing a reliable network of local suppliers, making links with local tourist guides; or the potential development of local gastronomy. This would support regional development, stimulate job creation through SME development and promote more inclusive growth.

The OECD (2013b) has identified that FDI investments in Mexico represent a potential market for Mexico's SME suppliers, leveraging new technology and managerial techniques, provided that linkages are built. Moreover, these local linkages can help diversify the offer of products, even within traditional sun-sand-sea destinations. A quality certification of suppliers can back up their integration in value chains, for example. FONATUR could potentially play a role in facilitating and promoting FDI investments that consider a development dimension and leverage local development, through the inclusion of SMEs in the value chain. There is also a potential role for

INADEM to provide non-financial support to local suppliers of multi-national tourism enterprises, and to link them with suitable finance instruments. Delivering on this will require co-ordination between these two institutions.

Box 5.6. Tourism Investment Programme in Australia

Tourism Australia and Austrade are working in partnership to deliver a tourism investment attraction programme. The partnership is delivering on its objective to generate strong international investment interest in tourism assets. The Australian Government offers a range of services to assist foreign investors identify new investment opportunities in Australia's tourism sector (www.tourisminvestment.com.au/), including: initial co-ordination of all investment enquiries and assistance; identification of suitable investment locations and partners in Australia; market and industry intelligence and investment opportunities; advice on Australian government programmes and approval processes; and information on the Australian business and regulatory environment.

Through the Tourism Major Project Facilitation (TMPF) service, established in 2012, significant tourism projects are assigned a case manager to assist with navigating the Australian Government approvals process. TMPF case managers can provide potential investors with guidance on: identifying the range of federal approvals required and facilitating introductions and meetings with the relevant approving agencies; providing support and expertise on government programmes and processes; assisting investors to access relevant Australian Government support programmes; and helping broker solutions to problems that arise during the course of obtaining approvals. Once an investor has an interest in a specific site, location or opportunity, State and Territory Governments can assist by providing investors with: detailed intelligence on specific sites within the state; advice and assistance on planning approvals and preferential zoning; and information on industry assistance programmes, employment and training incentives. Government and industry continue to work together to reduce investment barriers and streamline regulation in order to encourage investment interest and commitment to the Australian market.

Source: OECD (2016a).

Compared to the interventionist role played by FONATUR in tourism investment, the Australian Government's role has been more that of an investment facilitator. Australia's long-term national tourism strategy, Tourism 2020, contemplates integrating public and private finance, along with technical assistance, skills improvements and regulatory simplification to increase productivity and capacity to benefit from the growing demand from Asia. The tourism strategy has set up an action plan for each of these areas, with key deliverables and measurable instruments to assess the implementation of the plan (Australia Government, 2009). Following the initial phase of tourism facilitation of FDI inflows, Australia has started analysing the regional distribution of FDI (Box 5.6). Through the Australian example, FONATUR can assess and consider the move to a less interventionist role in tourism facilitation.

Other international experiences also show how public finance is being use to mobilise private sector investment and support big investment projects. The European Fund for Strategic Investments (EFSI) aims to unlock EUR 315 billion in additional investments over a three-year period, with an initial EUR 16 billion from the European Union and EUR 5 billion from the European Investment Bank. While tourism is not specifically identified under the plan, eligible tourism projects include transport infrastructure, energy efficiency of hotels and tourism resorts, the revitalisation of brownfield sites for recreational purposes, supporting tourism SMEs, and the setting up of investment platforms dedicated to tourism. Public funds are being used to finance tourism and mobilise private sector investment in the European Union, for example, where there is an initiative to foster infrastructure and innovation investment and support SMEs with indirect instruments (credit guarantees). The initiative incorporates ICTs to boost productivity and offers public support to finance tourism development.

Creating capital market instruments for tourism real-estate developments

The capital market offers a further instrument to attract private investment in tourism. Similar to the credit market, the capital market in Mexico is likewise underdeveloped compared to other economies of similar GDP per capita. That said, capital market finance has boomed in recent years due to internal and external reasons, including macroeconomic conditions, the finance reform and previous regulatory modifications. The underlying conditions for the development of capital market finance have been created by the public sector, but its uptake is private sector-led and sought after for its expected rate, not by its development objective.

As part of the initiatives to consolidate flexible financial instruments for infrastructure projects, the Mexican Stock Exchange has created two financial instruments primarily targeting institutional investors. While not tourism-specific, these new instruments have boosted the participation of domestic and foreign private investors in the tourism real-estate market.

The Infrastructure and Real Estate Trusts (FIBRAs) are along the lines of the US real-estate trusts and facilitate investment in real-estate by retirement funds, insurance companies and the general public. FIBRAs have a market capitalisation of USD 10 million, and have been used to invest in business hotels along the industrial and agro-industrial corridors in central Mexico. These investments are private sector-led and provide a monthly yield. The public sector has contributed to facilitating the underlying conditions supporting these instruments, including the capital market reform, ensuring equal treatment in terms of taxation, and providing judicial certainty.

Certificates of Capital Development (CKDs) are a financial security instrument intended to finance infrastructure development projects, or for the acquisition of companies. CKDs are sought by short-term investors. The Mexican Stock Exchange administers CKDs, and as with any security, their performance is linked to that of the underlying asset. As of 2015, Retirement Investment Funds (AFOREs) had invested MXN 80.9 million in 40 CKDs and MXN 42.5 billion in FIBRAs (Hinojosa, 2015; BMV, 2016).

A higher uptake of these instruments is reported in revitalising hotel developments, rather than in developing new niche markets. With debt instruments, the bank can absorb the risk through guarantees, but these capital market instruments transfer the risk to the investor. As a result, the use of CKDs to finance infrastructure construction (as opposed to infrastructure maintenance) is not widespread (Hinojosa, 2015). Other challenges include the potential for currency fluctuations to impact on yields, given the fact that business hotel transactions are usually conducted in Mexican pesos while the investors conduct their transactions in US dollars. Last, the instruments alone will not support tourism product diversification.

Against a backdrop of steady top-line growth, the hotel investment climate has resurged in recent years, with capital flowing into the sector and hotel transaction volumes topping USD 600 million in 2013, up from a low of under USD 100 million in 2009. For 2014, the volumes are USD 700 million in hotel acquisition from foreign investors, with FIBRAs and CKDs accounting for 25% and 50% of business hotel acquisition volume in 2012 and 2013 respectively.

Note, however, that FIBRAs and CKDs target investments where there is a homogeneous product and almost no segmentation of business activities (e.g. business hotels). They would be unsuitable to fund all-inclusive style hotels, where lodging, gastronomy, and other activities are combined in the room price. Moreover, the high fragmentation of Mexican hotel ownership, where about 60-70% of hotels do not belong to an international chain, prevents co-ordination of activities, policies and procedures, and the uptake of their portfolio by secondary instruments such as the FIBRAs.

Supporting access to financing for tourism SMEs

SMEs have a unique potential in the tourism sector, as the consumer comes to the producer enabling SMEs to be part of the global economy. According to the Sectoral Programme for Tourism 2013-18, small and micro-enterprises account for 99.8% of all firms in tourism-related activities in Mexico and generate 1.5 million jobs, or 86.3% of total employment in these sectors. TSA data shows that SMEs contribute 69% of total income in the tourism sector in Mexico, while the vast majority (87.4%) of tourism firms in Mexico employ five workers or less (Figure 5.3).

The proportion of self-employment is 64% indicating that for many, tourism entrepreneurship may be an economic necessity rather than a business opportunity. This suggests that there is room to improve productivity in the sector. Moreover, more than half of these firms operate in the informal sector and are therefore unable to access available finance sources. While tourism SMEs are in general less capital intensive (excluding connectivity infrastructure), the heterogeneity of the sector means that different SMEs face different financing challenges, ranging from the young and innovative firms such as application developers for city guides, to the more traditional hotel resorts, restaurants, or recreational services.

Tourism SMEs in Mexico thus face the constraints of being extremely small, with a significant portion operating in the shadow economy away from the existing credit opportunities including from the public sector. Other constraints in accessing external finance include the lack of a financial culture and difficulties justifying incomes streams as firms generally transact in cash and do not register business flows, as well as the high proportion of family businesses with limited management skills. A lack of financial knowledge to know what the most suitable financial instrument would be can also be a barrier. Tourism entrepreneurs often lack collateral to guarantee their borrowing needs, due to the intangible nature of their products, while the small scale of funding usually demanded may be insufficient to match the bank transaction costs due to screening and monitoring. Supply and demand side factors thus explain the finance constraints of tourism SMEs and entrepreneurs (ADB-OECD, 2014).

The characteristics of tourism SMEs in Mexico make them unlikely to be financed by the private sector. Therefore, the role of public development banks regains importance in this context, provided that viable tourism SME projects are financed at market interest rates. The use of subsidised rates brings the risk of crowding out the private sector on one hand, and of being a fiscal burden on the other if, for example, there are no available studies proving that such financing is optimal to other alternatives. Existing grant programmes for SMEs have so far lacked an institutionalised evidence-based evaluation system, which would allow for a gradual improvement of project targeting and selection. The term "viable" is also important, signalling that the only reason for the project not to be financed by the private sector is the high transaction costs.

Figure 5.3. Size of tourism enterprises by number of employees

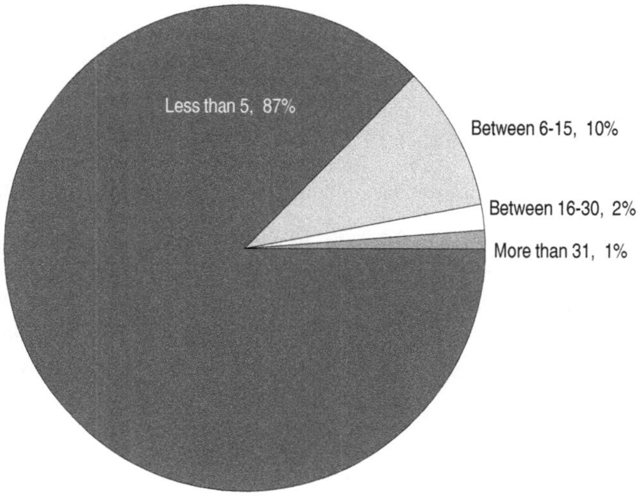

Source: Tourism Satellite Account (2016).

Financing instruments supporting tourism SMEs

The most common external finance instruments for SMEs and entrepreneurs are loans and credit guarantees. To solve the finance constraints of small firms, most OECD countries have a dedicated public institution to fund or channel funds for formal SMEs and entrepreneurs, bringing in financial or economic additionality. The public intervention can be direct (e.g. loans) or indirect (e.g. credit guarantees) and the form of the institution can vary depending on the context. For this public intervention to be sustainable and not crowd-out the private sector, the projects to be financed have to be viable at market rates (OECD, 2013b). The OECD is working to streamline and promote good institutional practices in this regard (Box 5.7). Within this framework, tourism SMEs generally have access to the same financial instruments available for all SMEs irrespective of their sector, sometimes supplemented by specific targeted initiatives.

The main public finance actors for tourism SMEs in Mexico are Bancomext, NAFIN, and FND. As part of the financial reform, development banks in Mexico have been given more scope and funds to lend to SMEs and entrepreneurs, including tourism firms. However, given that 97% of tourism SMEs in Mexico are of micro-size with finance needs well below the instruments offered by Bancomext and NAFIN, their financing needs are not sufficiently supported under the current framework.

Bancomext technically has the mandate to support tourism SMEs, which in theory can gain access to credit using the Bancomext modalities discussed previously through the commercial system under the modalities discussed previously (second-tier loans for up to USD 3 million through the commercial system, and direct lending for projects requiring more than USD 3 million). However, tourism SMEs finance needs, and micro-enterprises in particular, are smaller than those offered by Bancomext which in effect continues to support larger scale tourism investments and traditional product offering.

Box 5.7: Institutional and financial characteristics of public development banks

An OECD study on the role of public financial institutions (public development banks and investment agencies) in financing SMEs and entrepreneurs identified a set of good practices along two main dimensions:

Institutional

- The Institution should have a clear mandate, with local relevance, to reduce uncertainty for the private sector, which can expand activities without being concerned by unfair competition (provisions of funds at rates lower than the market).
- The Board of Governors should have expertise and knowledge. There should be transparent performance management. A government-appointed board presents the risk of political interference, and poses a set of conflicts for the government, which must navigate between its supervisory role and the business role of the institution, and between managerial incentives, and the pursuance of development activities.

Financial

- Regarding the financial dimension, the Institution should identify the binding market failure that prevents SMEs and entrepreneurs from accessing finance in the market, and decide on the provision (direct or indirect).
- The institution should have a risk management capacity team, able to identify the viable project to which to lend.
- There should be caps on the fiscal support for the development role of the Institution, with transparent disclosure of the source of funding (when subsidising activities), and consider charging fees instead of higher interest rates for riskier SMEs.
- The role of such Institution should be complementary to that of the private sector.

Source: ADB-OECD (2014).

One initiative which goes some way to addressing this limitation is the Improve Your Hotel (*Mejora tu hotel*) programme introduced in 2016. This programme offers long-term loans for up to 10 years at competitive rates, channelled through the commercial bank system, with the guarantee of Bancomext. It has been co-designed by the Ministry of Tourism, Bancomext, and the Ministry of Finance and Public Credit (SHCP) and aims to increase the productivity of the sector. At time of writing, eleven commercial banks participate in this programme.

NAFIN offers credit loans for tourism SMEs which have participated in FONATUR technical assistance programme and have a FONATUR-validated investment plan. Similar to the Improve Your Hotel programme, NAFIN foresees the launch of a programme targeting SMEs in the gastronomy sector.

Even where these finance instruments reach tourism SMEs, they remain focused on the existing model of hotel-related finance support. There is a need to actively promote and encourage instruments and supports which are suitable for new destinations, or support a more strategic approach targeting diversified tourism products.

The provision of micro-loans to support rural tourism initiatives provides an interesting example of how smaller-scale lending is supporting nature-based tourism in regional areas. FND provides both direct and indirect financing through non-bank institutions to small firms for small infrastructure development projects and alternative income generating activities such as services and trading. From 2009 to 2014, FND granted USD 26.7 million in credits to the development of rural tourism in Mexico. In 2013-14, 71% of the total disbursements have been directed to this sector.

Direct lending accounts for 65% of the resources, with the rest channelled through financial intermediaries. FND offers small loans up to USD 45 000 for entrepreneurs in rural communities will less than 50 000 inhabitants. The strategy has shown high repayment rates and an average loan of USD 40 565. These results signal that the target populations receive loans that are in accordance to their financial capacity and that loans are used to finance short-term operational needs.

These loans provide economic and financial additionality and enable the small firms to enter value chains as suppliers of local products. Entering value chains strengthens the institutional value of the SMEs and reinforces links with the formal sector. The Regional Development Programme 2014-18 for the South-southeast region has identified the need to develop local suppliers in the tourism market, which in general contribute to only 5% of tourism market inputs.

Beyond bank credit, asset-based finance is an alternative and more flexible technique which is widely used in tourism-related activities for working capital needs. Factoring, leasing, and purchase order discounting are also extensively used in Mexico, solving partially the lack of access to bank credit by many tourism SMEs, and enabling them to be part of a value chain, where the bigger firm is the guarantor for the SME credit. The OECD (2013b) notes that Mexican SMEs are overly dependent on trade credit, with 7 out of 10 Mexican pesos coming from that source; 1.7 from commercial banks and 1.6 from development banks. Young and innovative SMEs can benefit from equity instruments, although some business owners are reluctant to cede firm or ownership control (Table 5.2).

In Mexico, most of these instruments are available for tourism SMEs, which face special challenges due to the service-based nature of tourism, potential cash flow seasonality and lack of collateral. NAFIN offers alternative finance instruments as part of the "Value Chains Programme" (*Cadenas Productivas*), for firms belonging to a value chain and with annual turnover of more than MXN 250 million. Bancomext offers factoring services for exporting firms, along with letters of credit and export credit insurance for all firms, including tourism SMEs. Bancomext also offers hybrid instruments including syndicated, co-lending, and club deals loans for up to 50% of the total deal, to finance tourism development projects, but these are more appropriate for large firms.

Mexico thus offers tourism SMEs with the same range of finance instruments available in OECD countries. However, the characteristics of tourism SMEs make them unlikely to be financed by the private sector, while high levels of informality mean that a significant share of tourism businesses cannot access available financing supports. The relevance of these instruments for tourism SMEs depends on demand-side conditions, like the financial education of the firm manager, as well as firm size. It has also been noted that Bancomext loan thresholds are in practice not catering the needs of the smaller segment within tourism SMEs, whose finance needs are much smaller.

Table 5.2. Alternative external financing techniques for SMEs and entrepreneurs

Low Risk/Return		Medium Risk/Return	High Risk/Return
Asset-Based Finance	Alternative Debt	"Hybrid" Instruments	Equity Instruments
Asset-based lending	Corporate Bonds	Subordinated Loans/Bonds	Private Equity
Factoring	Securitised Debt	Silent Participations	Venture Capital
Purchase Order Finance	Covered Bonds	Participating Loans	Business Angels
Warehouse Receipts	Private Placements	Profit Participation Rights	Specialised Platforms for Public Listing of SMEs
Leasing	Crowdfunding (debt)	Convertible Bonds	Crowdfunding (equity)
		Bonds with Warrants	
		Mezzanine Finance	

Source: OECD (2014a).

Available supports also largely target the established tourism development model of financing hotel-related projects. More should be done to promote innovation and entrepreneurship to support product and destination diversification. For tourism SMEs, access to finance is only part of the story – non-financial supports are also important to facilitate uptake and support efficient use of available financing. The OECD (2013b) assessment of SME Policies in Mexico identified the need to increase awareness, take up and effectiveness of funding opportunities by Mexican SMEs.

Promoting tourism entrepreneurship

Established in 2012, the National Institute for Entrepreneurship (INADEM) is mandated to support and facilitate the development of SMEs, including micro-enterprises. It does this by raising awareness, linking firms to finance opportunities in the banking system and channelling federal funds through a broad range of finance instruments, including subsidies, debt, credit guarantees, and equity. INADEM provides a comprehensive support for SMEs in all sectors, including tourism, and also offers technical assistance and expertise for specific subsectors.

Although INADEM does not target tourism SMEs specifically, the aim of the institution is to boost productivity and entrepreneurship across all strategic sectors, including tourism-related activities if the project involves entrepreneurial skills, incorporation into value chains, or it is productivity enhancing (Figure 5.4). INADEM works with several states to support strategic SME projects identified under the National Development Plan 2013-18 and the Regional Development Programmes 2014-18. These include tourism projects such as the promotion of adventure tourism in Chiapas.

Figure 5.4. INADEM finance options for tourism entrepreneurial projects

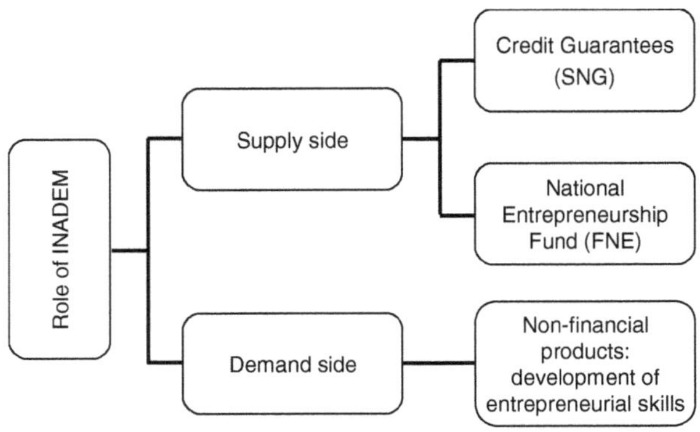

INADEM has successfully expanded access to entrepreneurship opportunities for the Mexican population. However, the INADEM annual budget allocation is insufficient to cater to the volume of viable projects that seek finance. In 2015, INADEM had a planned budget of MXN 8 billion, which was then cut to MXN 6.5 billion. The four modalities of public financing offered by INADEM include: funding contests, where SMEs apply for co-participation funds through subsidies; strategic partnerships between the federal and state governments to promote regional development programmes; co-funding activities at the request of states, provided the regional project is suitable and in concordance with the strategic national programme; and specific presidential initiatives, or initiatives from the Ministry of Economy.

Credit guarantees

One of the most important instruments in Mexico to finance SMEs and entrepreneurs including in tourism-related activities are credit guarantees. INADEM operates the National Guarantee System (SNG) through five development banks, offering public guarantees for up to 70% of the loan to new entrepreneurs who do not access finance through the private system. In this way, INADEM links projects in identified priority sectors, including tourism, to public financial institutions including Bancomext, FND and NAFIN which are in charge of administering and leveraging resources, and implementing programmes. The development bank system operates as second-tier, not lending directly to firms, but channelling projects to private financial institutions which use their own funding and receive the guarantee from the National Guarantee System. The private bank system is in charge of screening, lending to and monitoring SMEs and entrepreneurs.

Through this instrument, since 2007 the Ministry of Economy has allocated resources in guarantees for MXN 1.1 billion to facilitate access to finance for SMEs in the tourism sector, supporting 6 387 tourism firms. More than half (56%) of firms reached through the National Guarantee System are micro firms, 35% are small, and 9% are medium-sized. In particular, the instrument suits the needs of (formal) micro firms, which often lack collateral when applying for credit.

INADEM works with Bancomext, offering the National Guarantee System to tourism firms, irrespective of their size. During 2013-15, the programme benefited 3 416 SMEs from the tourism sector to the amount of USD 718 million. Loans of up to MXN 40 million can be used to finance working capital, assets, acquisition, expansion and remodelling of tourism hotels, sustainable technological improvements, branding campaigns, and the construction and equipment of hospitals and clinics in touristic areas. The programme interest rates for tourism firms are 10.8%, on average three percentage points lower than those observed in loans outside the programme. The amount of credit in the programme is tailored to the needs of each company. The target for 2015 was to benefit SMEs located in Magic Towns and strategic tourism resorts (see Chapter 4 for a discussion on the development of SME tourism clusters and promotion of cultural development in Magic Towns).

National Fund for Entrepreneurship and non-financial supports to increase SME productivity

INADEM also manages the National Fund for Entrepreneurship, driving the development of the venture capital industry through co-investment resources that have contributed to more than 30 new funds, which invest in high-impact projects in many industries, including the tourism sector, accounting for MXN 3.2 billion in 2014.

INADEM has allocated MXN 165 million through this fund to co-develop along with the Oaxaca state government the so-called Mescal Route (*Ruta del Mezcal*), promoting the regional integration of SMEs in the mescal value chain and its transformation into a touristic route. This programme highlights that a suitable approach for tourism SMEs in Mexico could be the provision of finance not only at the firm level but also at destination level, to allow for a strategic view and favouring the development of clusters that can help overcome economies of scale.

In addition to access to finance and credit, tourism product development and visitor services also require the development of entrepreneurial skills, training, sensitisation, and new forms of marketing. INADEM provides non-financial training and mentoring. A tourism-related example is the leverage of funding for the renovation of hotels in Ixtapa-Zihuatanejo in Guerrero for an amount of MXN 45 million. The support consisted of a diagnostic of the viability of the project for the firms, and personalised attention to entrepreneurs. In particular, since 2015 there is a project towards increasing productivity in small traditional firms by using ICTs. Such programme could be relevant for tourism SMEs (e.g. craft vendors or small food retail providers in tourism areas).

Mexico can also draw on the experience of other OECD countries in fostering entrepreneurship and innovation in tourism. Portugal, for example, is seeking to promote entrepreneurship and mitigate the barriers SMEs face in accessing credit. Turismo de Portugal has developed a diversified set of measures targeted at tourism, including participating in the Lisbon Challenge incubation programme, providing tourism-related tech start-ups with the opportunity to meet mentors and investors and participate in workshops, pitch sessions and networking events. Portugal has also introduced financial engineering instruments based on risk capital, an SME growth credit line and protocols with several credit institutions to make it easier for tourism businesses to access funding in a timely and cost-effective manner. Turismo de Portugal also organises awareness raising and information sessions on range of instruments for SMEs and entrepreneurs (Box 5.8).

Alternative financing approaches for tourism entrepreneurs

The internet and social media are driving rapid innovation, including in the SME financing space. Crowdfunding is a finance technique that uses the internet to match investors and borrowers for projects of common interest with an underlying social motive. Crowdfunding is a complement to bank finance and requires the banking system to operate: bank accounts, credit cards, an online payment system, and credit records are all necessary for the system to function. Not only can crowdfunding close the finance gap that firms observe, but also it can do it in a shorter time span than standard credit applications. It also brings non-financial benefits, like the validation of R&D outputs, an estimation of the potential demand for a product, and allows the borrower to benefit from the knowledge, network, and expertise from founders. Crowdfunding presents some risks, including project failure, fraud and lack of an exit option, as there is no secondary market to trade the investments (Robano, 2014).

Crowdfunding can be classified as non-financial (donations, rewards) and financial (peer-to-peer lending, or equity-related investments). In non-financial crowdfunding, investors are attracted by some characteristic of the project, such as local engagement or possible job creation, and donate money without pro-quo, sometimes in exchange of a pre-order of a product. This is the case with TravelStarter, for example, which is a global crowdfunding platform for entrepreneurs in the tourism sector, which received seed funding from the Slovenia Enterprise Fund and now operates in countries including France, Portugal, Spain and the United States. The platform helps individuals and local businesses raise funds for their tourism and travel related projects. Travellers select a destination and search for a project to fund, and claim an in-kind reward in return for funding a project (e.g. overnight stay in a guest house, bicycle rental).

Box 5.8. Fostering entrepreneurship and innovation in Portugal

Destinations are facing an increasingly competitive environment. There are three key ingredients for remaining successful in this industry: creativity, a wise use of technology and resilience. In this context, Turismo de Portugal has defined a framework to support travel start-ups, fostering entrepreneurship and innovation in the tourism sector and creating a dynamic entrepreneurship ecosystem in the country. This framework includes targets to: develop a more innovative and entrepreneurial culture in the travel sector; create and actively support initiatives accelerating and nurturing start-ups that can impact tourism; support travel start-ups in the critical phase of market development by mobilising marketing resources specifically for their needs; provide adequate public funding and attract private investment to the new travel businesses emerging from this movement; attract knowledge to Portugal, fostering the travel ecosystem and making the country a reference Travel Start-up Hub. Within this framework, the Portuguese Tourism Board established several partnerships and initiatives focused on entrepreneurship and innovation, which have been able to enhance a very active entrepreneurial tourism ecosystem. This includes:

- Encouraging tourism entrepreneurs to participate in horizontal accelerator programmes, notably the Lisbon Challenge (www.lisbon-challenge.com), in partnership with i-Beta. From nearly 100 start-ups accelerated the past two years, about 30 are from the tourism sector.
- Creating a vertical acceleration programme dedicated to tourism, the Discoveries Travel and Tourism Start-up Accelerator (www.startupdiscoveries.com), in partnership with Fabrica de Startups.
- Targeting projects that use or contribute to open data, notably Smart Open Lisboa (www.smartopenlisboa.com), a partnership with Lisbon City Hall, Portugal Telecom, Cisco and Beta-i.
- Including dedicated entrepreneurship programmes in the syllabus of Turismo de Portugal's Hotel Schools with a specific programme – Tourism Creative Factory.
- Attracting national and international investors to support these initiatives, through the Lisbon Investment Summit and Tech Tour.

Source: Turismo de Portugal

In financial crowdfunding, there is an expected monetary return. Financial crowdfunding can be classified in peer-to-peer lending and crowdinvesting (analogous to debt and equity finance, respectively). As of 2014 there were two crowdinvesting platforms in Mexico, Vakita Capital (offering domestic equity-based crowdfunding) and Crowdfunder (domestic borrowers raising money from international investors, under United States Securities regulation (MIF, 2014), and several crowd-lending platforms (Kiva, from the United States; Kubo Financiero, and Prestadero, both Mexican) along with two non-financial crowdfunding platforms: Fondeadora and Idea.

Box 5.9: Financing and supporting registered tourism businesses

The Federal Commission for Regulatory Improvement (COFEMER) is responsible for promoting and implementing regulatory improvement policies at federal level, and in federal entities and municipalities. In 2014, COFEMER and the Ministry of Tourism signed an agreement to co-ordinate the implementation of Tourism Enterprise Attention Centres (CAET) in priority tourism municipalities to stimulate tourism at local level. Under the agreement, the COFEMER Rapid Business Start-up System (SARE) is being used to promote tourism entrepreneurship and encourage the formalisation of tourism businesses, as well as provide advice and support with federal, state and local regulatory procedures. SARE allows low risk businesses that do not represent an environmental or health threat to obtain an operating license in less than 72 hours from a single window or one-stop-shop. Apart from regulatory simplification activities, the CAET will offer dissemination services from the Ministry of Tourism on the areas of mentoring, training, tourism statistics, and innovation and increase awareness of the availability of development funds.

This initiative operates through a pre-existing network of municipalities which have been certified under the Programme for Recognition and Operation of the Rapid Business Start-up System (PROSARE). Businesses which go through the rapid business start-up system are included in the National Tourism Registry. Tourism Enterprise Attention Centres are established following analysis of local regulations restricting tourism competition and installation of a *Punto para Mover a México del Sector Publico* promoted by the National Institute for Entrepreneurs (INADEM). COFEMER and the Ministry of Tourism are developing monitoring indicators to analyse progress in municipalities where Tourism Enterprise Attention Centres have been implemented, in order to find opportunity areas to improve the tourism service offering and encourage investment and employment in tourism.

Source: SECTUR (2015).

It has been argued that crowdfunding serves to monetise social media, as people invest in projects they care about, because of their social or local connections (Agrawal, Catalini, and Goldfarb, 2011). In that sense, crowdfunding can serve as an instrument to channel remittances to finance local development projects, in particular related to tourism. Mexico is second only to India as the country with most income remittance receipts (PWC, 2014). According to the World Bank's World Development Indicators' database, remittances to Mexico amounted in 2014 to USD 1 billion, or 1.9% of GDP.

There is also a range of other SME and micro-enterprise lending and development models created by governments, international donors and financial institutions, and social impact investors whose potential use in the Mexico context could be assessed when designing policies to fund SMEs. These include:

- Community shares: In communities that have investable capital, members purchase shares in community-owned tourism enterprises and receive a percentage of profits based upon their ownership stake, for example a community-owned ecolodge. It is similar in concept to equity-based crowdfunding. This type of share capital can typically only be issued by co-operative societies, community benefit societies, and charitable community organisations.
- Co-operatives: Not a new idea, particularly in Mexico, where land and sometimes community-wide economic activities are communally owned, particularly in the agricultural sector. However, it is not a widely adopted practice in Mexico's tourism sector and there would appear to be significant potential that can be explored, perhaps through pilot projects where tourism co-operatives can be formed

and potentially access start up or working capital through one of the alternative finance approaches discussed above, or more traditional government-backed programmes that might be expanded or created to increase support to communally-owned tourism enterprises. This model has the most obvious potential in remote communities, such as those in or near protected areas, where the land is already owned communally through the *ejido* system.

- Impact investment funds: Impact investing, or social investment, is a growing trend focused in the non-profit, international development assistance, and increasingly in the for-profit sector. Impact investments are defined as investments that deliver significant social and environmental benefits.
- Community tourism enterprise networks: The creation of networks of tourism-related small businesses and micro-enterprises that provide visitor services along the value chain on a local, region, and national basis. These networks not only have the potential create a pooled source of debt or equity financing, but can also be organised into marketing co-operatives and online marketing platforms that help to promote community tourism enterprises to visitors that might not otherwise be aware of them. One example is the Pearls of Uganda programme, which received start-up funding, grants and technical assistance from the United States Agency for International Development (USAID).
- Microfinance: Analogous to community shares, co-operatives, and community tourism enterprise networks, microfinance can provide a viable source of funding for small projects. Microfinance is a group lending technique for small-scale loans (the specific size varies with the context) that transfers the costs of loan screening and monitoring from the lender to the group of borrowers. The technique has been applied as a poverty-alleviation strategy and although there is no consensus on the net benefits it brings to the population, it has served to increase financial inclusion and empowerment of women, in particular in rural areas (Emran, Robano, and Smith, 2014). Microfinance can be a finance option for rural community tourism and Magic Town developments.

In Mexico, the National Commission for the Development of Indigenous Communities (CDI) has a specific programme to boost productivity in the indigenous communities through financing, training, and building social capital, which mirrors some characteristics of microfinance.

Alternatively, the provision of non-financial services should be considered. For example, the expansion of the use of private credit bureaux or public credit registries to build a financial history that can later allow for private funding. Related to this, the Tourism Enterprise Attention Centres and Rapid Business Start-up System (CAET-SARE) initiative is a starting point to build on financing Mexican tourism SMEs. This initiative is helping to address the issue of informality (Box 5.9). It can be envisaged the construction of a finance instrument to accompany the CAET-SARE initiative, analogous to microfinance (e.g. with the characteristics of group lending, sharing monitoring and screening costs, small amounts) as a public policy to support tourism SMEs in those destinations already identified as having tourism potential, including for indigenous communities.

References

ADB-OECD. (2014). ADB-OECD Study on Enhancing Financial Accessibility for SMEs: Lessons from Recent Crises, Chapter 2.5 available at http://www.oecd.org/cfe/smes/adb-oecd-study-enhancing-financial-accessibility-smes.pdf

Agrawal A., C. Catalini and A. Goldfarb. (2011). The Geography of Crowdfunding, NBER working paper 16820 available at http://www.nber.org/papers/w16820

Australia Government. (2009). « Tourism 2020 », Department of Resources, Energy and Tourism, available at: http://www.tourism.australia.com/documents/Tourism_2020_overview.pdf

Consejo Nacional Empresarial Turistico. (2014). Tourism Activity in Mexico 2014, Number 12, available at http://www.cnet.org.mx

Economist Intelligence Unit. (2014). *Evaluating the environment for public-private partnerships in Latin America and the Caribbean: The 2014 Infrascope.* EIU, New York, NY, available at: http://idbdocs.iadb.org/wsdocs/getDocument.aspx?DOCNUM=39560897

Emran, S., V. Robano and S. Smith. (2014). Assessing the Frontiers of Ultra-Poverty Reduction: Evidence from CFPR/TUP I, an Innovative Programme in Bangladesh, Economic Development and Cultural Change, vol. 62 N. 2, January 2014, pp 339-380

European Commission. (2016). Guide on EU Funding for the Tourism Sector. April 2016, available at: http://ec.europa.eu/growth/tourism-funding-guide

Faber B. and C. Gaubert. (2016). Tourism and Economic Development: Evidence from Mexico's Coastline. NBER Working Paper No. 22300, available at: http://www.nber.org/papers/w22300

Fernández C. and L. Villar. (2016). Heterogeneidad de la informalidad laboral y políticas para enfrentarla. available at http://focoeconomico.org/2016/06/07/heterogeneidad-de-la-informalidad-laboral-y-politicas-para-enfrentarla/

Fundación CODESPA. (2013). Programa rutas: la apuesta por un turismo inclusivo en Latinoamérica. Caracas: Fundación CODESPA. Retrieved from http://scioteca.caf.com/handle/123456789/564

Hinojosa, S. (2015) "Financiamiento de Infraestructura Publica con Mercado de Capitales en America Latina" Programa para el Impulso de Asociaciones Publico Privadas en Estados Mexicanos, available at: http://www.piappem.org/file.php?id=485

Industry Canada. (2011). Canada's Federal Tourism Strategy: Welcoming the World, ISBN 978-1-100-16807-4 available at: www.tourism.gc.ca

Multilateral Investment Fund. (2014). *Crowdfunding in Mexico: The Power of Digital Technologies to Transform Innovation, Entrepreneurship and Economic Inclusion,* MIF/FOMIN Access to markets and Skills, Washington, DC: Inter-American Development Bank

Nassr, I.K., V. Robano and G. Wehinger. (2016). Unleashing the Export Potential of SMEs in Greece, *OECD Working Papers on Finance, Insurance and Private Pensions*, No. 41, OECD Publishing, Paris. DOI: http://dx.doi.org/10.1787/5jm0qgt464f6-en

Nassr, I.K. and G. Wehinger. (2015) Unlocking SME finance through market-based debt: Securitisation, private placements and bonds. *OECD Journal: Financial Market Trends*, http://dx.doi.org/10.1787/fmt-2014-5js3bg1g53ln

OECD. (2016a). Innovative Financing Approaches for Tourism SMEs [CFE/TOU(2015)9/REV1]

OECD. (2016b). Financing SMEs and Entrepreneurs 2016: an OECD Scoreboard. Chapter on Mexico. DOI:10.1787/fin_sme_ent-2016-28-en

OECD. (2016c). *OECD Tourism Trends and Policies 2016.* OECD Publishing, Paris. http://dx.doi.org/10.1787/tour-2016-en

OECD. (2015a). OECD Economic Surveys: Mexico 2015, available at DOI:10.1787/eco_surveys-mex-2015-en

OECD. (2015b). *Policy Framework for Investment, 2015 Edition.* OECD Publishing, Paris DOI: http://dx.doi.org/10.1787/9789264208667-en

OECD. (2015c). New Approaches to SME and Entrepreneurship Financing: Broadening the Range of Instruments, OECD Publishing, Paris. http://dx.doi.org/10.1787/9789264240957-en

OECD. (2014a). Alternative financing instruments: The case of mezzanine finance, in OECD. , *Financing SMEs and Entrepreneurs 2014: An OECD Scoreboard*, OECD Publishing, Paris. DOI: http://dx.doi.org/10.1787/fin_sme_ent-2014-6-en

OECD. (2014b). Tourism trends and policy priorities, in OECD. *OECD Tourism Trends and Policies 2014*, OECD Publishing, Paris. DOI: http://dx.doi.org/10.1787/tour-2014-4-en

OECD/IDB.(2014). Public-private partnerships, in *Government at a Glance: Latin America and theCaribbean 2014: Towards Innovative Public Financial Management*, OECD Publishing, Paris. DOI: http://dx.doi.org/10.1787/9789264209480-32-en

OECD. (2013a). *OECD Investment Policy Reviews: Costa Rica 2013*, OECD Publishing. http://dx.doi.org/10.1787/9789264203952-en

OECD. (2013b). *Mexico: Key Issues and Policies*, OECD Publishing, Paris. DOI: http://dx.doi.org/10.1787/9789264187030-en

OECD. (2012). The Governance of Public-Private partnerships, OECD Publishing

PND 2013-18. National Development Plan 2013-18. Mexican Government

PricewaterhouseCoopers S.C. (2014). Doing Business in Mexico: Tourism. Febrero

PROSECTUR 2013-18. Tourism Sector Plan 2013-18. Mexican Government

PIT 2013-18. Institutional Programme of FONATUR, Mexican Government

Responsible Finance. (2015). Responsible Finance Industry Report, available at: http://responsiblefinance.org.uk

Robano V. (2014). New Approaches to SME Finance: Broadening the range of instruments. Case study of crowdfunding, OECD Publishing. DOI: 10.1787/9789264240957-en http://www.oecd.org/officialdocuments/publicdisplaydocumentpdf/?cote=CFE/SME(2013)7/ANN1/FINAL&docLanguage=En

Secretaria de Economía. (2016). Comisión Nacional de Inversiones Extranjeras: Informe Estadístico sobre el comportamiento de la Inversión Extranjera Directa en México Enero-Diciembre 2015, http://www.gob.mx/cms/uploads/attachment/file/58415/Informe_Congreso-2015-4T.pdf

Skidelsky, R., F. Martin, and C. Wigstrom. (2012). *Blueprint for a British Investment Bank.* London: Center for Global Studies, available at: http://globalstudies.org.uk/publications/blueprint-for-a-british-investment-bank/

UNCTAD. (2007). FDI in Tourism: The Development Dimension. New York and Geneva, available at: http://unctad.org/en/Docs/iteiia20075_en.pdf

World Bank. (2016). World Development Indicators, Accessed on 17 June 2016: http://data.worldbank.org/indicator/FS.AST.PRVT.GD.ZS.

ORGANISATION FOR ECONOMIC CO-OPERATION AND DEVELOPMENT

The OECD is a unique forum where governments work together to address the economic, social and environmental challenges of globalisation. The OECD is also at the forefront of efforts to understand and to help governments respond to new developments and concerns, such as corporate governance, the information economy and the challenges of an ageing population. The Organisation provides a setting where governments can compare policy experiences, seek answers to common problems, identify good practice and work to co-ordinate domestic and international policies.

The OECD member countries are: Australia, Austria, Belgium, Canada, Chile, the Czech Republic, Denmark, Estonia, Finland, France, Germany, Greece, Hungary, Iceland, Ireland, Israel, Italy, Japan, Korea, Latvia, Luxembourg, Mexico, the Netherlands, New Zealand, Norway, Poland, Portugal, the Slovak Republic, Slovenia, Spain, Sweden, Switzerland, Turkey, the United Kingdom and the United States. The European Union takes part in the work of the OECD.

OECD Publishing disseminates widely the results of the Organisation's statistics gathering and research on economic, social and environmental issues, as well as the conventions, guidelines and standards agreed by its members.

OECD PUBLISHING, 2, rue André-Pascal, 75775 PARIS CEDEX 16
(85 2016 05 1 P) ISBN 978-92-64-26656-8 – 2017

www.ingramcontent.com/pod-product-compliance
Lightning Source LLC
Chambersburg PA
CBHW061214240926
51846CB00006B/1219
* 9 7 8 9 2 6 4 2 6 6 5 6 8 *